CHEAPSIDE

In the Forest of Windsor

Christine Weightman

CHEAPSIDE

In the Forest of Windsor

This book is dedicated to all Cheapsiders, past, present and future

Published in 2000 for the Cheapside Millennium History
Exhibition and financed by the Durning Trust of Ascot.
All profits from the sale of this book go
to support the Cheapside Village Hall.

Published by Cheapside Publications
Heronsbrook Cottage · Ascot · SL5 7QG
Printed and bound in Great Britain by Antony Rowe
of Chippenham and Reading

CONTENTS

ILLUSTRATIONS AND MAPS

ACKNOWLEDGEMENTS OF ILLUSTRATIONS AND MAPS

The following have generously given us permission to reproduce their drawings, postcards, photographs, illustrations and maps:
Berkshire Record Office: No. 14
Eugene Burden: Nos. 9, 20, 22, 39
Michael Crutchley: Nos. 18, 19
John End: Covers, Nos. 26-31, 38
Rev. Tim Gunter: Nos. 14, 25
Mark Holloway: Nos. 3, 25
Angela Marshall: Nos. 36, 37
Royal Commission on Historical Monuments England: No. 17
J. and A. Singh: No. 40
John Weightman: Nos. 1, 2, 4, 6, 7, 15, 21, 23, 32-35, 41, 47
Suzy Williams tinted the back cover.
From G. M. Hughes, *"A History of Windsor Forest, Sunninghill and the Great Park"*, 1890: Nos. 5, 10, 11, 13, 16, 24

SOURCES AND ABBREVIATIONS

B.R.O.	Berkshire Record Office at Reading
C.C.	Chertsey Cartulary
C.C.R.	Calendar of Charter Rolls
C.F.R.	Calendar of Fine Rolls
C.L.R.	Calendar of Liberate Rolls
C.P.R.	Calendar of Patent Rolls
C.S.	Clifford Smith
Carlile	M. J. Carlile, *"Notes on Sunninghill Bog, the Red Stream and Silwood Lake"*, Imperial College, 1998
Carter	George Carter, Patrick Goode, Kedrum Laurie, *"Humphrey Repton, Landscape Gardener 1752-1818"*, Exhibition Norwich/London, 1983
Colvin	H. M. Colvin, edited, *"History of the King's Works"*, vol. II, 1963
Cooper King	Lieut-Col. Cooper King, *"History of Berkshire"*, 1887
Defoe	Daniel Defoe, *"A Tour through the Whole Island of Great Britain"*, ed. P. N. Furbanks, W. R. Owens and A. J. Coulson, 1991

D.L.	Durning Library Archive
E.B.	Eugene Burden's Collection
F.S.	Mrs Field Smith's notes
Hakewill	J. Hakewill, *"History of Windsor and Neighbourhood"*, 1813 (note "Hakewell" sic. on etchings)
Hathaway	Percy Hathaway, *"Some Ramblings of an Old Bogonian"*, 1995
Hodder	F. C. Hodder, *"A Short History of Sunningdale"*, 1937
Hughes	G. M. Hughes, *"A History of Windsor Forest, Sunninghill and the Great Park"*, 1890
I.C.A.	Imperial College Archive, London
J.E	John End's collection
J.F	Jack Franklin's History (unpublished)
Kelly	Kelly's Directories
Lysons	Daniel and Samuel Lyson, *"Magna Britannica, Berkshire"*, 1806
Marshall	Marshall's Directories
Morris	Reg Morris, *"Distant Views from Sunninghill"*, 1985
N.M.R.	Royal Commission on Historical Monuments England National Monuments Record
Over	Luke Over and Chris Tyrrell, *"The Royal Hundred of Cookham"*, 1994
Peake	H. Peake, *"Archaeology of Berkshire"*, 1931
P.R.O.	Public Record Office at Kew
Roberts,G.	G. Roberts, *"The Most Powerful Man in the World: The Life of Sir Henri Deterding"*, 1938, reprint 1976
Roberts	Jane Roberts, *"Royal Landscape: The Gardens and Parks of Windsor"*, 1997
R.S.P.	S. A. Rickwood, *"A Compilation"* by T. R. E. Southwood and J. S. Porter from Rickwood's manuscript
Searle	C. W. Searle, *"The Book of Sunninghill and Ascot"*, 1937
S.J.C.	St John's College Archive, Cambridge
Smart, P.	edited, *"Extracts From The Past, Ascot"*, The Durning Library Trust, Berks County Council, 1985
T.D.	R. R. Tighe and J. E. Davis, *"Annals of Windsor"*, 2 vols. 1858
Turner.	Frederick Turner, *"Egham, Surrey: A History of the Parish under Church and Crown"*, 1926
V.C.H.	Victoria County History for Berkshire, 3 volumes.

CHEAPSIDE IN THE FOREST OF WINDSOR

WHERE IS CHEAPSIDE?

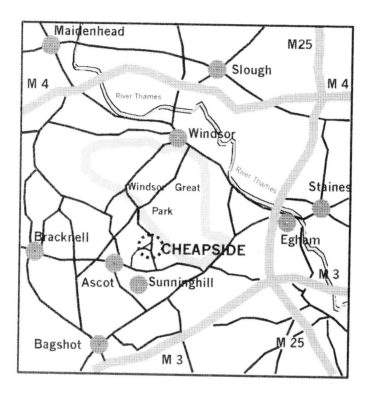

Cheapside is a small village within the Royal Borough of Windsor and Maidenhead at the eastern end of Berkshire. Now a part of Ascot it lies to the east of the racecourse and south-west of Windsor Great Park. Although mainly in the parish of Sunninghill it has always included a small part of the parish of Winkfield and has never fitted neatly into one administrative district.

The development of Cheapside was governed by the boundaries of Silwood Park, Sunninghill Park, Buckhurst Park and Windsor Great Park. We have therefore included the relevant histories of these estates and that of the Church of St Michael and All the Angels, a starting point for all the growth in our area.

Cheapside is one of the oldest parts of Sunninghill and was a settlement when most of modern Sunninghill and Ascot was still a mixture of marshy bogs and barren heaths. This book records its history.

PREFACE

This book was written in conjunction with the Cheapside Millennium History Exhibition first held in May and June 2000. This was the latest of a trio of history exhibitions held in the Cheapside Village Hall since 1977.

Five years ago, in 1995, the Cheapside Village Hall Committee, under its now sadly missed chairman, Barbara Mison, decided to celebrate the Millennium with a history exhibition. The Cheapside Millennium History Team was formed and embarked on a lengthy programme of research. The following have seen the project through to its completion: Brian Coupar, Pauline and David Drew, Sally Harker, Mark Holliday, Trevor Lewis, Silla and Sam Mossop, Anthony Wagg, Christine and John Weightman, Bob Williams and Edna Vidgen.

The team were resolved to provide something that would last, if not to the next millennium, at least for some tens of years. They decided to have all the display boards sealed and laminated for future use, to preserve the oral history on a video and to produce a book to record the information that might be collected and verified.

The whole project was given very generous financial backing from Daler-Rowney, who supplied all the boards; from the Kidwells Trust and the Council of Rural Action for the Environment who between them paid for all the expenses of research, photography and copying; from the Millennium Festival Awards for All Programme and Mrs A. Singh who covered all the costs of hiring stands, lamination and publicity; British Movietone News who helped with the video and from several private donors and the Cheapside Village Hall Trust for a multitude of other expenses. The video maker, author, publishers and the committee have worked steadily and for love for the whole five years. Without the support of all the above and many local people, who gave their time and services freely, the exhibition would not have been made.

The most permanent part of the Millennium Exhibition is this book, printed at the expense of the Durning Trust of Ascot. We are particularly grateful for their generous interest and funding without which this publication would have been impossible. In supporting this venture, the Durning Trustees, under their chairman, Catherine M. Stevenson, are fulfilling the wishes of their benefactor. Jemina Durning Smith founded the Durning

Library in 1882 and left a substantial legacy used to benefit the library and to promote the education of the inhabitants of Ascot and the district.

Our researchers were helped by the patience and skills of the staffs of the Royal Library, Prints Room and Archive at Windsor Castle, the Durning Library at Ascot, the Egham Museum, the Public Record Office, the Berkshire Record Office, the British Library and the British Museum, the Archives of All Souls College Oxford, St John's College Cambridge and Imperial College London, the BABTIE Archaeological Services at Reading, Shell International and the Royal Commission on the Historical Monuments of England.

Diana Anderson, Anne Barrett, Patricia Reader, and Stuart MacNeil of Imperial College, Malcolm Underwood of St John's College Cambridge, Judith Hunter of the Windsor Collection and Ann Darracott of the Maidenhead Civic Trust welcomed our enquiries and gave us every assistance.

Michael Carlile helped us in the field of environmental science, Gillian Clark provided information on eighteenth century orphans and Frank Gosling advised us on the geology of the area. Eugene Burden gave us the full use of his large map collection and his extensive library. John End gave us generous access to his comprehensive collection of old postcards and other local documents, Arthur Dance lent us his archaeological collection and Margaret and Norman Wendon allowed us to use their "*Bobby's Notebook*".

The Reverend Tim Gunter granted us full access to the parish records and to his pictures of the church. Cheapside School has also participated very fully in the project. They made some of the boards themselves and the headmistress, Hester Wooller, and Claire Lynch have been enthusiastically supportive.

All these are typical of the many residents who have helped so eagerly. We have had letters from ex-Cheapsiders living in the United States and Australia. Over a hundred and fifty people were directly involved in the research and the production of the exhibition, video and book. This is essentially their book as it was their exhibition.

THE ORIGINS OF A COMMUNITY
PREHISTORY TO 1660

"Once on this earth, once on this familiar spot of ground, walked other men and women, as actual as we are today, thinking their own thoughts, swayed by their own passions, but now all gone, one generation vanishing after another gone as utterly as we ourselves shall shortly be gone like ghosts at cockcrow."

(E. M. Trevelyan in *"Autobiography and Other Essays"*)

The Land

Cheapside is a small community of about 1,000 people. Grand parks rub shoulders with modest cottages and modern housing estates. There is a successful Church of England primary school and an active Village Hall. The local pub, the Thatched Tavern has a restaurant, which like the school draws its clientele from a wide area. Although there are no longer any shops and the church is a ten-minute walk away across the fields, Cheapside has always been a well-defined hamlet. It is isolated from the main centres of Ascot and Sunninghill by the very features that created Cheapside in the first place.

The Silwood Park estate belonging to Imperial College lies to the south. This was formerly the land and farms of Sunninghill Manor. The earliest manor house lay near to today's Cheapside. The evolution of the manor into the park affected the growth of the village and kept it apart from the modern village of Sunninghill and the church of St Michael and All the Angels. To the north and west of Cheapside lies the Sunninghill Park estate, the home of His Royal Highness Prince Andrew, the duke of York. This and the Ascot Racecourse form a green barrier between Cheapside and modern Ascot. To the east are Buckhurst Park estate and Windsor Great Park. In this direction a great expanse of woodland, parks and farms seals Cheapside away from the developments of Englefield Green and Virginia Water.

For most of its history Cheapside existed as a woodland and rural community within the Windsor Forest. This vast stretch of east Berkshire was the ancient hunting ground of Saxon, Norman and English kings. It was not a forest full of trees, as we imagine a forest today, but rather a heathy open region with scattered woodlands, farms and hamlets. Since the land was not very fertile the settlements were far apart and grew up in isolation. The

villagers depended on a few fertile fields and on the forest itself
for their livelihood. Cheapside was one of these small settlements.

Geological Map of the Cheapside Area

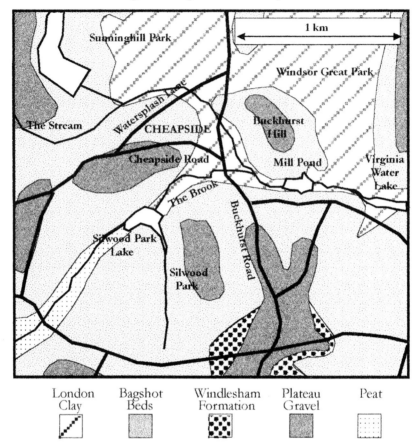

The first Cheapsiders settled on the deposits of London Clay
where there was a workable loam with thin beds of sandstone and
pebbles. The Clay stretches along the valley from Virginia Water
to the north east of Silwood Lake and towards Sunninghill Park.
The most fertile land in Cheapside and its last remaining farms at
Silwood Farm and Dairy Farm were on this Clay.

London Clay underlies all this part of the Thames Valley but in
most of the area this is covered by the Bagshot Beds. These
consist of finely grained sands, mainly yellow, pink and black with
some fine white sand beneath them. Within the Bagshot Beds
there are patches of gravel, flint and pebbles. There are also strips
of land where the Windlesham Formation (formerly called the
Bracklesham Bed) comes to the surface. In these deposits there

are larger rocks, heathstones, also known as greywethers or sarsens, which were used for building the first stone St Michael's Church.

The oldest known houses on the manor of Sunninghill were sited on deposits of Plateau Gravel. This gravel predominates on the hill in Silwood Park, Buckhurst Hill and, more importantly for the history of Cheapside, across the junction of Cheapside Road with Watersplash Lane. It was here that the old manor farm stood, surrounded by well-drained fields and close to the fertile land on the London Clay.

This complicated geological patchwork formed the basic structure for the settlement and growth of Cheapside and today's gardeners are also very well aware of the variations in the soil across the village. They grumble, as gardeners always do, that the ground suffers from being either too dry due to the fast draining sands or too wet where the clay and peat hamper drainage. But the land is seldom completely dry. Springs burst out wherever the porous sands and gravel meet with the underlying impermeable clay along the sides of the valley.

Another feature of the Cheapside landscape is the acidic soil. Camellias, rhododendrons and azaleas flourish in the local gardens. The woods are full of bluebells which are at their best on the Clay and so particularly splendid at the eastern end of the valley.

As a result of centuries of work by generation after generation Cheapside is a well-wooded area with an attractive skyline of large trees. The redwoods were mostly planted during the second half of the nineteenth century. They were tenacious in the face of the storms that brought down poplars, limes and oaks of the same age but are now dying back along Buckhurst Road. The elms that used to grace Cheapside Road were lost in the epidemic of the 1960s. Although many young trees still struggle along until they reach between ten and twenty years they then become colonised by the bark beetle which spreads a pathogenic fungus and they succumb without fail. The most ancient and sturdy survivors are the oaks. Some are up to nine hundred years old in Windsor Park and up to half that in Cheapside. They were always an important resource for Cheapsiders and they also flourished best on the Clay beds.

Working the trees was the basis for most of the settlements throughout the Windsor Forest. For many centuries trees were the main source for fuel, building and making tools and equipment. Branches of deciduous trees were cut in summer to be used with holly as winter fodder for deer and domestic animals. Oak bark was harvested in late spring for use in tanneries. Trees were pollarded and repollarded. This involved cutting out the main leaders at a convenient height above the ground. Others were coppiced, cutting the trees right back to the ground to encourage multiple re-growths. Since timber was the main material used in local house building up to the late eighteenth century very few of the earlier cottages have survived.

Two small rivers flow through Cheapside and the earliest Cheapside Green was probably close to their junction. The Stream runs out of Sunninghill Park and joins the Brook that comes from Silwood Park Lake. Together they pass into the Millpond and on to Virginia Water Lake. The Brook used to be known as the *"Red Brook"* because of its distinctive colour. Eighteenth century naturalists called it a chalybeate or iron-bearing stream (chalybeate derives from *"khalub"* or *"khalups"* in Greek, meaning steel). It was the presence of soluble ferrous iron that attracted the Stuart and Georgian gentry to take the waters at the Wells Inn, where the springs were traditionally known as *"Old Charley"*.

The soluble ferrous iron enters the Brook from the Sunninghill Bog and this stimulates the growth of bacteria such as *Leptothrix*. These bacteria appear as fine ochre coloured strands festooning plants, clustering along the banks and forming small mats on the surface. For centuries this was known as ruddle and used for marking sheep. The Brook is at its reddest before it enters Silwood Lake but the red stain is still visible at the eastern end of Cheapside. By then the Brook passes over the Clay and, since no more iron enters the water, it gradually clears; when it reaches the Millpond the redness has disappeared (Carlile).

In spite of its muddy colour the Brook is a healthy stream and supports a rich wildlife. There are fresh water mussels, roach, rudd, gudgeon and sticklebacks and even the occasional soft-shelled European crayfish. These used to be much more common than they are now. Another river inhabitant that has declined recently is the water vole.

The valley of the Brook is the haunt of more than seventeen species of dragonfly and over a hundred and four species of beetles and flies. As a result it is a good habitat for birds, amphibians, reptiles and wild mammals. Edward Green has listed a hundred species of wild birds sighted in this area. Along the Brook, herons, mallards, water-hens, kingfishers and mandarin ducks can be seen regularly and in the woods, parks and gardens there are many song-birds, game-birds and birds of prey. As well as the mandarin ducks, exotic and enchanting birds which have spread widely across the district from private pools and lakes, there are green parakeets which sail high over Cheapside in flocks of up to fifty birds or more and gather to eat the buds on the fruit trees. They have now been breeding nearby in the Thames valley for more than fifty years.

Cheapside is also well endowed with reptiles especially grass snakes with their golden crowns and toads and frogs. There are many foxes and badgers, a few weasels and stoats and plenty of their prey, rabbits, mice and shrews. Deer are frequently seen in the woods and gardens, even walking up the road in mid-morning. Fallow deer are seldom seen but the native roe deer and the feral muntjak wander through Cheapside leaving the evidence for their presence on damaged roses, trees and shrubs.

The People

People have been living in and around Cheapside for thousands of years. None of the country lying south of the Thames was directly affected by the last Ice Age so it is possible that people have been moving through the forest and staying beside our Brook from the earliest days of human habitation.

The oldest known sign of human presence dates from about 10,000 years ago in the Mesolithic or Middle Stone Age era. These people made camps along the streams in the Thames valley, then part of the Rhine river system. Some may well have stayed beside our Brook. They found food in the forest and the streams. They cut down trees and reeds to provide their shelters and used the skins of the animals for their clothes. Two of their finely crafted flint tranchet axes have been found, one at Manor Farm Ascot in 1896 (N.M.R. part i, SU 9268), and another in a garden opposite the Thatched Tavern in 1992 (below, actual size 130x45x25 mms).

This was dated to between 8,000 and 12,000 years old. It was dug up about a hundred yards from Cheapside Road lying on top of the silver sand marking the course of an ancient river.

By 3,300 BC Neolithic or New Stone Age farmers may have settled near here taking advantage of the lighter soils of the Bagshot Beds. A flint chert or celt, i.e. a cream coloured axe of that period, was found at Silwood Park in about 1850 by the owner, Michie Forbes (ibid, SU 9468). One of their stone maceheads, used for ceremonial purposes, was found down a well in Sunninghill (ibid, SU 9367). Another stone axe and stone clubhead were found near Ascot Station (ibid, SU 9268) probably in connection with a barrow that was destroyed during building works (ibid, SU 96NW7).

In the Bronze Age, 2,300 to 800 BC, there were enough people settled here to build a number of bell or round barrows such as the one containing twenty-three urns which was excavated in 1901, near Sunningdale Station. The urns are now in Reading Museum. There were four more barrows in the grounds of the present-day Heatherwood Hospital. In the late eighteenth century the Soldiers' Pillar was set up on one of these barrows to mark the junction of several forest rides. It had disappeared by 1890, by which date most of the barrows had also vanished (Hughes, p. 321). Only one barrow has survived and now lies among the hospital wards. It is well marked and worth a visit.

The people who built these barrows must have lived in the area for several generations. They had both the organisation and the leisure to construct major funeral and religious monuments. They were farmers who cleared parts of the forest and also hunters, supplementing the food they could grow with fish and fresh water mussels from the streams and game from the forest. They would farm the light, dry and fertile soils on the south east of the heath, i.e. in Sunninghill and Cheapside.

After the climatic deterioration of about 1,000 BC the sandy land, which had been denuded of trees, became even more heathy and less fertile. As a result settlement declined right across this region. Only on the Clay deposits did the land remain suitable for farming.

By the late second century BC we are on the threshold of written history. The Celtic population of southern Britain had again grown in numbers and was more economically active. New ideas were adopted from abroad, such as the iron ploughshare, making it easier to farm the heavier clay of the Thames valley and settlements spread extensively across the valleys of Berkshire.

By the time of Julius Caesar's invasion of Britain in 55 BC, the Atrebates were living in modern Berkshire occupying all the lands on the south bank of the Thames while the Catuvellauni lived on the north bank. In the century after Caesar's departure the Atrebates adopted many Roman ideas and customs. All kinds of Roman goods were welcomed by the aristocracy and merchants traded throughout the tribal lands. Eppillus, a chief of the Atrebates, issued Roman style coinage bearing the word *"Rex"* i.e. king.

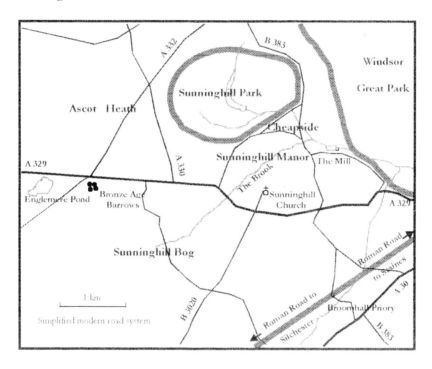

Sketch map of the Early History

Calleva Atrebatum was one of the chief centres of the Atrebates. *"Calleva"* meant *"the place in the woods"*. Later this centre would be known by the Saxon name of Silchester, *"sil"* (as in Silwood), derives from *"siele"*, meaning willow in old English. Silchester was thus *"the camp in the willows"*.

In Roman Britain Calleva Atrebates was an important centre. From there the new Roman roads radiated out across southern England. Their main road to London crossed the Thames on a bridge near Staines. Its route near to Sunninghill has been largely destroyed by later developments but can still be traced near the present Broomhall Farm and Wardour Lodge. From Broomhall it went through Cowarth Park and across the eastern end of Virginia Water.

Saxon Sunninghill

After the withdrawal of the Roman legions in 410, Saxon raiders and settlers flooded into the Thames valley. By 450 the bridge at Staines was destroyed, though a Saxon silver penny, minted in East Anglia about 700 and found near the site of the old Roman road by Arthur Dance, shows that merchants and travellers were still using the road for many centuries.

It used to be thought that the Saxons completely overwhelmed the Romano-Britons in the south of England and eliminated all of them. Today's historians agree that there was some Celtic survival, especially in the female line and in the more isolated wooded areas. Nevertheless the Saxons dominated the language and the culture of this region. There are very few surviving Romano-British place names though the name of Datchet, the legend of Herne the Hunter and names of local rivers such as the Thames and the Lodden are of British origin.

Sunninghill itself was a Saxon settlement. Its name derives from the Sunna or Sonna people who were, according to the Chertsey Abbey foundation charter, a *"Saxon tribe settled in these parts"*. Their territory lay right across East Berkshire. The main settlements of the Sunna lay to the west. Sunninghill was probably one of the last hills that they occupied on the eastern edge of their territory.

By the early sixth century the lands of the Sunnings had became part of the kingdom of Wessex under its first king, Cedric. The Thames, the old boundary between the Atrebates and the Catuvellauni, was now the boundary between the Anglo-Saxon kingdoms of Wessex and Mercia. During the next two centuries the kingdom of Wessex was divided into administrative areas called hundreds. Each hundred was originally 100 hides, about 12,000 acres. By the time of the Domesday Survey of 1086 Sunninghill, not mentioned in the survey, was in the hundred of Beynhurst (which later became the Cookham hundred).

The Church of St Michael and All the Angels

St Michael's Church is where the written history of Sunninghill and Cheapside begins but exactly when the church was first founded is not entirely clear. The conversion of the Saxons and the establishment of the Saxon Church in this part of England started in the mid-seventh century. In 597 St Augustine's mission had arrived at Canterbury and by 635 Bishop Birinus, whose see was at Dorchester, had baptised Cynegils, king of Wessex. Chertsey Abbey, the nearest monastic settlement to Sunninghill, was founded in 666 by monks from Canterbury and Cookham Abbey was established by about 700. Sunninghill Church could have been founded either under the aegis of the bishop or through the missionary work of the monks of Chertsey or Cookham Abbeys.

Both G. M. Hughes and the Victoria History of Berkshire give 890 as the date for the foundation of St. Michael's but there seems to be no surviving documentary or archaeological evidence to support this date. If this is indeed the correct date, then the church was founded in a brief period of peace during the Viking invasions. The Treaty of Chippenham was negotiated in 878 between King Alfred and the Vikings. Some new churches may have been founded just after this treaty and St Michael's may be one of these. However it was not long before the Vikings resumed their raids on this part of the Saxon kingdom. Many settlements along the Thames valley were destroyed. Chertsey Abbey was sacked and the abbot and ninety monks were killed (Turner). As late as 993 there were three hundred and ninety Viking ships on the Thames at Staines and Oxford was taken by a Danish army in 1009. The last two centuries of the first millennium were dangerous and disturbed and not the best time for the foundation of churches.

The dedication to St Michael and All the Angels gives some indication as to the origin of our church. Hughes thought it was dedicated to St Michael because it was built on a hill like St Michael's Mount but many early churches were built on hills and not dedicated to St Michael. He also suggested that it might have been dedicated to St Michael after the Norman Conquest because William the Conqueror had landed on St Michael's Day but of course many churches were dedicated to the great Archangel long before 1066.

The most significant fact in the dedication is that the Archangel Michael was honoured as the conqueror of the devil of paganism. He is thus particularly associated with churches built at a time of conversion to Christianity. There is a cluster of churches all dedicated to St Michael in this part of Berkshire including those at Easthamstead, Bray and Warfield. The church at Warfield was in existence by 1016 when Queen Emma granted the *"vill and chapel"* of Warfield to the bishop of Winchester. Easthamstead church is also thought to be over 1000 years old and St Michael's at Bray was founded before the Domesday record. So we have here three churches, all dedicated to the Archangel Michael and all founded well before 1000, presumably at the time when the Saxons of this region were converted to Christianity.

The ancient yew tree in the churchyard may offer yet another clue to the date of the original church but it also offers as many problems as solutions. The dating of an old and hollow yew is not a very accurate science. It is calculated by considering the placement and the girth of the tree. V. Cornish in *"The Churchyard Yew and Immortality"*, 1946, described St Michael's yew as *"a wreck situated N. W. of the church"* and suggested it was 1,000 years old. In the 1980s it was assessed at about 1,200 years old and in 1994 in *"The Sacred Yew"*, Arnand Chetan and Diana Brueton gave its age as 1,100 years old. There it is described as being *"very hollow and having a girth of 18 feet"*. Until the late eighteenth century, when the church was extended, the yew was of course further away from the church. The fact that it is on the north side of the church may have retarded its growth.

The yew may have been originally part of a circle planted around the first church and associated with ancient beliefs in immortality and the protection of the dead. However yews are not only associated with Christian churchyards. They were also planted beside pagan holy places and these were often associated with water. There was once a spring about a hundred and fifty metres north-west of the church. Today this spring lies beneath the pretty rustic dairy in the garden of The Cedars. The fact that this spring erupted on a hillside would certainly have been considered miraculous in ancient times and may have given rise to a sacred site venerated in the pre-Christian era.

Indeed all the ingredients necessary for a pagan shrine are in the vicinity, a spring on a hill, oaks, yews and mistletoe. So it is possible that our ancient yew was once part of a grove associated with a pagan water shrine and the dedication to St Michael was intended to counter the pagan influences. If the yew tree predates the church we are still no wiser as to the foundation date of St Michael's. Paganism survived in parts of southern England up to 1050 so in theory the church could have been founded at any time between the eighth and the eleventh centuries.

Up to the nineteenth century there was yet another piece of evidence relevant to the dating of the church. This was an inscription on one of the arches of the old church. It is no longer in existence and is known only from the reports of earlier local historians (Hughes, p. 174-5). The inscription commemorated the death of *"Livingus, presbyter"* on the *"11th kalends March"*. It may refer either to Bishop Livingus of Crediton who died in 1046 and who had been a monk at Winchester or to Abbot Livingus who ruled Chertsey Abbey from 993 to 1024. It may also of course commemorate another unknown priest of the same name who had some connection with the church. Since the inscription was in stone it suggests that it was associated with the Norman church unless parts of the Saxon church were already in stone.

The Norman Church seen from the South-West (Hughes)

Considering all the evidence, none of which is exactly conclusive, it is possible that the first St Michael's was built near the site of a pagan sanctuary between the late seventh and ninth centuries. This would fit with the traditional date for the church, the age of the yew tree and the dedication to St Michael. If it was not founded as early as this then it might date to the period of the conversions of the Danes in the tenth century but it surely existed well before the Normans arrived in England.

St Michael's was reconstructed in stone during the reign of King Henry I, 1120 to 1130. By that time there must have been a small community of woodlanders to warrant a newly built church. Other local churches at Easthamstead and Warfield were also built in stone at about the same time, Warfield in 1135 and Easthamstead by 1159.

Local dark grey-brown heathstone was used for St Michael's. There was an outcrop on the hill near the church and along the ridge of Sunninghill. The house near the church, close to today's Ashurst Park, was originally called *"Stoneylands"*. The same stone occurs in various outcrops across the area and was quarried for building up to the mid-eighteenth century. *"Heathstone from Cranbourne Chase"* was listed in bills for the repair of Windsor Castle and it was also used to make the great waterfall at Virginia Water.

The Norman church survived intact up to the late eighteenth century. It had a barrel roof decorated to represent the starry heavens. Remains of this were found in the 1880s when the chancel was rebuilt. A watercolour made in the nineteenth century shows a small church with a chancel, nave and central tower. The entry porch was on the south side and there was a fine west window. This sturdy little church served the parish for seven hundred years.

Broomhall Priory

In 1199, a couple of generations after the stone church had been built, King John granted the advowson of St Michael's to the priory of St Margaret at *"Bromhal"* or Broomhall. The advowson is the right to appoint the priest and the responsibility for the care of the church. The king gave the nuns a piece of land from the royal forest to support the maintenance of both the priory and the church (V.C.H., vol. II, p. 80).

Perhaps the king thought it appropriate that Saint Margaret who kills dragons should be associated with the Archangel Michael who slays devils. (On the other hand it has been suggested that our church was originally dedicated to St Margaret and changed to St Michael's later). St Margaret's Priory is first mentioned on a Pipe Roll of 1157-8 (Thompson, p. 219). It had been founded by the middle of the twelfth century by the De Warenne family, who were the Norman earls of Surrey and it was on their land. The first abbess whose name we know was Joanna in 1249 (Hughes lists the known abbesses, 1266-1522, on p. 350). The present day Broomhall Farm is on or very near the site of this ancient priory, marked on the Norden map of 1607 as *"Bromwell"*.

There is little documentary evidence for the history of the priory and the church. Sadly, few of the priory's records survived the fires of 1321 and 1462. St Margaret's was however mentioned several times in the Chertsey Abbey records of the twelfth and thirteenth centuries (Turner). In 1158, for example, the abbot of Chertsey granted land to the Broomhall Priory (C.C., xlv). More of its history can be traced in crown charters and in documents at St John's College Cambridge, which eventually acquired all the possessions of the priory.

Broomhall Farm close to the Site of the Priory

Broomhall Priory enjoyed royal patronage throughout the thirteenth century and the abbess and nuns became the major landowners in our region. King John's son and successor, Henry III, 1216-1272, was a particularly pious man and regarded the priory with special favour. In 1228 he ordered Jordan, the forester of Windsor Forest, to give the nuns full access to a hundred acres of waste which had been granted to them earlier (C.C.R., Henry III). Three years later the nuns were excused from paying the pannage fees for thirty-six pigs (pannage was the right to graze pigs in the forest and a tax was charged for exercising this right). They were also granted three beams of timber to repair the shingles on the refectory roof and an oak tree to use in other building work. In 1244/5 the nuns of Broomhall were excused a corn levy (C.L.R., Henry III and V.C.H., vol. II, pp 80-81).

In three successive years from 1240 to 1242, the king gave money from the revenues of Windsor Castle to *"the nuns of Bromhal and the lepers of Windles"* (*Windles* is Windsor). This money was to be used by the nuns as alms for the poor. In 1242 the two priories of Broomhall and Ankerwyck (Ankerwyck lay across the Thames, south-east of today's Magna Carta island) were each granted alms enough for a thousand poor (C.L.R., 1240-1242).

This was a very generous gift and was part of a donation made by the king on behalf of the soul of his recently dead sister, the Empress Isabella, wife of the Holy Roman Emperor Frederick II. A gift of this size was intended as a diplomatic gesture to impress the Emperor. With this grant the nuns could have given bread and shelter to all the poor in their district and to all those who were passing through. The priory was obviously a thriving community providing a safe refuge on a well-travelled route. Four years later the nuns were permitted to build a new bridge over a nearby stream (Hodder) and the priory increased its landholding at this *"NewBrugge"* site, probably near Coworth Park and Blacknest Gate.

Gradually the priory acquired land and influence further afield. By 1269 Broomhall held the advowson of the church at Aldworth, Berkshire, and the use of all the lands belonging to that church (S.J.C.). Royal benevolence towards the priory continued into the reign of King Edward I, 1272-1307, who confirmed their rights over Aldworth in 1308. Between 1270 and 1294 there were at least nine royal writs all confirming the rights and possessions of Broomhall (S.J.C., D 14).

In 1281 the bishop of Salisbury agreed to the accession of the new abbess, Margery Wycombe, chosen by Queen Eleanor who had the right to make the appointment (S.J.C.). Two years later Abbess Margery was given the right to enclose the hundred acres of priory waste since it was now under cultivation. The nuns were instructed to enclose it with a ditch and a fence low enough for the deer to be able to enter and leave. This must have left them with the sort of problem very familiar to the present inhabitants of Cheapside.

By the end of the thirteenth century the priory was flourishing. A tiny bronze figure with traces of gilt and enamel was found in a field near Broomhall farm by Arthur Dance. It may give some indication of the precious objects possessed by the priory. It is the figure of a saint and has become detached from a casket of the type made at Limoges in the early thirteenth century. The figure would have been set against a highly coloured enamelled background. One of these caskets may be seen in the British Museum. How this little figure came to be detached from its casket and buried we shall never know, but its existence so close to the site of the priory suggests that it may have belonged to St Margaret's and that the priory was rich enough to possess such luxury items.

Documents in the archive of St John's College reinforce the theory that Broomhall was a prosperous priory. Various indentures record both gifts to the priory and leases by the abbess and the sisters to local men who farmed the priory land in Sunninghill, Chertsey and Coworth (S.J.C., D 14). In about 1250 the abbess was given land in Egham by Gilbert de la Barre of Chertsey and this grant was confirmed to the Abbess Agnes in 1271. Ten years later Agnes also received lands on behalf of the priory from Richard de Thorpe and Robert de Scotho of Chertsey (Turner). A charter of 1256 confirmed a lease to one Pentecost of Farnham for a yearly rental of thirty shillings. This was witnessed by several local men including Richard, son of Hugh West of Sunninghill and his son, another Richard along with Richard Batayle and Henry of the Mill (Turner). This is one of the earliest documents to give names for local residents.

In 1285 Henry de Lacy, earl of Lincoln, and his wife granted the nuns a further hundred acres of waste in *"Asserigge in the Parish of Wokingham lying along the highway between Bracknell and Reading"*, today's Ashridge (this property was sold by St John's College before 1814). The priory thus built up a large landholding including lands in Sunninghill and Winkfield, Chobham, Hurley and Bagshot (S.J.C., D 14).

Up to the sixteenth century the nuns appointed the priests to St Michael's Church. Clement Debenham is the first priest whose name we still know. He served from 1297 to 1316. Some of the early priests were local men such as Simon of Tappelewe (Taplow) who held the living from 1338 to 1348, and others came from further afield such as John Peckere of Swindon who followed Simon (see Appendix Three). The priests probably lived at a house near the church and served as chaplains and confessors at the priory.

From later maps and from the Cookham manorial records (see later) it is possible to build up a vague picture of the settlement around the medieval church. St Michael's stood in the centre of a piece of glebe land given to the church from the royal forest. Since the land was an assart, i.e. enclosed from the royal waste, a quit-rent was due annually. This land included the original Church Green. Beside the church there was the priest's house and some cottages for the labourers who worked the glebe land. Cart tracks went past the church towards the farming land where Silwood Park is today and other tracks led from the church to the priory and to the mill.

The abbess who was contemporary with Clement Debenham was Isabella of Sunninghill, 1295-1310. By the early fourteenth century the priory was important and valuable enough to be involved in political arguments between the king, the bishop of Salisbury and the abbot of Chertsey, all of whom had an interest in it. After the resignation of Isabella, Maud of Broughton was elected and appointed by the king but she was forced to yield her place to Clarisa de Cotes after an intervention by the bishop. The priory recovered from this crisis and continued to expand. In 1327 the Abbess Brummhilda de Bokham held a manorial court at Windlesham indicating that Windlesham was under their control.

From the middle of the fourteenth century the fortunes of the priory began to decline. They may have been hard hit by the Black Death, very likely to affect a priory sheltering travellers from London. There are some signs of economic problems at this time. In the late fourteenth century the nuns granted away two houses and ninety acres in *"Potnall"* (or *"Portnall"*) to John Raynold and John Batelmewe of Egham and in 1372 they had to give up some of their lands to Chertsey Abbey. The economic decline was accompanied by scandal. In 1404/5 the Abbess Juliana *"alias Dunne"* had to resign because of her *"evil life"* (Cooper King).

However the decline of the priory should not be exaggerated. One of the very few surviving seals of the priory was attached to a document of 1392. The seal shows St Margaret crowned and standing on the dragon thrusting a spear into its mouth. Two heads, which may represent the nuns, are turned towards her. This sealed a promise by the Abbess Eleanor of *"Bromhall nunnery"* to pay an annual rent of three shillings and four pence to the dean and chapter of Lincoln on account of their possession of the church of North Stoke in Oxfordshire (P.R.O., A.S. 401). The priory was still leasing out land in the late fifteenth century (S.J.C., D 16). It is however no coincidence that the decline of the priory of Broomhall was matched by the emergence in the area of more important pieces of secular property. These were Sunninghill Park and Sunninghill Manor.

Sunninghill Park

The fact that there was no mention of Sunninghill in the Domesday Book and there is no evidence of an early manor or village supports the idea that the first church may have been in a wild pagan place. The population in the Thames valley dropped during and after the Saxon settlement and those who survived or who settled here would have lived an isolated woodland life cultivating a few fields. From the tenth century the Saxon kings used all these heathy lands south of the Thames as a hunting forest. Sunninghill lay well within this royal hunting ground close to the Saxon palace at Old Windsor, visited regularly by the court from the seventh to the eleventh centuries. Some have suggested that St Michael's Church was in fact a chapel in the forest used by the court as a place of refuge and as a landmark.

The royal hunting area was known as *"the forest"* meaning *"the land outside"* from the Latin *"foris"*, i.e. land outside fences and enclosures. By the Norman forest laws, all game and especially the deer, red, roe and fallow, belonged to the crown. Everywhere in the royal forest, stags, harts, boars and hares could only be killed by royal permission. All these animals were reserved for the *"delight of kings"*.

At the time of the Domesday Book William Fitzother was the Warden of Windsor Forest. He was a local landowner and the Constable of the new Norman castle on Clewer hill. The wardenship of the forest and the governorship of the castle were combined into a senior court appointment. The seal of the office was a castle and a stag's head. It remained customary for these two offices to be vested in one person right up to 1813 (Roberts, p. 9). The duty of the Warden was to preserve the vert (the greenery) and the venison which fed upon it.

Windsor Forest was divided into a series of bailiwicks and each of these was an administrative and judicial district of the forest under a bailiff. Our corner of the Forest was covered by the bailiwicks of Fynes, Finchampstead and Battles. Battles included Sunninghill, Winkfield and Binfield. Richard de Battaille (or Battaye) was the chief forester of Windsor around 1266 and our bailiwick was probably named after him. The Battles aisle at Winkfield Church and the Battles field near St Michael's also derived their names from him or from his bailiwick.

Each bailiwick was subdivided into walks and these were managed by a keeper or under-keeper. The keepers had to report any wrongdoing to the bailiff at the forest court which supervised the administration of all the forest rights and levies such as the payments for pannage and assarts. Small timber, peat for fuel and branches, acorns and mast for animals might be taken from the forest, but only with royal consent. Parts of the forest might be enclosed for farming, but again only with royal permission. This was the right of assart and purpresture. Quit-rents had to be paid on these assarted lands. At the bailiwick court in 1266/7 Richard de Bataille's son was permitted to make a ten-acre assart at Sunninghill. He had to pay a quit-rent for the privilege.

The whole forest was guarded and protected by the royal foresters who policed their designated areas. In the late thirteenth century Richard de Battaille granted John de Sunninghill a quittance (i.e. a pardon) for the offence that his dogs had been found in the forest (Hughes, p. 109). Many men were employed to maintain the forest and its deer. As was the custom, some of these men became known by their occupation. In 1376 a Sunninghill estate was transferred to Wills le Venour. Venour and venery meant dealing with deer. Some of the earliest residents of Sunninghill would have come here as foresters and huntsmen.

In addition to controlling the whole vast hunting ground, the kings enclosed or *"emparked"* parts of the forest to improve their access to the game, hence Windsor Great Park and later Sunninghill Park. The earliest Parks in Windsor Forest were created in 1130 and more were made in the thirteenth and fourteenth centuries. Sunninghill Park was one of the latest. It was created during the tenure of Sir Simon de Burley who was the Chief Forester of Windsor Forest in 1377. The fourteenth century Park was basically the same as that shown on the 1607 Norden map (see page 39). Its boundary on the south-east ran along what is now Watersplash Lane.

The south-west of Sunninghill Park was in Sunninghill parish, the larger north-east section across the Stream was in the parish of Winkfield. Thus the Park lay astride two administrative areas but was independent of them because it was directly administered by the crown. Sunninghill Park was also independent of Cookham Manor (see later). However the lord of Cookham and the bailiff of Sunninghill Park might well be the same, as with Sir John and Sir William Norris in the fifteenth century.

All deer parks followed a similar pattern. A large, usually circular, space was surrounded by a ditch and a paling fence. Within the park there would be a lodge for the parker or keeper and a series of fishponds. The fishponds were needed for the long periods when meat could not be eaten for religious reasons. Holly was planted as winter fodder for the deer. The Park was the main focus of royal interest in Sunninghill providing as it did both food and entertainment for the royal household. Of course the crown still had the right to all deer outside the Park as well.

Fourteenth and fifteenth century kings would visit the lodge in Sunninghill Park while out hunting but they were not likely to stay there. In addition to Windsor Castle they already had another major residence in this part of the forest. This had been built between 1244 to 1246 and was known as the Windsor Manor. It stood between two streams on the north side of today's Virginia Water. Its construction had cost £1,100, a huge amount at the time, and it was a very fine house indeed, with glass windows, a great hall, a chapel and royal chambers decorated with wall paintings. This mansion was surrounded by a moat and a small deer-park (Colvin).

Windsor Manor was often used by the kings and their courts. Important alterations and extensions were made there between 1394 and 1396 under the orders of King Richard II. Seven new fireplaces were needed, five chambers were painted and a new chapel, gatehouse and drawbridge were added. It was visited by Henry IV in 1406 and continued in extensive use to the end of the reign of Henry VI. The house was less used by the Yorkist and Tudor kings but it must have been maintained because it was still in occasional use in the seventeenth century (it was marked on Norden's map of the forest). Certainly the most important royal residence in our part of the forest, this was where the king stayed when hunting nearby.

The bailiffs who managed Windsor Forest including Sunninghill Park were generally substantial local men with lands in the region (see Appendix One). In 1447 Sir William Perkins was the bailiff of Sunninghill Park and after his death Sir John Norris of Yattenden and Ockwells took over. Beneath these men were the parkers or keepers who actually lived in the Sunninghill Park. These men were usually chosen from among the royal servants. At the end of the fourteenth century, the Sunninghill parker, who was also the riding forester of Battles Walk, lived in a lodge, near the site of the present Lower Farm. In 1484 the last Yorkist king, Richard III, appointed William Bolton a *"yeoman of the crown"* as *"the parker of Sunninghill and the riding forester of Windsor forest"*, his salary was to be paid out of the revenue of Windsor Castle. A year later William Stafferton was made keeper of both Sunninghill Park and Swinley Rides (C.P.R., Richard III).

After the Tudor king had defeated and killed Richard III at Bosworth in 1485, *"our rebelle William Stafferton"* was removed and replaced by Henry Jewet, one of the new king's servants. He was appointed on the same terms with wages of three pence a day as forester and four pence a day as parker. It was he who gave his name to *"Jewitt's Lodge"* which was enlarged and repaired in 1535 when Thomas Ward was the controller of the accounts. Jewet himself was replaced in 1498 by John Basket, another royal servant, who held the office until his death in 1503 when Richard Weston took over (C.P.R., Henry VII).

During Henry VII's and Henry VIII's reigns, from 1485 to 1547, Jewitt's Lodge and other lodges and houses in the Windsor parks were repaired, rebuilt and replaced. The Crown Exchequer paid out £300 to renew the Sunninghill Park rails or fences and to build a new mansion in Sunninghill Park to the north of the old lodge. This was the forerunner of today's Sunninghill Park house. The new house lay on the hill, very close to the parish boundary between Sunninghill and Winkfield. It is possible that the ornamental grounds were also developed then. There was an avenue of limes, more fishponds and a fountain, hence *"Fountain Close"* which was marked on the earlier maps.

In 1499 Prince Arthur, (1486-1502), wrote from *"the manor of Sunninghill"* to All Souls College at Oxford to support an applicant for whom his mother wanted an appointment (archive of All Souls, CTM. 302, no. 15; see Appendix Four). Some local historians (including Hughes) have suggested that this letter was written from the manor of Sunninghill, i.e. Silwood Park today. This is most unlikely since Sunninghill Manor was then a series of undistinguished working farms sub-tenanted under the Norris family. Kings and princes did not stay with sub-tenants. As far as the crown was concerned Sunninghill Manor was merely an administrative district within the Manor of Cookham. An alternative could be the old royal Windsor Manor. Henry VI had signed several charters and letters from *"our old manor at Windsor"*, but it seems unlikely that Prince Arthur or his secretary would call this Sunninghill Manor by mistake.

Prince Arthur was the heir of King Henry VII, the elder brother of King Henry VIII, and he died in 1502. The *"manor of Sunninghill"* was mentioned in the last line and the letter was headed *"By the Prince"*. It is more than likely that this letter was sent from Sunninghill Park. The presence of a prince at the Sunninghill Park house would also explain why there was so much expensive development in the Park at this time.

Ten years later, Henry VIII, who became heir after the death of his brother Arthur, also wrote from what he called *"Sunninghill Manor"*. It was one of the first letters of his reign written on the first of August, the day after his father's death. Like all kings, Henry regularly combined business and pleasure. In 1542 the king held a council meeting at Sunninghill, also presumably at the Sunninghill Park house.

Henry VIII especially enjoyed hunting. By the 1530s he had a pack of buckhounds which were specifically associated with the Windsor hunt. From the reign of King Edward II to that of Queen Elizabeth I, the Brocas family provided the hereditary Masters of the Royal Buckhounds (Hughes, p. 35). Sir Bernard Brocas had a chantry in Clewer Church. Ascot Heath became one of the meeting places for the buckhound pack.

From the 1540s to 1619, the Nevilles were bailiffs of Sunninghill Park. From time to time they were in residence at the Park House and some of the Neville children's births and burials are recorded in the Sunninghill parish registers. Sir Henry Neville I, who died in 1593, was a gentleman of the chamber to both Henry VIII and to his son Edward VI. During Queen Mary's reign he lost his estates and offices because, as a fervent supporter of the reformed religion, he had supported the succession of Lady Jane Grey. When Mary restored Catholicism, Sir Henry thought it wiser to leave the country and he was at Padua between 1554 and 1556. In his absence his property was granted to the bishop of Winchester but his lands and offices were restored by Queen Elizabeth and he was reinstated as forester of the bailiwicks of Battles and Fiennes and as keeper of Sunninghill Park. Sir Henry worked closely with the queen's favourite, Robert Dudley, earl of Leicester, who was the Constable of Windsor Castle, the Keeper of Windsor Forest and the Master of the Buckhounds.

Sir Henry was in high favour throughout Elizabeth's reign. He held property all over the country, in Kent, Yorkshire and Wiltshire with a large holding in Berkshire including Waltham St Lawrence, Warfield and Wargrave. There are frequent references to his presence in the locality. In 1560 he requested permission to use timber from the Windsor Forest to repair his stables at Sunninghill Park. Four years later his infant son Richard was buried at St. Michael's and a year later another son Alexander was also buried (B.R.O., D/P 126 1/1). It does seem that he and his family made regular and lengthy visits to the Sunninghill Park House.

Sir Henry Neville II, 1564-1614, was a protégé of Elizabeth's chief advisor, Lord Burghley. He succeeded his father in 1593 and was appointed Master of Game, Bailiff of Sunninghill Park and Mote Park and Riding Forester of Battles Walk. Elizabeth wrote to him in January 1599 giving him orders to ensure the protection of the game and deer in Sunninghill Park during his absence as ambassador in France. By 1601 he was back at the Park House. Towards the end of Elizabeth's reign, Sir Henry was foolish enough to become involved with the rebellion of the earl of Essex. As a result he lost all his offices, was fined heavily, £5,000 was no small sum, and he spent some time in the Tower. He was restored to his offices and titles on the succession of King James I, but was still short of money when he died.

Sunninghill Manor

The development of Cheapside is closely associated with both Sunninghill Park and the manor of Sunninghill. The latter has evolved from a working manor in Tudor and Stuart times into a gentleman's park in the eighteenth century and finally into the Field Station of Imperial College today. In the course of its long history its boundaries and limits have changed but the core of the manorial lands have remained within the circle formed by today's Cheapside Road, Buckhurst Road and the London Road. Cheapside first emerges into written history as part of the Sunninghill Manor.

In Norman times St Michael's Church, Broomhall Priory and the administration for the Royal Forest were all in existence but there is no evidence for a manor here until the fourteenth century. Those who lived here were on scattered, isolated holdings within the royal forest. Their homes were made of the timber, which was plentiful, with mud and thatch, all perishable materials leaving little trace. Indeed as late as the eighteenth century only the largest houses were in brick. So we have little surviving material evidence of the earliest buildings here.

There is however written evidence that there were people living here. The earliest reference to a transfer of property at Sunninghill, written as "*Sunigehill*", dates from 1183. A few years later in 1197, lands in "*Sunninghull*" were granted to Gilbert, son of Blackman, by William de Cumba (Hughes, p. 107). Neither of these were men of any great substance. It was probably because there was no local family of any importance that King John gave the advowson of St Michael's to the priory of Broomhall.

A generation later, in 1220, John de "*Suningehulle*" witnessed a grant to St George's Chapel at Windsor (St George's Chapel Archive). He or his namesake had died by 1246 when "*Ricardo de Pesemer*" was entitled to inherit his lands. In 1252 Robert of

26

Sunninghill was a royal huntsman expected to provide venison for the feast of the Ascension. It is quite likely that the earliest owners of the property which became Sunninghill Manor were royal gamekeepers and huntsmen (C.C.R., Henry III and Edward II).

By 1296 all of Sunninghill, which was not in the hands of Broomhall Priory or Sunninghill Park, was administered by Cookham Manor, an administrative grouping succeeding the Cookham hundred and created by the royal exchequer. It gathered together all the smaller hamlets in this part of the royal forest. The royal manor of Cookham eventually included Cookham Town, Woodside, Maidenhead Town, North Town, Binfield, Woodwards and Sunninghill.

Winkfield was not included in the same hundred or in the same manor as Sunninghill. It was in the Ripplesmere hundred and both Winkfield and Ascot were dependent on the royal manor of Follyjohn. In Cheapside the boundary between the Winkfield and Sunninghill parishes and between Ripplesmere and Cookham hundreds was the Stream that crosses Watersplash Lane and Buckhurst Road (V.C.H., I, p.327, II, p.117). This ancient division has survived up to the present day and is now the boundary between the Royal Borough of Windsor and Maidenhead and the Borough of Bracknell Forest.

The crown either kept the income from Cookham Manor or endowed other members of the royal family with the property. Cookham was part of the dower of several queens including Isabella, the wife of Edward II, 1307-1327, and Philippa, wife of Edward III, 1327-1377. In 1399 it was settled on Humphrey, duke of Gloucester, the brother of Henry V and the founder of the great library which is now the core of the Bodleian at Oxford. He owned Cookham up to his death in 1447 and Sunninghill is often mentioned in the lists of his endowments.

The individual manors on the Cookham estate were sub-tenanted and the tenants could transfer them to others and pass them to their heirs with royal permission. Sunninghill was named in a few charters recording land transfers and in wills such as that of 1326/7 when John Podenhale of London is recorded as having land in Coworth and Sunninghill. Podenhale is marked on old maps near Shrubs Hill. Potnol Park near Virginia Water takes its name from this estate.

The first reference to Sunninghill as a property with a *"messuage"*, that is a substantial house as opposed to a mere cottage, appears in 1362/3 (C.F.R., Edward III). The manor then owned twenty acres of wood and one carucate of land, some under the plough and some waste, in all about 120 acres. A carucate was originally the amount of land that eight oxen could plough each year but by the fourteenth century it was merely a unit of taxation. The manor was in the hands of John de Sunninghill and Joanna his wife and they had bought it from John Holm. Holm's Close was still known four hundred years later according to Hughes. In the 1362/3 charter Sunninghill was listed as part of the Cookham Manor and it owed £20 rent per year to the king. By this date then, there was a main house, farmland and some cottages. The land of the manor was bounded on the south by the Broomhall Priory lands and on all other sides by the Royal Forest and Sunninghill Park. St Michael's Church, the priest's house and the land around them belonged to the priory so the main house on the manor naturally developed some distance away.

In 1372, William Derenford of Coworth and Joanna his wife transferred lands in Coworth and Sunninghill (C.F.R., Edward II and III). Dornford, deriving from Derenford, was the old name for the ford at Blacknest Gate (also called Blackness Beeches). Derenford was later listed as a lord of Sunninghill Manor (see Appendix One). In 1410, John Wantele was listed as lord of Sunninghill in the Cookham manorial court rolls. By 1438 Thomas Haseley, a tenant under Humphrey duke of Gloucester, had left Sunninghill Manor to his trustees (C.F.R., Henry VI). He had had a large landholding with possessions scattered across England and in the city of London.

The chief value of the Sunninghill lands lay in its venison and timber. Throughout the fifteenth century the timber was taken by the crown for the building at Windsor Castle. Oak from Sunninghill was used to build the first St George's Chapel (which was remodelled in Victorian times as the Albert Chapel), the Knights' Houses (in the lower bailey on the south side of the chapel), and Eton College (Tighe and Davis, vol. I, pp. 338, 375). In 1475/6 Sunninghill Manor provided more timber for the glorious new St George's Chapel, built by King Edward IV (V.C.H., pp. 374-5). Local stone from Cranbourne Chase was also used. All this felling, quarrying and carting would have employed labourers from the manor of Sunninghill.

The manor was also expected to pay its share towards the building and maintenance of the crown property at Windsor. In 1422 a charge of a hundred marks was taken from the income of the manor of Cookham to pay for repairs and rebuilding at the castle. Five years later Sunninghill Manor together with the manors of Bray and Binfield had to contribute to another levy and again in 1454 there was another similar charge (C.C.R., Henry V and VI).

In 1447 after the death of Duke Humphrey, the manors of Cookham, Bray "*Benyfield and Sondynghill*" were committed to Sir John Norris and Sir Edward Grimston to hold for seven years (C.F.R., Henry V1). Duke Humphrey's death was part of a national political crisis and there followed a period of great weakness for the Lancastrian monarchy. King Henry VI suffered bouts of insanity and his wife Margaret of Anjou who expected to act as regent was challenged by the Yorkists led by Richard, duke of York. This led to the period of history known as the Wars of the Roses. The political instability was compounded by the loss of the lands the English Crown had held in France and a coincident period of inflation that lasted throughout the second half of the fifteenth century. As a result of all the political struggles, crown lands changed hands frequently.

In 1448/9, Henry VI confirmed the transfer of Thomas Haseley's holdings including those in Sunninghill, Winkfield, Ascot, Old and New Windsor to a group of trustees including the Archbishop of York (C.P.R., 1449). They were then reallocated to a group of knights who had both local interests and court favour: Sir Edmund Hungerford, Sir John Norris (or Norrys) of Yattendon, his son William, his brother Roger Norris and Thomas Bakham.

Later all the income from the local lands of the late Humphrey duke of Gloucester was designated by the young Yorkist King Edward IV for the support of his Queen, Elizabeth Woodville. This grant lapsed under King Richard III but was renewed by King Henry VII and later this income was transferred to his queen, who was Elizabeth Woodville's daughter, Elizabeth of York.

Sir John Norris secured a charter confirming his rights over the manor of Sunninghill and he was still holding it when he died in 1466 (B.R.O., D/E Fa L1). The Norris family had extensive property in the county of Berkshire. Throughout the later fifteenth century and for much of the sixteenth century they dominated the county as sheriffs and major landowners with influence at court. Sir William Norris (1433-1506) had been knighted in 1460 and, during the reign of King Edward IV, he succeeded his father Sir John (1405-1466) as the steward of the manors of Cookham and Bray and as keeper of the royal manor of Follyjohn. His most splendid local property was at Ockwells near Maidenhead where the magnificent glass windows placed in the hall to commemorate the marriage of King Henry VI and Margaret of Anjou in 1445 can still be admired.

Sir William supported the Buckingham rising against King Richard III but escaped serious punishment and recovered his lands under King Henry VII. Like his father, Sir William was also the bailiff of Sunninghill Park. In 1501 one of his sons Sir Edward Norris held the stewardship of Windsor Forest. Sir Edward's son, Henry, was less fortunate. He became a close friend of King Henry VIII and was part of the glittering court around Queen Anne Boleyn with whom he was accused of adultery. He was beheaded in 1536.

His son another Henry, born in 1525, had his main residence in Berkshire at Wytham. He was regarded with favour by Queen Elizabeth who restored all the property that had been lost when his father was found guilty of treason. This included his stewardship of Cookham and Sunninghill Manor. He died in 1601 and was buried in the church of St Michael and All the Angels at Rycote. He and his wife have a very elaborate memorial in Westminster Abbey surrounded by the stone effigies of their *"warlike sons"*.

In the sixteenth century some of the local Sunninghill families began to emerge into prominence. The Lanes prospered due to their connection with the Norris family. George Lane of Coworth, whose family had been there for over 200 years (Hodder), had served under Sir John Norris (one of Sir Henry's warlike sons) in Ireland when Sir John had been Lord President of Munster.

George Lane's son, Henry, married Ann, one of Sir John Norris's daughters and in 1567 he bought Sunninghill Manor from Sir Henry Norris. Four years later a son of Henry Lane and Ann Norris was baptised at St Michael's Church (B.R.O., D/P 126 1/1).

The Lanes held the manor for fifteen years and then sold it to William Day, Provost of Eton, for £210. A year later William Day also bought Ockwells from the Norris family and shortly afterwards he became bishop of Winchester. A copy of the indenture of the Lane/Day sale is preserved in the archive of Imperial College. Dated the 1st August 1582 it provides us with our first full description of our manor:

"all that manor of Sunninghill late parcel and inheritance or possessions of the right honourable Henry Lord Norreys and all and singular lands

tenements and hereditaments in Sunninghill and Winkfield known by the name of Eastmore and Assarts". *"Eastmore"* the old manor house is here named for the first time. *"Assarts"* were pieces of land taken in from the forest or waste.

The manor's copyhold or customary lands, which were the lands held by a written copy or charter or by established custom with the right of inheritance, were listed as:

"four acres in a certain field there called Crofte also Le Crofte now in the occupation of John Slann". The Croft was land near today's Cannon Inn crossroads.

"one acre in the same field in the tenure of Richard Hodd"

"And all the close of land called Middlewell five acres in the tenure of Robert May" (a close is an enclosed field)

"And all three closes of land called Eastmore six acres now in the tenure of Henry Slann, a brook passes through the said Eastmore and is the stream which drives the mill now in the tenure of Robert May". The lands of Eastmore were sited along the Brook on the south side of Cheapside Road and Robert May's mill was where today's Mill House stands in Mill Lane.

"And all that close called Meade plotte three acres now in the tenure of Lawrence Slann"

"And all those two acres called Heyworth now in the tenure of Thomas Milton".

This made twenty-one acres in all.

In addition the manor owned land which was rented out on a yearly basis as follows:

5s 6d from *"one messuage ten acres of land and one close of meadows and woods three acres in the tenure of John Smith"*

9s 5d from *"two closes of land called Bleknest containing nine acres"* and *"that close called Haddbrooke five acres in the tenure of Robert May"*

5d from *"two closes of pasture in the parish of Winkfield six acres in the tenure of Henry Sawyer the younger"*

20d from *"one acre of arable land in Winkfield called Mylfield in tenure of Alice Newnham widow"*

4d from *"six acres of arable land in Winkfield in the tenure of John Lybord"*. The Winkfield land was across the stream in what became known as Bucket Hill, in today's Buckhurst Park or near the Mill House.

10d from *"one close of arable land one and a half acres in the tenure of Henry Milton"*

3s 6d from *"a messuage and eight acres in the tenure of Robert Gill and Margaret, his wife"*

4s from *"one tenement, one cottage and eight acres called Roves in the tenure of Robert Gill"*. A tenement was larger than a cottage and smaller than a messuage.

3½d from one and a half acres *"of arable land in a field called Lycrofte in the tenure of Richard Slann"*

9s 4d from *"one messuage and lands in the tenure of George Woodward Esquire"*.

This made fifty-nine acres used for arable and pasture bringing in a rent of thirty-five shillings and three and a half pence. The total area of the listed manorial lands was eighty acres.

Here then is the earliest existing description of the manor of Sunninghill. There are only four named houses including Eastmore, one tenement and one cottage. The water mill which becomes such a prominent feature and landmark already exists and is owned by the Mays. It was known as the Lord's Mill or the King's Mill. Of the families mentioned we shall meet the Mays, the Slanns (or Slaans), the Smiths and the Miltons in the following centuries. It is also already clear that the lands of the manor included parts in the parish of Sunninghill and parts in the parish of Winkfield.

Sunninghill Manor was not a prosperous manor. In another late sixteenth century document concerning the quit-rents due to Cookham for assarts, there are only five enclosures on Sunninghill Manor (B.R.O., D Esk m1-178). This is far less than in any other part of the Cookham administration. Those who had taken in land from the waste included Francis Broughton and Henry Sawyer. The latter was named in the Lane/Day sale document of 1582. Francis Broughton is also named on the Nicholson survey of 1613. Moreover in a list of marketable goods which were produced within the manor of Cookham, Sunninghill Manor is mentioned once only as producing and selling *"furze"* or gorse, hardly a profitable crop. It was clearly the poorest manor in the Cookham list at that time.

The Dissolution of Broomhall Priory

The major event here in the Tudor period was the dissolution of Broomhall Priory. This happened over a decade before the major dissolution of the monasteries that resulted from King Henry VIII's breach with Rome. The larger priory of Ankerwyck was not closed until this dissolution in 1536. The excuse for shutting down Broomhall was that there were only four nuns and the prioress left. Its closure was to the advantage of Sir John Fisher, bishop of Rochester but it was the work of the chancellor, Cardinal Wolsey and his secretary Thomas Cromwell. They were trying to increase royal income by acquiring the lands and possessions of the smaller religious houses.

Sir John Fisher was the chaplain, advisor, biographer and executor of Margaret Beaufort, the mother of Henry VII and the grandmother of Henry VIII. In 1511, two years after Margaret Beaufort's death, her executors secured a charter for the foundation of St John's College at Cambridge. Bishop Fisher began searching for suitable land with which the college could be endowed. Broomhall was probably brought to his attention by Wolsey though he may have known the priory from his visits to Margaret Beaufort's palace at Woking. Fisher accepted the closure of the smaller religious houses but he did not assent to the wholesale dissolution of the monasteries. This only began in full force after his death. Sir John was executed in 1535 because he refused to take the Oath of Succession, which set aside Mary as heir in favour of Elizabeth and asserted the independence of the church in England from Rome.

In 1520 the bishop of Salisbury was instructed to close Broomhall Priory. Johanna Rawlins, abbess since 1511, was offered twenty nobles as a golden goodbye and the remaining nuns were to be moved to other religious houses. They seem to have been very reluctant to go and Richard Archpriest, a lawyer appointed by the bishop, tried to hurry them along. Nicolas Metcalf, the first master of St John's College, also took a keen interest in the matter. When sweet words did not suffice, harsh threats and slanders followed and there is a reference to the nuns being removed *"for such enormities as by them practised"* (Turner). They finally left the priory in 1524. Johanna Rawlins was granted a pension of £5 a year. She acknowledged the payment of half her pension: *"50 shillings of good and lawful money of England for half a year"* but she does not seem to have been paid the rest. Her nuns were given some articles from the priory and resettled in other convents (S.J.C., D 13). Richard Archpriest wrote that *"with great adoe the nuns are got from Broomhall"* (Turner).

The closure was confirmed by a papal bull of 1524. All the 566 acres of Broomhall Priory, together with its rights over the churches at Sunninghill and Aldworth, its forest rights and all its houses and manors reverted to the crown. About the same time another priory was closed down at Lilliechurch in Kent. This was close to Bishop Fisher's own see at Rochester. The property of both these priories was sold to Fisher for £300 and four years later all the possessions and advowsons belonging to both the priories were granted to St John's College.

As a result of these transactions St John's College owned and still owns extensive property in the district. They were soon to be seen making use of their endowments. In 1579 they leased a piece of their land to Michael Slade. It was *"a tenement and a piece of land abutting on ferme field"* (i.e. the field belonging to the manor farm) *"on the north side and on the churchyard on the south side and upon a little lane over against the church on the west"*. This was the land around today's Cedars. It was then leased out for twenty years at a rent of ten shillings a year (S.J.C.).

St John's College became responsible for the appointment of the priest and for the maintenance of the church. Their first appointee in 1535 was the Reverend Joseph Gates but he was deprived of his living before 1557, during the reign of Queen Mary I, because he had married. Thomas Ranard was made vicar in his place. Although he was appointed under Mary and was chosen to restore the Catholic practices and liturgy he survived up to 1564. In that year Robert Sherrington was appointed vicar and he was followed by Maurice Serill (or Sorrill) who was vicar up to 1594. Towards the end of Queen Elizabeth' reign, in 1594, John Robinson became vicar. This heralded a lengthy period of stability since he remained vicar up to 1626 and was followed by his son, another John Robinson who served throughout the civil war right up to 1654.

The Reformation was a difficult period for St Michael's church as can be seen by the removal of the Reverend Joseph Gates. Even before this, towards the end of the reign of King Edward VI, when the Puritans were powerful at court, commissioners were sent out to confiscate all church plate and other *"frivolous and Popish"* valuables. The Crown Commissioners arrived in Berkshire in 1553 and were very active here for a couple of years. They had been ordered to ensure that all the churches complied with the new reformed religion and to remove any unsuitable items. The list made by the commissioners registering their confiscations at St Michael's included:

"a chalice of silver worth 40 shillings,
three bells,
a cope of red damask,
two vestments of satin,
two altar cloths,
one towel,

a draper towel,
a sepulchre of timber" i.e. a model of Christ in the tomb for
Easter display
"two brass candlesticks and two cruets" (B.R.O., D/P 126 1/1)
The valuables were taken away, the wooden sepulchre was broken
up, the painted walls were whitewashed and all the decorations
had to be removed. This was the most dramatic and destructive
change at St Michael's until the later rebuilding swept the original
church away altogether.

During Tudor times the administrative responsibilities of the
vicar and the parish began to grow rapidly. By an Act of
Parliament of 1538 each parish was responsible for keeping a
register of baptisms, marriages and funerals. The earliest surviving
records of St Michael's Parish date from 1561 and are now in the
Berkshire Record Office (B.R.O., D/P 126). Further legislation,
passed between 1597 and 1601 and popularly known as the Poor
Law Acts, made each parish responsible for looking after their
own poor. The administration of this law was a duty of the parish
up to 1834. A vestry committee was appointed with overseers and
other officials whose duty it was to levy and administer the poor
rate charged on all the landowners. As a result of this legislation
there was increased documentation and from this time onwards
we are able to learn more about the villagers of Sunninghill.

Another Tudor change still visible in Cheapside was the
planting of the Tudor oaks. The 1580s saw the first known
deliberate plantations here. Lord Burghley, Elizabeth's chief
minister, was lord of the manor of Ascot. He ordered the
enclosure of thirteen acres at Cranbourne to be used for oak
planting and his example was followed by other local landowners.
At least two oaks of this age have survived in Cheapside, one in
the grounds of Silwood Park and the other in the garden of
Heronsbrook Cottage. These trees were intended to provide
materials for building ships.

Apart from these oak plantations there was little visible change
in the landscape during the Tudor period. There was some
economic growth and more land was taken in from the waste.
This development is recorded in the surveys made early in the
seventeenth century.

By the end of the reign of Queen Elizabeth I, Sunninghill was
an area of scattered hamlets and Cheapside was one of these.
Others lay around the church, between the church and the mill,
around today's Upper Village Road in Sunninghill and around
today's Wells Lane. Administratively speaking there were three

powers here: Cookham Manor, Sunninghill Park directly owned by the crown, and St John's College. Cheapside would develop on the cusp of these administrations, a small pebble between the two great millstones of Sunninghill Manor and Sunninghill Park.

The First Cheapside

The first written record of Cheapside appears in a list of rents due to the manor of *"Sonyngehill"* on Ladyday 1584 in the Cookham Manor papers (B.R.O., D/E fa Li.) Some of these Cookham documents are duplicated in the Imperial College Archive, copied when John Pitt was contesting the rights of Cookham Manor over Sunninghill in the eighteenth century. The large collection at the Berkshire Record Office is in a very poor state. Only one scholar has tackled these papers. This was the late John Brooks who worked on the documents for many years but unfortunately he did not cover Sunninghill and a great deal of time and skill would be needed to research them thoroughly.

The 1584 rental referred to Eastmore as the main house on the manor, and named properties at Silmore, Darnford (Blacknest) and Buckhurst Hill. John Aldridge is mentioned as having land on the manor. His family will feature largely in the following two centuries.

Phillip Farrant was in occupation of Eastmore and its lands, presumably as a subtenant of William Day. Farrant had other property in Sunninghill. In 1586 he sold the leasehold of twenty acres to John Myller of Binfield for £50 (J.E.). Farrant must have retained the freehold since he transferred all or part of the plot called *"Long Deane"* to Richard Wapshott in 1617. In the land transfer of 1586 two of the arable fields were called *"Stoney Close"* and *"Broomfield Close"*. There was also a meadow called *"New Meade"* and another field called *"Shepperde Close"*. These fields were located as lying east of the *"Heathe Moors"*, south and west of other lands belonging to Phillip Farrant (i.e. Eastmore), and north of *"Leecroft"* which belonged to John Slann. This was named as *"Lycrofte"* in the 1582 Day/Lane sale indenture and belonged to Richard Slann. From this description the land in question was the old *"Healthy Hall"* estate opposite the Wells.

Cheapside was named in the 1584 document as an area *"voc. (called) Cheapside or Mill Green"* i.e. connected with a Green or Common close to the Mill. There were no named tenants nor any specific property mentioned. Nor did the document give any indication for the origin of the name Cheapside.

The name may derive either simply from being a poorer part of the manor or from *"cheape"* meaning trader or peddler. The latter is unlikely since there is no evidence for a market here, though it is possible that *"chapmen"* or peddlers would call on their way from Windsor to Bagshot or Egham. However the word *"cheape"* also meant an inn-keeper and there was certainly an old inn called *"The Tun"* on *"Cheape Green"* though this is not recorded until the end of the seventeenth century. So the origin of the name remains a mystery.

G. M. Hughes claimed that the Lammas lands of the manor were in Cheapside (Hughes, p. 116). Lammas lands were used both as arable strips and as common pasture. Animals could be pastured here between Lammas Day when the harvest was in, which was the 1st of August (the 12th of August after the calendar revision of 1752), and the spring sowing in February or March. These fields were reckoned to be about seventeen acres and this just about covers the suitable land available in Cheapside. Slight signs of the furrow-and-ridge strip system may still be traced in the gardens at the eastern end of Cheapside. Cottagers would want to live near these fields so that they could take advantage of both the arable and the common grazing.

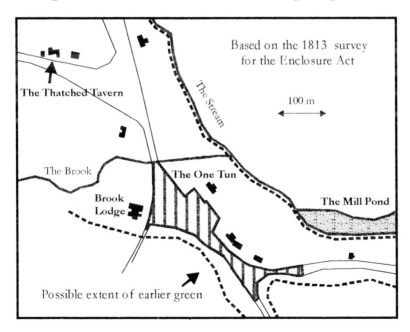

Sketch map of the Old Cheapside Green

There were probably less than a dozen families in Tudor Cheapside, and possibly a few squatters who, if permitted, would settle and obtain customary rights. Their small enclosures were predominantly rough pasture with some fields under the plough, small kitchen gardens and some copses or coppices where the timber was exploited for fuel and for building. All their fields or closes had been assarted from either the manor waste or from the royal forest.

Cheapside was identified with the *"Mill Green"*, also called the *"Lord's Green"* and *"Cheape Green"*, later *"Cheapside Green"* and *"Tun Green"*. This multi-named piece of common straggled along what is now the Buckhurst Road from the corner of Cheapside Road and along Mill Lane towards the Mill. Fragments of the ancient green remain, the large triangle at the junction of Mill Lane and Buckhurst Road, the small triangle between the Cheapside and Buckhurst Roads and the patch of land in front of Tall Pines and Culvert Cottage opposite to Tun Cottage. The rest has all been enclosed within the gardens of the adjoining houses.

Up to the middle of the fourteenth century most of the inhabitants would owe labour services to their overlord but after the Black Death, as labour became scarce, many of these services were commuted to money payments. The nuns of Broomhall, however, continued to stipulate working days as part of their tenancy agreements as late as 1494/5 (S.J.C., D 16). All the settled inhabitants had customary rights in the manor lands such as the right to graze their animals on the Lammas lands and to gather fuel from the wastelands.

As the population grew more land was taken in from the waste. Generally speaking up to the Black Death in the middle of the fourteenth century more land went under the plough and more land was assarted. After the Black Death there was less use of marginal land and less assarts. Sunninghill was relatively isolated with no major trading centres nearby so it may have escaped the worst of the plague. Cheapside included some of the best land in the manor and was probably under the plough throughout most of this period.

Sunninghill Surveyed

In the archive of Imperial College London there is a large bundle of seventeenth and eighteenth century manorial court barons, indentures of sales and leases and a few wills mostly copied out in the eighteenth century. The court barons recorded payments due to the lord of the manor and registered all transfers of copyhold land. They are generally in Latin though there are a few in English. Most of the indentures and wills are in English. The earliest entry dates from 1612 registering Matthew Day as holder of the manor with twelve tenants. Read alongside the Cookham manorial documents in the Berkshire Record Office these documents provide a clear picture of Sunninghill Manor.

One of the main reasons for the increase in documentation in the seventeenth century was the accession of King James VI of Scotland as James I of England in 1603. This shrewd king, who was already well experienced in government, ordered a scrutiny of all the crown possessions. This, of course, encompassed Windsor Forest and included an enquiry about all the assarts made with or without permission. In these documents there are more references to Cheapside itself and many references to the Sunninghill families: the Pithers, Mays, Searles, Slanns, Bakers, Miltons and Lanes.

In addition to the documents, we have the first known map of our area, made in 1607. John Norden, the Surveyor in the Royal Office of Woods and Forests, was paid £200 for his surveys and maps of the Windsor Forest and Parks.

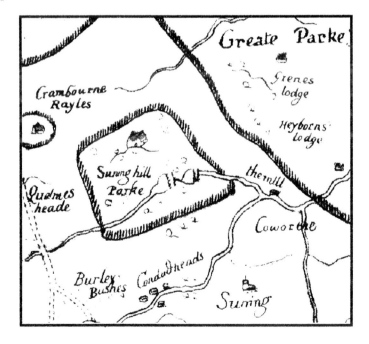

Detail of the Norden Map of 1607

Two complete copies were made, one for King James and one for his heir, Henry, Prince of Wales. They were essentially about crown property so Sunninghill Manor was neglected while Sunninghill Park was thoroughly described (copy at the Durning Library, originals at Windsor Castle Library and British Library).

According to John Norden: *"Sunning hill Parke"* possessed *"450 acres of good ground, with three and a quarter miles of pale"* (i.e. fence) and two fishponds one of which was called *"Brewers Pond"* and was sited near the *"Redditch Gate"* and the *"Redditch Wood"*. Within the park there were 260 fallow deer with 80 antlers and 30 bucks. The keeper was Sir Henry Neville. The Norden map at Windsor Castle shows the Park House as a substantial courtyard mansion with a gateway entrance in the south wing looking across to the larger fishpond or lake.

Norden marked houses close to the conduit heads near Engelmere pond. These conduits supplied water to Windsor Castle from the sixteenth century onwards. He also shows this stream flowing into the Millpond, which is not correct. Although Norden drew in the church at *"Suning"* he did not indicate any houses on the Sunninghill Manor. He was after all only surveying the royal possessions.

The most important of all the early Stuart documents was the *"Survey of Assarts Purprestures and Other Lands within the Forest of Windsor"* made in 1613 by another royal surveyor, Otho Nicholson (B.R.O., 126/28/2). This provided the first extensive review of the whole of Sunninghill.

Nicholson described a district made up of scattered holdings lying within a vast area of waste from which many assarts had been made. His *"Soninghill"* covered a total acreage of about 3,200 acres, of which almost 2,000 acres was listed as waste or uncultivated land. The enclosures were a mixture of arable, pasture, meadowlands and coppices. There were forty-six landowners including the king, St John's College and the church. The parish owned at least one cottage in Cheapside. Seven of the owners held land but had no houses or cottages here and four owners had more than two houses in their possession. Eleven cottages, two mills and twenty-seven houses were listed. From this we can guess that there were between 100 and 150 people in the whole area.

Six of the inhabitants were given the title of *"Mr"* signifying a higher status than the rest. One of these was a Mr Minburne who leased the 294 acres of Broomhall and *"Tetness"* from St John's College. There was a house at Broomhall but none at Titness.

Another was Mr Robinson the vicar, who had the vicarage with fourteen acres of glebe land and another house with a one-acre field. This was probably the site of the Church House and the Church Green.

Two other men of means were Mr Francis Broughton and Mr Robert Hodge. Broughton had twenty-one acres and a house at a place called *"Dene upon the bounds of Sunninghill"* and Hodge had fifty-four acres in several holdings, some on Eastmore Moor and Hawks Fields, some woodland with part in Winkfield and another of pasture and meadow called *"Picknest moor and Blackwater"*.

Mr Matthew Day of Eton had sixty-three acres in *"twelve closes of pasture and meadow ground and a house called Eastmore"*. Bishop William Day had passed his Sunninghill lands on to his son Matthew who would be mayor of Windsor for five terms. In 1625, Eastmore with two closes was sublet to John Leaver and by 1653 Matthew Day's wife still owned most of the property. Shortly afterwards Richard Day, who was probably one of Matthew's sons, petitioned James I to support the planting of more acorns in the forest and he reminded the king about Lord Burghley's plantation acres at Cranbourne which was by that date *"tall young oaks"*. Do we have our first keen local ecologist here or was Richard hoping to get a subsidy from the crown for planting oak trees?

Phillip Farrant had fifty-three acres and three houses at *"Denbrook"* and *"Adams"* near *"Tetnes Hill"*, Denbrook being the name of the stream which now feeds Silwood Lake from the Bog. He was plain Phillip Farrant with no *"Mr"* although he was one of the wealthiest men in the parish.

The king owned Sunninghill Park which *"with the part that lyeth within Winkfield parish"* contained 472 acres. The house and lodges were not mentioned. The king also owned all the Sunninghill waste estimated at 1,985 acres and this was administered through Cookham Manor.

After these major landowners there was a group of families who would become the core of the population of Sunninghill right up to this century. Only three of the families named in 1613 do not appear in the 1653 record which shows a solid continuity in the troubled times of the civil war. These are the local yeomen who would, throughout the seventeenth and early eighteenth century, act as the parish officers. The most important of these yeoman families were the Mays, the Miltons and the Slanns.

"Homfry" May owned the two water mills clearly named by Nicholson. One was *"part in Winkfield with water mill"*, the Lord's

Mill as it was sometimes called, and today's Mill House. The other was listed in the survey between the entry for Eastmore and that for Cheapside and described as *"one water mill and pond"*. This probably lay on the Cheapside Brook between today's April Place and Heronsbrook House and was fed by ponds of which there may still be traces in the garden of Heronsbrook Cottage. Even in the driest of summers there is a constant flow in the Brook. It is unlikely that this was a flourmill, the other being so close, perhaps it was a timber mill or for crushing bark at a tannery.

Nicholas May, Humphrey's son, had *"two closes of arable and meadow grounds called Medhill"* in all six acres. They also had a house with seven acres elsewhere in the parish. Altogether the May family had twenty-five acres. By 1653 Robert May owned all this property. In 1625 William Pursell and his wife were subtenants at the mill with *"one close of arable land of fifteen acres and a watermill and some of his land is in Winkfield"*. A document of 1608 also named Pursell and stated that the mill-owner paid a rent of one red rose a year to the crown for his assart of royal land, a sweet form of a peppercorn rent. In the Nicholson survey William Pursell had twelve acres near Titness *"called Newlands"*.

The Mays of Sunninghill may have been related to Hugh and Baptist May who, a couple of generations later, moved in very high social circles indeed. Baptist was a friend, servant and architect for King Charles II. He became Keeper of Windsor Park. Hugh was in exile with Charles and after the Restoration, in 1668, he was made controller of the Royal Works and designed the Long Walk.

The five members of the Milton family named in the 1613 survey had a large holding totalling six houses and seventy-two acres. Nicholas Milton had a house and two arable fields, in all three acres. Henry Milton had two houses and forty-six acres of mostly arable land. He was a farmer of almost the same standing as Phillip Farrant. Robert Milton had a house and two plots of land, six acres in all. Thomas Milton had a house and fourteen acres in five arable and meadow fields and Widow Milton, the matriarch of the family, had a house and three acres. Robert, Nicholas and Henry Milton were still local landowners in 1625. In 1653 a Robert Milton owned the properties which Henry and Nicholas had held in 1613 and 1625.

The Miltons had been in Sunninghill for some time. Back in 1494 a Robert Milton leased the tenement called NewBrygas (Newbrigge) in Sunninghill which belonged to Broomhall Priory. He agreed to pay for the lease and to perform two working days every autumn (S.J.C., D 16). They would remain in the Sunninghill area for many years. On the William Eden map of 1800 (B.R.O., T/M 26) *"Miltons Lodge"* was marked near where Ascot Gate is today, and *"Miltons Walk"* was shown north of Sunninghill Park.

Four members of the Slann family owned land in 1613. They had thirty-seven acres altogether with two houses and two cottages. William Slann had a house and land of seven acres. Richard Slann had three fields near Sunninghill Park of seven acres and another seventeen acres elsewhere. Daniel had a cottage and two acres and Henry had a house and four acres. William and Henry Slann still had property here in 1625 and, in 1653, John and William Slann still owned land. Judging by their position in the survey some of their property was in modern Cheapside. According to a document in the Imperial College Archive, Henry Slann also had a timber-mill. This is the first mention of such an enterprise in this district. By 1706 one William Slann had a timber and carpentry business at Beggars' Bush near today's Cannon Inn crossroads. By 1800 *"Slans Hill"* was marked within Windsor Great Park to the west of Smith's Lawn.

Four other familiar families are named. William Pither and John Searle each had three acres, the latter had a house as well. Haman Attlee had a house and two pieces of land. A Robert Attlee was mentioned as a tenant of Broomhall Priory in 1262 when he leased some arable land in Winkfield (S.J.C.). The Lane family still owned some land in Sunninghill even though they had sold the manor to William Day. Henry Lane, succeeded by his son Edward in 1653, had *"wood ground adjoining the Lord's Green"*, i.e. Cheapside Green. John and Elizabeth Lane leased the Coworth lands from St John's College in 1662 (I.C.A.) and thereafter the Lanes were to continue to hold property in Coworth for more than a century.

The Nicholson survey is especially important for Cheapside which was described for the first time as:

"certain cottages and small backsides to them belonging, called Cheapside in the occupation of Edmund Baker, Francis Key, John Elliot, the Parish, Mr Edward Nevelle containing one small pasture ground near adjoining Humphrey May".

The Bakers were a family who would be connected with Cheapside for some time. William Baker had *"one house and 6 closes of arable pasture and meadow ground lying to the corner of Sunninghill Park"*. This was a plot of thirteen acres and Jacob Baker had it in 1653 (B.R.O., D/E AR m11). Mr Edward Neville was probably one of the Neville family, still the bailiffs of Sunninghill Park. The reference to the parish suggests that there was already an almshouse here.

Cheapside appears in Nicholson's survey between the entries for Homfry May and Robert Hodge on one side and Homfry May and Phillip Farrant on the other. The Hodge land was partly in Winkfield, near Mill Lane and Buckhurst Road. On the other side of the Cheapside entry lay the second mill and Eastmore. Thus it seems that in 1613 Cheapside lay between today's Mill House and today's junction of Buckhurst Road and Cheapside Road. It was one of the several hamlets making up the parish of Sunninghill.

By the time of the 1613 survey the centre of Sunninghill probably lay between St Michael's and the main Mill. From a study of later maps it is clear that a track ran from the Church towards the Mill cutting across today's Silwood Park. Cottagers lived along this track and worked the manor and church lands and their own strips of arable and pasture. They coppiced the woods and provided labour for the royal park.

The Farrants and the Days

In 1613 Phillip Farrant owned *"three houses and 2 meadowgrounds Adams and Denbrook"*. Five years later this *"yeoman of Sunninghill"* transferred the Long Deane land to Richard Wapshott. This was the same land which had been transferred to John Myller in 1586 (I.C.A. and J.E.). The Wapshott family had held lands here and on the edge of Chobham for a very long time. They were said to have descended from one Reginald Wapshott, King Alfred's bowman.

One of the most interesting documents from the early seventeenth century is the will of Phillip Farrant dated March 1621 (I.C.A., 6/B 11). Phillip declares that he is a *"yeoman being sick in body but whole in mind and of perfect memory"*. He was a substantial landowner with property both in Sunninghill and in Thorpe in Surrey. He left ten shillings to the poor of Sunninghill and two shillings and sixpence to the church box. He left his wife Agnes:

"my newe house" (known as Farrants) *wherein Mr Hevinength lately dwelt situate in Sunninghill and the barne, stable garden, orchard and backside thereunto belonging and my own parcel of arable land one acre"*.

She was also to have an annuity of seven pounds a year, her clothes, the best feather-bed, some linen, other household goods and two ewes, two lambs and a cow. The household goods were modest. There were no silver items.

The main legacy was for his son, also called Phillip. For clarity's sake we will call him Phillip II. He was to inherit:

> *"my capitall messuage wherein I dwell being in Sunninghill all the barnes, stable buildings and edifices, garden and orchard and all my other messuages tenements lands meadows, coppices rents and services in Sunninghill and in Thorpe in the county of Surrey"*

and all the residue of his goods and chattels. Phillip II's three sons were also provided for. There was a piece of property in Thorpe for one grandson Phillip. Another grandson, John, was to have the Long Deane which was eight acres and yet another grandson, Henry, was to have a *"grove containing four acres adjoining to the borne in Sunninghill"*.

Phillip Farrant's two married daughters were also beneficiaries. Priscilla was to have a cow, a ewe and a lamb and an annuity of twenty shillings. His other daughter Agnes, the wife of John Lovell, had a smaller annuity of two shillings and sixpence but she was to inherit his property:

> *"in Sunninghill now in the occupation of Nicholas Baker and the parcel of my piece of meadow and coppice ground commonly called the Lower Grove bounded out on the south side thereof from the corner of my plot hedge, overthwart to a beech standing in the hedge adjoining a parcel of ground of Nicholas May's called Mead-hit abutting upon the land boarding my new dwelling house into the green called Mill green on the west part and abutting the King's waste called Mill green on the north part".*

This seems to have been around today's Heronsbrook House and Harewood Park.

All Priscilla's and Agnes's daughters were to have a ewe and all his godchildren were to have an annuity of twelve pence. He also left his granddaughter Agnes, the daughter of his deceased son Thomas, a ewe, a lamb and thirty pounds. Agnes' money was to be paid over to *"Robert Gunner her mother's father for her use and benefit"*. Finally he left a lamb to his servant Margery Slann, an indication perhaps of the social levels between the Farrants and the Slanns. The will shows that the land was used for mixed farming with a predominance of sheep, exactly what would be expected at that time.

Phillip Farrant appointed his son as his sole executor and to oversee the will he named Edward Rogers a friend from Chertsey and Henry Lee a friend from Old Windsor. The witnesses included Edward Baker who was named in the Nicholson survey as owning land and a cottage in Cheapside.

In 1629 Matthew Day was recorded as transferring the lordship of Sunninghill Manor to Phillip Farrant II and in the late 1630s Farrant also leased Eastmore with eighty acres. However Matthew Day still owned large parts of the manor land since in 1654 he raised a £500 mortgage on Sunninghill Manor which was then recorded as consisting of 218 acres and nine houses (R.S.P.). The mortgage may have included some of Day's lands outside Sunninghill. Matthew Day died in 1661 aged 88 years. It was a timely death since he had been a strong supporter of Parliament and with the 1660 Restoration he must have felt very uneasy. He was buried at St Michael's and his table tomb was moved when the old church was pulled down (Hughes, chapter XX).

The Farrants like the Lanes before them both owned parts of the manor and lived on it. As local men they were aware of local problems. In 1634 Phillip Farrant II headed a petition against the proportion of manorial charges born by Sunninghill. They argued that Sunninghill Manor should not be charged as a sixth of Cookham Manor but as a twelfth since Cookham had 5,201 acres and Binfield 2,907 acres of *"manured land"*. Both of these had men of great estate whereas Sunninghill had only 799 acres of *"manured land"* and had *"mean men, their grounds barren and the deer seldom out of them"*.

The petition was fairly successful. In 1637 it was agreed that Sunninghill should be charged as only one tenth of the manor of Cookham since Sunninghill Manor was indeed *"barren land overlaid with deer"*. Perhaps we might try to appeal against our local taxes today on the same grounds.

Even though it had grown substantially since Tudor times, seventeenth century Sunninghill was certainly not a wealthy area. A Parliamentary survey of 1650 reported that Sunninghill and Binfield lay within the Cookham Manor but *"since they are in the forest they have not been surveyed"*. Cookham viewed the Sunninghill lands as only a small part of its jurisdiction but they kept a fairly close eye on what went on. In 1654 the lord of Sunninghill was fined for failing to keep the manor pound for stray animals in good repair (B.R.O., D/E Fa Li.).

In 1668, *"Farrants"* built by Phillip Farrant I, was bought by Thomas Rawlings of Middlesex from *"Alice Farrant of Colchester in Essex late wife of Thomas Farrant, citizen and tallowhandler of London"*. She also sold Rawlings all her dower rights and titles over all the lands of her late husband in Sunninghill and in Thorpe (I.C.A.).

Thomas Farrant was the son of Phillip Farrant II. At the time of this sale Selmore or Silmore Farm was rented by William Edsall from Judith Jefcoat who was the only daughter of Thomas Farrant, and the family still had the land known as Long Deane (I.C.A.).

During the seventeenth century there were three larger houses mentioned on the manor lands: Eastmore, Selmore Farm and the new Farrants. By the middle of the following century the name Farrants had disappeared from the records. What happened to Farrants and where were these houses?

According to Hughes writing in the 1880s: *"North of the Church Green lay Eastmore, the ancient manor house, Farrants another old mansion and a farmhouse standing in the valley, and west lay Tetworth"* (Hughes, p. 217). In other words Eastmore, Farrants and the farm were all close together north of the Church. Beyond Eastmore lay Cheapside and Lord's Green, later called Cheapside Green. Farrants was not far from Eastmore and: *"had sixty acres of which Silmere Hill and Long Denes were a part, and two fields lying between the great coppice and Eastmore"* (ibid). The *"great coppice"* was Silwood, part of this still exists to the south of the Brook and is now known as Nash's Copse. It was from this wood that the eighteenth century estate of Silwood Park took its name.

Eastmore was the oldest house on the manor. Hughes suggested that it stood between today's Silwood Farm and Tetworth Hall. He described its site as near to an old garden with two ancient yews and a famous vine, which still flourished in 1880 when he wrote his book. Old yews can still be found in the wood on the hill above Silwood Farm. Some foundations of a brick wall and bits of pottery which were found near here by John End show that a house once stood on this hill. Was this Eastmore or was it the Jacobean house called Farrants? The presence of brick suggests that it may well have been the latter.

On Jean Rocque's map of 1752 there are two houses in an enclosure at the Cheapside end of the Sunninghill Manor lands, i.e. north of the church where Hughes sited Eastmore. Although they are shown rather far to the east, they are presumably Selmore Farm and beside it Farrants or Eastmore. Further west there are five buildings near today's Tetworth Hall. Among these lies Parsonage Lane which led across the Brook to the church.

On the William Faden survey of 1788/91 (P.R.O., MR 687) and the William Eden survey of 1800 (B.R.O., T/M 26) there were buildings marked close to the Brook. These may be Selmore Farm and higher up the hill, Farrants. They are so close together that they may have become a main house and its dependency. There is also a clump of trees higher up the hill which may mark the site of an earlier house, Eastmore perhaps.

Detail of Jean Rocque Map showing the Manor Area

By 1813 when the Enclosure map was made, James Mann owned Tetworth then known as *"Healthy Hall"*. His house was no longer on the old site opposite the Wells but at the north side where Tetworth Hall is today. Hughes looking at this map may well have seen this as north of the Church due to its orientation. Is it possible that when Sibbald built his new house, the old Eastmore was taken over by Mann and Eastmore became his new house to be called Tetworth much later? Or was Eastmore on the hill where today's Imperial College telecommunications tower is? In either case it was called Eastmore because it lay on the east of the great moor or heath where Ascot Racecourse is today.

Farrants and Selmore Farm were both close to Pound Hill where the parish pound was kept for taking in stray animals. This name survived into the late nineteenth century when all the houses to the west of the old Cheapside Post Office (today's "Thatchers" hairdressers) were described as being on Pound Hill. The Pound was near to today's junction of Watersplash Lane and Cheapside Road. Farrants and Selmore Farm were sited close to each other and Farrants may well have replaced the old Selmore which survived only as farm buildings. The name Farrants simply disappeared when the family who built it had left and the house took the name of Selmore Farm.

The Sale of Sunninghill Park

The Nicholson survey enabled the crown to assess how much was due in quit-rents. This was all part of an effort to increase the crown income. The most dramatic local effect of their search for revenue was the sale of Sunninghill Park. Both James I and his successor Charles I used Bagshot Lodge as their main base for hunting in Windsor Forest. Hunting within parks was by this date less fashionable and there are no references to their use of Sunninghill Park House, which had probably become quite dilapidated. Sir Henry Neville III lost control of Sunninghill Park in 1619 when Alexander Levingstone, the tutor to Henry, Prince of Wales was appointed in his place. Nine years later Sir Henry was still trying to recover his offices at Sunninghill Park claiming that his family had had rights there for 300 years. He died two years later and in the same year his son, Sir Henry Neville IV, sought permission to fell 600 trees to rebuild the Park House so he must still have had some interests in the Park.

Sir Henry Neville IV married Elizabeth, a daughter of Richard Staverton of Warfield, the keeper of Cranbourne Chase. Sir Henry was a colourful character who wrote several radical books and pamphlets and was accused of atheism. During the Civil War, he was a Roundhead and his brother Sir Richard was a Royalist, a division common in many families that often enabled the family property to survive intact. In 1663, after the restoration of King Charles II, Sir Henry was imprisoned but he managed to escape and left the country. He eventually returned and lived on unmolested to 1694. When he died he was buried at Warfield.

At the time Henry Neville IV was applying to rebuild the house, the crown interest in Sunninghill Park was almost at an end. Both the first two Stuart kings sold off parts of the royal forest and some of the royal parks. Sunninghill Park was sold when King Charles I wanted to raise money without having to consult Parliament. Another way to make money was to farm out the quit-rents levied on encroachments on the wasteland. In 1606 James I sold the quit-rents from the Sunninghill portion of waste for a limited term to William Daresen for £629.10s.

In November 1630, Sunninghill Park with its 472 acres of land ceased to be a royal possession. It was sold to Sir Thomas Carey (or Carew) for £2,700. Carey was Groom of the Chamber to King Charles I and was distantly connected to the Boleyns, courtiers under King Henry VIII and Queen Elizabeth I. Carey seems to have bought the Park purely as an investment. The land was disparked, subdivided and let out to tenants, the bulk being leased to Thomas Draper. Carey died at Whitehall in 1634 and was buried in Westminster Abbey. On his death he left three daughters. They continued to lease out the park to Thomas Draper who finally bought it in 1654 for £3,300.

Thomas Draper was already a resident in Sunninghill. He had built a new brick house south east of the church near the London Road at *"Stoneylands"*. This was called *"Ashurst"* a generation later when it was owned by Draper's son-in-law Sir Henry Ashurst and it was the first entirely brick house in Sunninghill. Was it made of local brick? We shall never know. Ashurst was rebuilt and resited over the centuries.

Thomas Draper pulled down what was left of the old Sunninghill Park House and built himself a new brick house in the late Jacobean style. This house had a central part and two wings. He made major changes to the gardens possibly planting an avenue of limes. Hughes referred to a plan of 1662 which showed the *"Dutch style of gardening at Sunninghill Park"* (Hughes, chapter XIX). This new garden style was influenced by the ideas brought back to England from the Netherlands by the royalists who returned home with King Charles II in 1660.

Thomas Draper was one of those who benefited from the restoration of the monarchy. He became the Sheriff of Berkshire and was made a baronet in 1660. Five years later he married Ellen Baber at Sunninghill Church. By that time Sir Thomas had friends in very high places. Through his marriage he was connected to Sir John Baber, one of the royal physicians and as a result he moved in court circles. In 1665 he was named along with Sir Edward Hyde, the Chancellor and later Lord Clarendon, as licensees for a monopoly to dig for coal in Windsor Park. There was however, and perhaps fortunately, no coal there.

Sir Edward Hyde also had local interests. He had married a daughter of Sir Thomas Aylesbury who had been the keeper at Cranbourne in the 1640s. Hyde's daughter, Anne, was born at Cranbourne Lodge and in 1660 she married James, duke of York who later became King James II. This Anne Hyde was the mother of Queen Mary II and Queen Anne and her connection with Cranbourne brought both James II and Anne into the area. In 1668 James, duke of York and his brother the king visited Sir Thomas Draper and his wife at Sunninghill Park. They stayed there to hunt and to dine. Ten years later Sir Thomas Draper showed his patriotism by contributing to the rebuilding of St Paul's Cathedral. The only other Sunninghill resident who did so was a Mrs Dawson.

The Civil War

As well as ensuring the collection of the old manorial taxes and selling off surplus estates the Stuart kings also tried to raise money by enforcing fines due from any infringements of forest law. In 1631 Henry Rich, earl of Holland, Constable of the Castle and Keeper of the Windsor Forest, began enforcing the ancient forest laws with great severity. His aim was to maximise royal income and to stop poaching and trespassing.

According to the earl's 1636 report on encroachments into the royal forest, the Miltons were fined for having cottages on the royal waste and soldiers were brought in to eject four squatters who were living under the roots of trees. Three years later Holland had all the locks on the park gates changed and the fences repaired to keep the deer in and the poachers out. He seems to have been successful in building up the herds of deer. In 1640 the Grand Jury of Berkshire protested against the *"innumerable increase of deer"*.

As a result of Holland's heavy handed approach and with the worsening national crisis the whole forest region erupted into rebellion. In 1642 a report to the House of Lords stated that there was:

"great destruction and killing of His Majesty's deer in the Forest of Windsor where the people of the country in a riotous and tumultuous manner have lately killed a hundred of His Majesty's Fallow Deer and besides Red Deer and do threaten to pull down the pales of the Great Park".

Members of the Smith family of Sunninghill were named among the leaders of these rebels. Anger over the enforcement of the forest laws was one of the reasons why the people of this region were generally hostile to the crown and supported Parliament in the Civil War.

The earl of Holland left the area in 1642. This was the year when King Charles I raised the royal standard at Nottingham and the Civil War began. Windsor became a garrison town for the Parliamentary army. The venison and vert became food and fuel for the troops. The keepers who continued to fight the poachers were often harmed themselves. In 1647 the keeper Symonds complained to the Parliament that all the parks in Windsor Forest were destroyed. He had been wounded by poachers and his son had been killed in the Great Park (Roberts, p. 13).

When King Charles I was executed in January 1649, a Parliamentary report claimed that there were no deer left in the Great Park, that the forest lodges were being ruined and timber was being cut. A certain Captain Aldridge was accused of taking trees from the forest. From their profits the family was able to buy up Sunninghill manor after the wars. The Aldridge family had already been around here for some time. Richard and Margaret Aldridge were at Binfield in 1504.

The value of the timber in the forest can be measured by the various attempts made to catalogue the trees themselves. In one report 992 trees were counted, *"mainly old dotteroll"*. A dotterel was a pollarded or elderly tree. The management of the forest was important enough for it to be discussed in Parliament and the value of the Great Park was assessed at £1,371. There was a proposal that all crown lands should be sold and the money used to settle the arrears of army pay. It was probably alarm at this prospect that led the Sunninghill parishioners to file their 1653 claim of rights. In their petition they laid claim to all the assarted lands which had formerly belonged to the crown. They also recorded their rights in the royal waste: the right of common pasture, *"turbary"* the right to dig peat, *"yeate heath"* to take heather, and *"pannage"* to graze pigs, and their rights to dig and take gravel, sand and loam. They were not granted their petition which simply joined the huge pile of similar requests coming into Parliament from all over the country.

Sunninghill and Cheapside were certainly seriously affected by the Civil War even though there was no major fighting here. The parish registers record that from 1641 to 1653 there had been *"no care in registering any births, burials or marriages in this Parish by reason of the tumults and confusions of the Civil War"* (B.R.O., D/P 126 1/1).

During the war, Windsor and the surrounding area were generally on the side of Parliament but there were many local disagreements. The Days of Eton and Windsor supported Parliament, while the Mays and Glynns of Sunninghill were Royalists. In 1655 William Glynn of Sunninghill was fined

£112.13s for attending King Charles I at Oxford. He had to mortgage his lands to pay the fine (Hughes, p. 128).

Sir Thomas Fairfax, the great Parliamentary general, made Windsor Castle his headquarters for a time and Oliver Cromwell visited him there in 1645. The Parliamentary army occupied the Great Park, deer were eaten, timber was cut, farms were robbed and travel was dangerous. After Colonel Thomas Pride purged the House of Commons in October 1648, the king was taken to Windsor where he stayed until shortly before his execution in January 1649. In the 1650s unpaid Parliamentary soldiers were living in Windsor Park and Forest, pieces of land were debentured to them and some of them acquired sizeable holdings. Those who could, took advantage of the anarchy to increase their property.

The years of the civil war were indeed tumultuous but there were real economic opportunities. There was a great demand for timber and also for leather for harness, saddles and heavy clothing. The Slann's timber yards flourished, the Aldridges were making their money, and a leather industry developed in Cheapside. It would be a rather different Cheapside by the time of the Restoration.

The Yew Tree in St Michael's Churchyard (Hughes)

THE MAKING OF A COMMUNITY : 1660 - 1800

*"The country people who lived there, far from the towns
and main roads, remained for a long time without a voice
of their own or anyone to speak for them. They were
nevertheless there; they did things, cared about things, and
thus had their effect, without anyone realising it, on the
heart and soul of the nation."*

Daniel Halevy in *"Visites aux Paysons du Centre"*

Under Royal Patronage

The last years of the Interregnum were memorable for the
great storm of 1658 that uprooted trees and damaged houses
throughout Windsor Forest. Many people regarded this as a sign
that the republican regime had outlived its usefulness and 1660
brought the restoration of King Charles II. He appointed his
nephew the talented Prince Rupert of the Palatinate as Ranger of
the Royal Forest and Great Park. A survey of the Great Park was
made to assess the extent of damage and Charles took a personal
interest in restoring the Windsor parks. Prince Rupert brought in
red deer from Germany to replenish the stock.

Two years later an Act of Settlement was passed regulating the
conditions under which a poor person might become legally
settled on wasteland. This may have marginally increased the
numbers acquiring permanent rights of settlement but there was
still a vast and empty waste all around the little hamlet of
Sunninghill. The famous diarist Samuel Pepys commented on this
emptiness. In 1664 he was lost in the forest on his way to visit his
chief at the Admiralty Office, Lord George Carteret, who was
then living at Cranbourne Lodge. He wrote that he passed
through *"a very meloncholy place and little variety save trees"* (Pepys, vi,
p. 159).

The literati of the later Stuart period were not favourably
impressed by our region. Daniel Defoe visiting in 1703 wrote
*"One may frequently be put in mind of the Arabia Deserta where winds raise
the sands"* (Defoe, p. 59). He compared Bagshot heath with the
Barnsley moors, *"all black"*. These town dwellers were alarmed by
the wildness and by the winds which lashed the forest from time
to time. After the Great Fire of London, Pepys received a letter
from Lady Carteret telling him that pieces of burnt official papers
had been swept out of London by the strong east wind and had
fallen to the ground at Cranbourne.

Although Pepys found the forest a gloomy place and Defoe regarded it as a black desert, the late seventeenth century was a period of increased activity and the sort of houses that they would have enjoyed visiting were being built. Defoe himself noticed that *"the lodges in those parks, are no more lodges, though they may retain the name, but palaces"* (ibid). In the half century from 1660 to 1714, there was a considerable growth in the number of larger houses and for the first time Sunninghill became a fashionable address. The reign of Queen Anne brought the arrival of the Royal Races on Ascot Heath and taking the waters at the *"Sunninghill Wells"* was a major attraction. By 1714 almost all the features which would stimulate the development of Cheapside were in place: the big houses for the gentry, the Racecourse and the Wells.

Queen Anne spent more time at Windsor than any earlier monarch. Her mother had been born at Cranbourne Lodge and she had a special interest in the area. Her very poor eyesight made the usual feminine occupations of reading and embroidery difficult so Anne preferred outdoor occupations. After her marriage to Prince George of Denmark, she passed most of her summers at Windsor Castle and was always there in the hunting season.

In keeping with the new fashion the queen preferred to hunt in the Forest rather than within a Park. Kennels were built for the royal buckhounds near Swinley Bottom where they remained until relocated in 1790 to new buildings west of Ascot Heath (hence today's Kennel Avenue and Kennel Ride). When Anne could no longer ride on horseback due to her many miscarriages, her increasing obesity and her continuous ill health, she drove out in a chariot. In 1702 Swift reported seeing her in Windsor Forest where she *"hunts in a chaise with one horse which she drives herself and drives furiously like Jehu and is a mighty hunter like Nimrod"*. A series of carriage drives were made such as Queen Anne's Ride which provided a direct route from Windsor Castle to Sunninghill. Eventually there was an attractive network of carriage rides including nine drives radiating from the barrows at Ascot (today's Heatherwood Hospital). This work was completed during the late eighteenth century partly by the troops who were stationed nearby.

The royal presence brought the court and the nobility into the region. In 1702 Anne appointed John Churchill, later the duke of Marlborough, as Ranger of the Forest and the Parks. Seven years later the office was passed on to his wife, Sarah duchess of

Marlborough, for many years the queen's closest friend. The fiery duchess was very protective of the forest and is quoted as saying *"I will never cut down a tree so long as it will bear a leaf"* (Roberts, p. 29).

It was as a result of Queen Anne's frequent residence at Windsor that the Royal Ascot Races began. They were inaugurated on Saturday the eleventh of August in 1711 in the presence of the queen, and were recorded by Dean Swift. The queen had been encouraged to use Ascot Heath for horse races by the duke of Somerset who was the Master of the Buckhounds and by his wife who was Mistress of the Robes. A racecourse was constructed near to the Buckhounds' kennels at Swinley and it became a practice that only horses used for hunting with the Royal Buckhounds were allowed to race. There was a stylish start to the proceedings with a royal procession up the course thus establishing a long-lasting tradition continuing to the present day. On the third day of the races the queen offered a prize of plate worth 100 guineas. Many less royal activities went on during the races such as cock-fighting, bare-fist boxing and gambling on cards as well as horses.

This 1711 meeting was not the start of a continuous series of Royal Ascot Races. After the queen's death they were only sporadically revived under her immediate successors. Nor did the races bring any development around the Heath. Apart from Ascot Heath House and an inn called the Stag and Hounds there was no significant settlement in modern Ascot for many years and no large properties there until the nineteenth century. Indeed it was not until the late nineteenth century that Ascot came to life for more than a week each year.

The first reference to the Sunninghill Waters *"which are of the finest kind"* appeared in a pamphlet by Francis Brokesley, the vicar of Shottesbroke written in 1711. The Wells was not mentioned in an earlier pamphlet on chalybeate wells so their public notice coincides with the start of the Ascot Races. The Wells Inn also became better known due to the annual Race-Week and its *"health-giving"* springs soon made it a most fashionable watering place and a popular inn.

However the Wells Inn had existed long before 1711. The building had probably begun life as a farmhouse. The date 1557 was carved over the kitchen chimney of the old inn that was pulled down in 1885. The first innkeeper we know of by name was John Hatch in 1721 but again the Hatch family had been in the parish for several generations before him. He was followed by a Mr Davis in 1754, Richard Hodges in 1770, David Bronsvelt who *"failed"* and J. Marshall who had it at the height of its popularity in the 1780s and 1790s (Hughes).

In the mid-eighteenth century the spa was the only feature of Sunninghill to be mentioned by Jean Rocque in his preamble to his maps of Berkshire: *"Sunninghill Well is much resorted to by the nobility on account of its mineral waters"* (E.B.). The Wells Inn was frequently enlarged to provide more accommodation for the increasing number of guests and for their entertainment. By the 1750s there was a long ballroom or breakfast room opening on to the garden used for balls, music and public breakfasts. During the 1790s and 1800s when the army was billeted nearby the inn became a convivial meeting place for the officers. Sunninghill houses were advertised as *"near the celebrated Wells"*. In 1792 the Reading Mercury claimed that the Wells Inn was as good as any German spa. Its waters gradually went out of fashion in the nineteenth century but the Inn was still *"much Frequented"* for the Races.

The Old Wells Inn (Hughes)

The Wells and the Races attracted the court and the gentry to build or to rent houses in Sunninghill. In 1700 there was only a handful of larger houses. As well as the oldest houses such as Eastmore, Selmore Farm, Farrants, and Sunninghill Park House, there were the newer Healthy Hall opposite the Wells and the forerunner of the Tetworth estate, Brook Lodge, Beechgrove, Ashurst or Oakleigh and The Cedars. Most of these properties were not known by their modern names and were generally called after their occupier.

A few local place names like The Wells were consistently used by the late 1600s but the majority were still constantly changed both in documents and on plans. Buckhurst is a good example of this. Sometimes it was called Bucket Hill and sometimes Buckhurst Hill. This variation went on for more than a century. In the fourteenth century Blacknest ford was called the *"Domford gate on the street"*, a reference to the old Roman stone road which ran close by. Domford referred to the Darenford family. In 1667 John, son of Richard Darenford was baptised at St Michael's (Hodder). The family lived on in Sunninghill for at least two centuries.

In 1677 The Cedars was the property of Mr William Buckle, who probably built the first large house on the site, and early in the eighteenth century he sold it to Elizabeth Squires. She leased the vicarage meadows from Dr Palmer, the vicar, who also allowed her to divert Parsonage Lane away from her garden. This lane which ran between today's Sunninghill crossroads and Cheapside was to become the source of a long running controversy between the later vicars and their neighbours. After Elizabeth Squires died the property was owned by a Mrs Scott who leased it to Sir David Lindsay. His daughter, Elizabeth, married Augustus Schultz of Ashurst and became a generous local patron.

The first large house to be built in Cheapside appeared at this time. This was Brook Lodge, now called Heronsbrook House. Brook Lodge was probably built by Robert Russell and Elizabeth Gale of Woking who were given the land as part of their marriage settlement in 1693. In the deed it was described as a plot of several acres lying west of Cheape Green. The same piece of land had changed hands three years earlier. The house has a wood and plaster centre compatible with this date with a brick front added probably in the early eighteenth century. Land beside Cheape Green was mentioned in another land transfer of 1719 when a coppice or wood lying on the north and east of the Green was up for sale.

By 1700 Cheape Green was a well-known place often used to identify pieces of land when they were sold or leased. It was described as close to the boundary between Winkfield and Sunninghill parishes and astride the Brook. The use of the name Cheape Green rather than Cheapside Green lends weight to the theory that the name comes from *"cheape"* meaning innkeeper.

Although there is no clear evidence it does seem that by the 1690s the Tun Inn was already on one side of the Green.

Since Cheape Green was on the distant edge of two parishes the residents were able to make small enclosures from the waste and their properties grew at the expense of the surrounding forest. Queen Anne's Cheape Green was already a mixed community. It included paupers in the parish cottage, labourers, small farmers like the Slanns and the Butlers, yeoman farmers like the Farrants and the Miltons and landowners like the new owners of Brook Lodge or the Cowderys who built the largest house here. This was *"Sunninghill House"* built in 1713 (now known as Harewood Park). It was described by G. M. Hughes as being *"in Mill Lane on the border of Beggars' Bush Heath overlooking the Mill in the valley and across the common towards Silwood"* (Hughes, p. 256).

The Aldridge Family

In the 1670s the Aldridge family who were to dominate local affairs for more than a hundred years took over the manorial lands. The family had been living in and around Sunninghill for some time, the earliest reference to an Aldridge here occurring in 1585. Members of the family were farmers, and in the Parliamentary army. They seem to have prospered from the Civil War and by the 1660s they were timber-merchants, farmers and tanners.

Throughout the period that the Aldridges were at Sunninghill Manor, the family lost many of their infant children. The record of these losses in the parish registers gives some indication of the personal sorrow and pain that is so often absent from history. In 1715, Abel, the son of John II and his wife Elizabeth, was buried at St Michael's. Eleven years later Samuel and Thomas Aldridge were buried in September and October. Three years later Robert Aldridge was buried in the November and, in the year of John II's death, young Stephen Aldridge was buried in March (B.R.O., D/P 126 1/2).

The first John Aldridge bought Selmore Farm from Thomas Rawlings in 1673 and in the same year he acquired Eastmore and the manor estate of about ninety acres from Matthew Day for £552 10s (I.C.A.). He soon settled into his role as lord of the manor holding regular manorial courts starting in 1675 and taking an active role in parish affairs. The court barons for this and for subsequent courts held by the Aldridges are in the archive at Imperial College.

The Aldridge family tree is very confusing since there was at least one John and one Henry in successive generations.

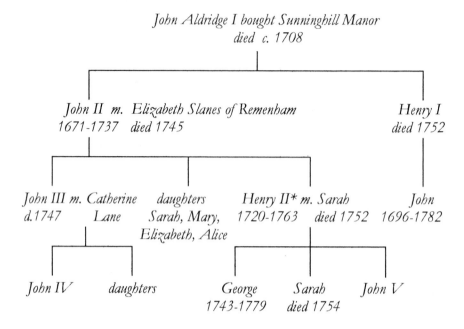

John Aldridge I bought Sunninghill Manor
died c. 1708

John II m. Elizabeth Slanes of Remenham
1671-1737   died 1745

Henry I
died 1752

John III m. Catherine
d.1747   Lane

daughters
Sarah, Mary,
Elizabeth, Alice

Henry II* m. Sarah
1720-1763   died 1752

John
1696-1782

John IV   daughters

George
1743-1779

Sarah
died 1754

John V

*His grave is near the east end of St Michael's Church under the organ.

At the time of John Aldridge's purchase, quit-rents of £2 13s were due from the owner of Eastmore to Cookham Manor. Farrants was not mentioned in either of these transactions but it was named in a 1670s list of the *"Charges for Rails to enclose Churchyard and Church"* which recorded all the parishioners of Sunninghill who were responsible for maintaining the fences around the churchyard. According to the 1670 list:

the Parson was responsible for the gate

Francis Broughton for 3 panels

Sir Thomas Draper for (his tenants) the Robinsons and for Richard Attlee 3 panels and for the Brick House he owed another 3 panels

Mr Thomas Rawlings for Farrants, now owned by Mr Aldridge, for 7 panels

Edward Lane of Coworth (for land he held in Sunninghill) for 1 panel,

the Broomhall estate for 6 panels   (B.R.O., D/P 126 8/1).

It seems that John I may have owned or rented Farrants even before he bought the rest of the manor.

The unimportance of Sunninghill Manor at this time is indicated by the fact that it is not marked on any of the maps made before 1770. In 1712 Henry Wise made *"An Accurate Plan of Windsor Parks and Part of the Forest"*. On this, Sunninghill is shown as a cluster of fields lying south-east of Sunninghill Park along the road from Windsor (Royal Collections, RL 29579). Only thirteen small buildings are indicated and no manor house. Wise was of course mapping the royal estates and he was not concerned with the surrounding villages but he would surely have marked any significant building.

From the 1721 list of those who paid towards the maintenance of the church rails it is clear that the Aldridges were far less wealthy than Sir John Baber at Sunninghill Park. The latter paid for eighteen panels on account of the park and for seven more on account of his tenancy of the Tittenhurst and Broomhall lands of St John's College. Aldridge paid for only four panels on account of Selmore Farm and for five more on account of Eastmore (no mention of Farrants here). Others paying for the church fencing included Sir Henry Ashurst who paid for two panels on account of *"the Brick House or Stoneylands"* and two more panels on account of his ownership of *"New Bridge"*.

Sir Henry Ashurst owned less land than Aldridge but he was of a higher social status. The Ashurst estate extended across the present London Road and included the land now occupied by the Marist Convent (E.B.). In 1715 the two families were political rivals when Sir Henry Ashurst contested the seat at Windsor as a Whig and was opposed by John Aldridge II who supported the Tory Church party (Hughes, pp.217-219).

John II was in the business of farming and leasing land. In 1725 *"Silmore"* was let to the Buckworth family. Sir Edward Buckworth was Master of the Horse to the daughters of George III, and Assistant Gentleman Usher to the king. Several members of this family were buried in the vault under St Michael's Church. Ten years later, *"Sellmore farm and land was let to John Verry, a farmer from Hampton in Middlesex"* (I.C.A., Cat. No. 31/B11). John Verry had married Mary Lane at Upton Nervet in 1731 so there may have been a family connection with Sunninghill. (Interestingly a John Verry lived in Watersplash Lane from 1988 and his father Hugh Verry has lived there since 1998. They are related to Aldridge's tenant).

Silmore, Selmore or Silwood Farm (Hughes)

The contract for a three-year lease of the farm was signed on 14th October 1735. It was very detailed and showed that a great deal of work was needed on the farm and its outbuildings. Aldridge agreed to repair the fence and the windows, to *"new lay"* the barn floor, to whitewash the house and to allow *"timber lath plaister for a necessary house and John Verry to cover it"*. He would also allow Verry forty shillings and Verry was to put twenty shillings of his own money *"twards parting the stairhead chamber and making a partition below to enclose a place under the stairs for an ale cellar"*.

Aldridge was allowed to keep the use of the barn until Mayday for threshing his corn and for storing his hay and he could also continue to use the grazing on *"14 acres of the old grass till John Verry plows it up"*. Verry was to have *"one more load of bushe this winter"* and he agreed to *"spend all the unthreshed straw on the premises before May Day next and leave the dung there for the benefit of the farm"*. In addition John Verry was to pay Aldridge:

one pound and one shilling for the clover seed already sown,
ten shillings and sixpence for the *"Rea* (rye) *Grass Sewed"*,
thirteen shillings and sixpence for *"3 bushels of tufs carried in"*,
one pound sixteen shillings for eight acres of ploughing,
and *"all to be paid by november next"*

As well as being a farmer and landlord, John II was a tanner and a supplier of other tanneries. At least four generations of Aldridges had tanneries along the Brook. Tanneries were a major industry from the seventeenth to the nineteenth centuries and employed a sizeable proportion of the population. They needed only a modest capital to set them up. Hides were soaked first in a lime solution to remove the hair, then scoured in pits containing dung and water and finally steeped in pits containing ground-up oak bark and water. Since they were extremely smelly, tanneries were usually sited at a suitable distance from the houses of the gentry.

The Aldridges had access to plenty of oak bark. In March 1725 John II wrote from *"Sellmore"* (so he was living at the farm then) to the bursar of St John's College enclosing a payment of seventeen pounds fifteen shillings and three pence for bark. He had taken the trees from their land and was asking for a further allocation of timber (S.J.C., D 108 187). He explained that although the *"proper season is at hand"* he had *"received no trees so far"*. He added that *"Barke is shaved and hatched and sold to two tanners in Southwarke"* but floods and snow had delayed his transports sent via Egham. He wanted ten pounds in all, or two shillings and sixpence per pound of the total money, for his work. He had a commission drawn up by his son, John III, who was, he proudly wrote, a *"Notary Publick at the Admiralty Office in Doctors Commons"* and *"though a tanner he was the lawyer of the parish and used to act for Mrs Squires in that capacity"* (S.J.C., D 74). He also asked the College to send letters to him via the Bagshot bag since *"My letters lye at Windsor sometime a weeke before I have em"* (S.J.C., D 108/185/188).

It is clear from this letter that John II regularly used oak from the Broomhall estates and that he sold bark on behalf of the College to the London tanneries. He was a self-educated business man who took a keen interest in his estates holding manorial courts both at Sunninghill and at Windlesham, the latter on behalf of St John's College (I.C.A.; S.J.C. D 109).

John Aldridge II was sixty-six years old when he died on the 27th April 1737. The memorial to him and his wife is at St Michael's Church. His will, written a year earlier, gives a clear picture of his estates (I.C.A.). Eastmore the *"chief mansion"* on the manor was left to his eldest son, John III the lawyer, who was also to have all the property in Taplow and Beaconsfield, which John II had inherited from his father.

"Sellmore Farm and Coppices towards further Long Deanes" went to his son Henry II, to whom he also left the *"home wherin I now dwell ... with yards, orchards, tan yards and piece of ground called School House Platt and two meadows after the death of my wife"*. If Verry was still at Selmore under his three-year lease then there were two other habitable houses on the manor both mentioned here. Was the

"home wherin I now dwell" which he left to his wife Elizabeth and afterwards to Henry in fact Farrants?

He also left a *"house in Sunninghill"* and *"a close called Church close now in possession of Mrs Elizabeth Northcote"* to his daughter Alice. *"Money and 2 closes called Further Long Deanes adjacent to William Wapshot on the south and to Selmore Farm on the north and two further closes occupied by John Correy lying between Sellmore Mead and a lane"* went to another daughter, Elizabeth. A third daughter, Mary who was still under 21 years, was to receive money. (She died and was buried in 1740 and probate was granted on her will in 1741, also in I.C.A.). John II also left an unspecified amount of money to the poor.

From this will it is clear that John Aldridge II was both richer and better educated than Phillip Farrant had been. Among the personal items mentioned were a silver tumbler, a best pair of pistols and a two volume history of England which were to go to John III. A watch, a second best pair of pistols and silver spurs went to Henry II with *"all my mathematical instruments and books except such books as my dear wife shall choose for her own use during her natural life and my glass bookcase"*. A silver tankard, a silver pint mug and silver spoons were left to his daughters (I.C.A.).

According to one of the few court barons in English, rather than Latin, in the Imperial College Archive, John II's widow, Elizabeth Slanes Aldridge, acted as the lady of the manor with John Sawyer as her steward. Was this John Sawyer a descendant of Henry Sawyer mentioned in 1582 and a member of the family who gave their name to what is now the Ascot Gate of Windsor Great Park? It was called Sawyer's Gate well into the twentieth century. In the eighteenth century John and Samuel Sawyer both owned land close to this gate.

John III, the lawyer, survived his father by only ten years dying on the 26th April 1747. An indenture concerning his will referred to *"John Aldridge of Doctors Commons gentleman and his wife Catherine"*, to his brother *"Henry Aldridge, tanner and Sarah his wife"* and to *"his son and heir John Aldridge gentleman"*. This last was John Aldridge IV who eventually inherited most of the Aldridge estates.

Henry II, the younger son, was, like his father, a tanner, an amateur mathematician and a scientist. He lived on to 1763 and features in various local land transactions. In February 1762 he sold *"two closes known as Further Long Deanes occupied by John Slann and another five and a half closes by the church"*. This land had passed from John II to Mary Aldridge and thence to John III who sold it to his brother Henry. The land was described as abutting *"towards the east on the common or King's waste, towards the south and south-east land of John Wapshott occupied by Richard Byrnes, west land of Henry Aldridge and north, land of Thomas Charlwood".* This land, near today's Tetworth Hall, was part of a later deed of sale, 1792, made between the vicar and James Sibbald. In 1763, John Wapshott leased 20 acres and a cottage to Sarah, Henry's widow, and before his death Henry had bought some land from Wapshott.

**Table by John Aldridge II, entered in the Parish Records
to determine the days of the week and Easter**

Henry II had a son, most originally called George. He left Sunninghill and went to India. His fate is revealed in a 1799 copy of a certificate in the Imperial College Archive. *"George Aldridge of Eastmore in the parish of Sunninghill, the son of John Aldridge's younger brother"* was an East India Company soldier. He had been born in 1743 and was described as a tanner by trade. He had a *"dark complexion, brown hair and was deeply pock-marked he measured 5 foot 9 or 10 inches and had a deep long scar from his left eye, good sight and hand".* For five years he had been with the East India Company, no doubt hoping to make his fortune as many young men did in the service of the Company. He left from Fort St George at Madras to go to Calcutta but his ship was wrecked in the *"Balasore Roads"* and he perished at sea.

This information was collected by John Aldridge IV in 1781. He added that George had made his will in November 1763 and had appointed *"his brother John Aldridge of Holborn, William Pitt of Chappel Street in the Parish of St Margaret in the city of Westminster and John Nicolls"* as joint executors. The will was proved in 1779.

All these documents were collected and transcribed for John Pitt who bought the Sunninghill Manor estate from the Aldridges and fought a lengthy case contesting the right of Cookham Manor to levy charges on Sunninghill.

Parish Government

The Aldridges featured prominently in the affairs of Sunninghill parish from the 1670s to the 1770s. The population of Sunninghill has been estimated at only 225 in 1705 but reading through the vestry books and overseers papers which exist from 1713 it is amazing how much activity there was (vestry books are B.R.O., D/P 126, 8/1-6 and the overseers papers are ibid, 13/1-5). The vestry or parish committee had to maintain the church and uphold law and order. Among their many other responsibilities, they had to stop strangers from cutting the king's peat and to register any assarts and any new building on the royal and parish wastes.

Each parish had a chief constable; the Aldridges served in this position throughout the first half of the 18th century. John II also wrote the vestry accounts for which he was paid a shilling a year in 1708. There were nine petty constables, eight tithingmen responsible for reporting on the misdemeanours of their neighbours, two churchwardens, two overseers of the Poor Law and two surveyors. These unpaid offices were all filled by local men including Mays, Miltons, Bakers, Slanns, Wapshotts, etc. Only Aldridge was normally written down as *Mr* Aldridge. The rest were known simply as John Baker or William May etc.

A major task facing the vestry was to provide for the poor of the parish. An indenture of 1680 recorded the conveyance of a cottage and garden in Mill Lane near Cheape Green to the trustees of the parish. It was to be let and the income used for the poor. This may be the same cottage mentioned in the 1613

Nicholson survey. Signatories on behalf of the parish included John Attlee, William Slann, Edward Lane and John Wapshott. The Cheape Green cottage was the first of the parish almshouses. A small plot of land near Sunninghill Park called Pound Hill Plat (plat means place) was also let to raise money for the poor. This was mentioned again in 1708 and is marked on the enclosure documents of 1817. Today this is part of Silwood Park, close to the junction of Watersplash Lane and Cheapside Road.

The expense of maintaining the poor could be very high. For example the parish paid out three pounds to a surgeon brought from Egham to treat one of the paupers. Moreover the responsibility grew throughout the eighteenth century. In 1708 the parish was maintaining only five paupers but by the 1790s there were more than twenty dependants. Orphans were lodged with local women and apprenticeships were arranged for the boys. There was a heavy expenditure on clothing, a major expense in those days. In 1707 a coat had to be provided for John Avons. Its cost was not to exceed six shillings and he was also to have a pair of stockings not to exceed one shilling. Were they fitting him up to send him into service? Another man was to have shoes and stockings not exceeding thirteen shillings and sixpence.

The vestry was also responsible for many of the church expenses. In 1707 the parish paid two shillings for ringing the bells to celebrate the Union of Scotland and England and seven shillings and sixpence to celebrate the failure of Guy Fawkes. They paid too for the organist and the choristers, for the bread and wine for the Eucharist, for washing church linen and for candles and cleaning. In addition they paid out eight shillings for glazing the windows and two shillings and three pence to the man who removed the ivy from the tower.

Above all the vestry had to maintain law and order and they did this with ferocity. In 1707 the vestry paid four shillings and sixpence for a mound to be made for the whipping post and for mending the stocks. They paid out another two shillings and nine pence on the stocks in 1708 and one pound twelve shillings and sixpence after their use for poor Goody Hudson. There is no written evidence as to the site of the stocks and whipping post. They may have been on the Church Green or on the Cheape Green. Local tradition places them on the latter along Buckhurst Road and some of the older people remember the remnants of the stocks near the triangle between Mill Lane and Buckhurst Road.

The parish also had to pay money for the maintenance of parishioners sent to prison in Windsor or Reading. In order to control the population and prevent vagrancy the vestry issued certificates for parishioners who needed to travel, for example Edward Milton was permitted to go to Hanworth in 1709.

In spite of the ferocity of the punishments, the late seventeenth and early eighteenth centuries were a very lawless era. In 1685 William Smith, whose family members had been regularly arrested for poaching and trespassing, was convicted of stealing three horses and sentenced to death.

Apart from familiar crime such as theft and murder there were also highwaymen to contend with. Wealthy travellers and residents attracted thieves. In 1670 Claud Duval, ex-page to the duke of Richmond, was hanged at Tyburn. He had terrorised travellers throughout Windsor Forest. Edward Lane, the son of John Lane of Coworth, was shot in 1683 while trying to arrest two highwaymen at the Wells Inn. In 1704 *"A certain highwayman, whose name we know not"* but *"probably a member of the Dibley Gang"* (Hughes p. 18), *"attempted to rob the Salisbury Stage near Kingswick Beech but he was shot through with a brace of bullets by a gentleman of this parish"*. He was buried in St Michael's Churchyard (B.R.O., D/P 126 1/2).

Highway robberies were of course rare incidents in an age when natural disasters were far more perilous. In November 1703 there was another great storm which was so severe that a coachman at Windsor was blown out of his seat and had his neck broken. When we consider that most of the inhabitants of Cheapside would then be living in fragile, thatched, wood and plaster cottages its effects must have been terrifying.

St Michael's Church: its Land and Income

After almost a hundred years of religious argument, the Restoration of King Charles II ushered in an era of relative stability for the Church of England. St Michael's Church had settled into an easy relationship with its patron, St John's College. Each vicar entered into an agreement to lease the vicarage and church lands or glebe at a peppercorn rent and in return the College would support the vicar and the church. Any major improvements to the vicarage were paid for by St John's College and they also provided the timber.

The Reverend John Robinson senior, 1594-1626, signed an agreement with the college in 1618 to lease the rectory and four acres of *"moorland called Priest's Moor and five acres of arable land"*. St John's retained the rights over all the timber on these lands (S.J.C., D 16). A college visitor to Sunninghill reported that Mr Robinson had nine acres of glebe and eighteen acres as well as a *"bad house adjoining the church yard"*, and he had *"a church house let at 20s per annum to a poor man"* (S.J.C., D 94). This definition of the glebe differs from the fourteen acres listed in the Nicholson survey and in the church terrier of 1677 (a terrier is a register of income from land and tithes).

In 1677 the Reverend Dawson, 1664-1700, recorded that the church property included a vicarage, stable and a hay-house. He defined the church land as being:

"bounded: to the west by the house and land of John Aldridge" (the manor land)

"on the south by the lands of Sir Thomas Draper" (Stoneylands later Ashurst and Oakleigh)

"on the east by a lane leading to Church Green and on the north by the land of William Buckle" (The Cedars)

"and by the lane leading out into the heath by the house of John Aldridge" (Parsonage Lane).

John Aldridge had to pay the parson *"a fat pig at Christmas for the use of the lane"* and William Buckle had to pay for *"land by the Brook which had been added to his meadow"* (B.R.O., D/P 126 6/1).

The different sizes of the church land in these various accounts arises out of the fact that as well as the glebe, the vicars often owned other pieces of land in the parish and in addition there was land which belonged to the parish. In 1606 and 1613 two pieces of royal waste had been given to the vicar to hold in trust for the parish. The document of 1606 signed and sealed by one of the Norris family confirmed the donation of a cottage and half an acre of waste which was located between the church-yard and the land belonging to Robert Milton. This was part of the Church Green. In 1613 a further three acres were given increasing the size of the Church Green. Since all the Green was assarted from the royal waste a quit-rent of four pence a year was due (ibid D/E).

During the first half of the seventeenth century there was the house on the Church Green let at a rent of twenty shillings a year to Mr Gwynn and another cottage, the *"bad house"* of 1618, also known as the *"church house"* by 1704. One of its rooms was used for vestry meetings, for a night class and possibly for a Sunday

School which was under the supervision of the parish clerk. The *"church house"* was an insubstantial building not directly attached to the church and often in need of repair. It was rebuilt in 1719 and again in 1732 at the expense of the parish.

Apart from the land and the rental from Mr Gwynn's house, the vicar had an income from the church charges. In 1634 John Robinson junior listed these as sixpence for a burial, a shilling for a marriage and sixpence for a churching. By 1702 when John Morris was vicar, the charges had increased to one shilling and sixpence for a marriage, a shilling for publishing banns, sixpence for churching a woman or for a burial, and four pence for registration as a parishioner. The fee for a burial within the church was six shillings and eight pence and ten shillings in the chancel. The churchwarden had to be paid extra for *"breaking the ground"* (ibid D/P 126 1/2). The vicars themselves had to pay out one shilling and sixpence a year in Synod charges to the Church.

Another part of the vicar's income came from tithes, a tenth part of all the hay, wool, lambs, calves, milk, coppices, honey, geese, eggs, pigs and fruit produced in the parish with an extra penny a year on the herbs of the garden. These were very difficult to assess and even harder to collect. In practice they were mostly commuted into cash. Unfortunately for the vicars some of the richest estates such as the St John's College farms at Titness and Broomhall and the erstwhile royal land at Sunninghill Park were exempt from tithe so other arrangements had to be made. In 1634 forty shillings was due from a farm at Broomhall which was described as *"is in our parish but not of our parish"* (ibid 6/1).

In 1638 Robinson junior questioned the position as regards Sunninghill Park. He noted that:

> *"before the King parted with Sunninghill Park to Mr Carey, His Majesty, when it was full of deer gave the vicar of Sunninghill 20 shillings for one lodge and 3s 4d for the other one and the keeper knowing the vicarage to be worth but 20 marks allowed the vicar the grazing of a nag for nothing and six or eight cows for 6d per week."*

Since the sale in 1630 the estate no longer kept deer and had discontinued the payments to the vicar. Robinson must also have missed the use of grazing for his nag. Eventually Mr Draper agreed to pay the vicar 13s 4d per year (ibid 6/1). The Mill paid 5s 8d a year to be exempt from tithe. In 1705 the total tithes were worth less than £10 a year (ibid 1/2). Without the *"bounty of its patron"* the living was *"worth little or nothing"* wrote the Reverend Morris in 1702. As a comparison, the tithes at Egham were worth £40 a year in 1656.

Some small improvements were made to St Michael's in this period. The church tower had been silent since the three bells had been removed by the royal commissioners in 1563/4. The first of the modern bells was cast by William Eldridge of Wokingham in 1662 during the incumbency of Francis Sayer, 1654-1664. In 1705 the second and third bells of St Michael's were cast by John Warner and in 1712, six new pews were installed on the north side of the church paid for by Edward Watson. The parishioners also began to replace the church plate that had been confiscated along with the bells for being *"popish"*. The earliest dish which still exists today dates from 1703 and there is also a chalice given by a patron in 1711 marked with the initials *"HC"* which has a cover of the same date. Another piece of silver plate was given to the church in 1716.

The 1766 list of payments for the church fence shows that there were many more parishioners than in 1721 and also that the church fence had grown in length. Sunninghill Park headed the list paying for eighteen panels measuring a total of 144 feet and 4 inches, Broomhall and Tittenhurst paid for seven panels covering 54 feet and 5 inches. Mr John Aldridge IV paid:

for *"Bronsvelt"* (Bronsvelt was at one time the innkeeper at the Wells) two panels at 10 feet 10 inches,

for *"Sylmore"* four panels of 28 feet 4 inches,

for land which had belonged to Whapshots one panel of 9 feet 5 inches,

for land which had belonged to Edward Lane he paid for one more panel of 6 feet 1 inch.

Aldridge no longer paid for Eastmore since it now belonged to John Pitt who paid for five panels a total of 36 feet 3 inches. *"Stonylands"* which had belonged to Ashurst was now owned by William Farrell who paid for 2 panels of 14 feet 6 inches and he also paid for *"New Bridge"*, another 2 panels at 13 feet 10 inches. Edmund Cook Esq paid for 5 panels of 14 feet ten inches and George Hatch of the Wells Inn paid for 3 panels of 19 feet 10 inches.

The rest of the list ran as follows:

late Atlee now John Bartholomew 3 panels making 19 ft 9 ins

late Worth now Cooke a little gate etc leading into the Church Green, 2 panels making 13 ft 2 ins

late Jacob Edwards now John Johnson, J Pearman and Samuel Sawyer 1 panel making 8 ft 1 ins

Mr Deane and John Simons 1 panel making 8 ft 6 ins

Thomas Elliot and John Fernhead 1 panel making 7 ft 10 ins

George Cacutt 2 panels making 18 ft 8 ins
William Slann and Mr William Davis 1 panel making 8 ft 5 ins
Widow Ann Staples 2 panels making 11 ft 10 ins
John Baker and others 1 panel making 8 ft 6 ins
Edward Atfield 1 panel making 7 ft 9 ins
Widow Dee and James Grace 1 panel making 10 ft 6 ins
Sir John Ellwill Bart. 1 panel making 10 ft 7 ins
Mrs Schutz panel and stye (stile) *1 panel making 7 ft*
Mrs Lane Hatch for Careless 1 panel making 8 ft 6 ins
John Skillings 2 panels making 14 ft 10 ins
Thomas Tilbury and others 1 panel making 8 ft 2 ins
Thomas Platt's landlord 2 panels making 14 ft
Mrs Lane or Ed Lane 4 panels making 23 ft 4 ins
*George Hatch and John Johnson paid for 1 panel making 8 feet 3
inches*
Rev J. Thistlethwaite for the gate.

This was a total of 79 panels making 594 feet and 9 inches in all
(B.R.O., D/P 126 8/3).

There were several differences between this list and the earlier
ones. The church fencing had been increased by twenty-five
panels to include the *"church house and vestry room"* as well as the
"little gate" to the Church Green. The length of the list and its
detail may be due to the character of the vicar. The Reverend
Joseph Thistlethwaite was certainly more inclined than his
predecessor to extract every last penny in dues and also to see
that he personally paid out as little as possible, hence his non-
payment for the three panels paid for by the earlier vicar. But
most noticeably by 1766 there were more people in the parish
considered capable of contributing to the costs of the rails.

The vicars themselves were not always resident in the parish.
When Dr Robert Palmer became vicar in 1722, a position he
occupied until his death in 1748, he chose not to live here. As a
scholar and a gentleman he did not find Sunninghill an attractive
place. Most of the gentry only spent the summer season here and
some probably only came for the Races. The vicarage was leased
out but it was not neglected and in the year he died, Dr Palmer
was having it rebuilt. A date found during later renovations in one
of the lower rooms of the vicarage confirmed that a main
rebuilding took place at this time. Palmer employed a curate to
hold the services and he returned his vicar's fees. He also doubled
the Queen Anne's bounty of £200 and enabled the parish to buy
fields known as Long Deanes and Searle's meadow. They were let
out and the income used to support the poor helping to keep the

poor rate down. Both Palmer and his successor Thistlethwaite commented on the very great contrast in wealth among their parishioners.

Joseph Thistlethwaite replaced Dr Palmer. He did indeed reside in the parish serving for almost sixty years and dying in 1807. His colourful career merits a chapter in any history of the parish church. After his death the new vicar was the Reverend Samuel Freeman Montague Hebelthwaite, another *"gentleman"* who never lived at the vicarage. He died in 1817 in Bridlington. Once more the parish was run by curates.

The Problems of Joseph Thistlethwaite

It has been written of the Reverend Thistlethwaite that he had *"no tact or knowledge of the world"* and was *"too fond of the right to pursue the expedient"* (Sunninghill Parish Magazine 1958). The judgement may be deemed somewhat unchristian for a parish magazine and is surely a little harsh. Since his predecessor had not lived in the parish the local worthies had been able to run things very much as they chose. Thistlethwaite who lived here throughout his incumbency was a determined man with the courage of his convictions. As a result he was very likely to come into conflict with the more powerful parishioners. He himself was not a rich man though his wife was wealthy. In his early years here he let out the vicarage and its three-quarter acre garden on a six-year tenancy for £80. When he and his wife moved into it later they spent a considerable amount in having it improved.

Thistlethwaite thought that the wealthy men of the parish failed to pay their share of the church costs. He claimed augmented tithes and extracted as much as possible in the payments for the church fences. In the 1790s he wrote to St John's College, that there were 200 acres of arable land in the parish, half of which was held by James Sibbald at the manor and he added: *"If any person's tithe could be increased it is he ... he has perhaps 150 acres beside water and woodland and he pays £55:8s. All the rest of the parish is in little patches the largest 40 acres the soil is decidedly poor"* (S.J.C.). In the same letter he also noted that Sunninghill Park gave a paltry thirteen and four pence a year in place of tithes.

Here was a man who took his own responsibilities very seriously and expected the same from others. Throughout his incumbency orphan children were brought from London to be placed with nurses or foster mothers in the parish. In 1763 nine such children were being cared for in Sunninghill. A letter of 1759 from Mrs Blencoe who was one of the inspectors for the Berkshire Foundlings Hospital showed his involvement in the care of the children and her opinion of him as a worthy man:

> *"I was at Sunning Hill Wells in Berkshire when your letter came to Mr Thistlethwaite, the minister of that place, who at my request first took care of the children there. He is a very sencible, good sort of man and has a good income for he married a lady of fashion and fortune. The gentleman consulted me upon what you wrote to him as to allowing the nurses 3d a week more, and they to clothe the children. I gave him my opinion that I had rather do it myself, very few nurses are fit to be entrusted with more and fewer capable of keeping any account Many of them I'me affraed wold live better and dress themselves finer and let the poor infants go ragged and dirty."*

("*Correspondence of the Foundling Hospital Inspectors in Berkshire 1757-68*", edited Gillian Clark, 1994, pp. 75, 173).

The disparaging remarks about Thistlethwaite in the 1958 Parish Magazine were due to the large amount of litigation that is recorded during his tenure. He had lengthy arguments with his neighbours over the lanes running from the London Road to the church and from the church across the fields to Eastmore and Cheapside. This was not a new issue.

There had been an investigation about the track to Cheapside in 1745 when Dr Palmer was the vicar. At this enquiry John Pickering of Cheapside, who was born in 1724 and worked as a coachman for Mr Baber, said that he usually went to church through Brook Lane, as today's London Road was called before it became a turnpike.

The Parsonage Lane, which went between the Parsonage and The Cedars, north of the glebe meadow, over the stream and then upwards towards Eastmore and Cheapside, was shorter but it had a locked gate at the bridge and he had to get the key from Mr Bentley's. In 1745 his father's coffin had to be carried from Cheapside to be buried and they were forced to go through Brook Lane *"a worse way and much muddier"* because they could not use Parsonage Lane (B.R.O., D/P 126 8/2). Perhaps the gate at the bridge was locked because the bridge was unsafe. In a letter to St John's College Thistlethwaite reported on the need to repair the bridge in Parsonage Lane and he asked permission to use timber from the Titness lands belonging to the college and sublet to Sir John Baber (S.J.C., D 74).

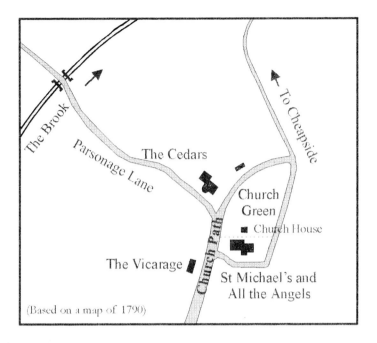

Sketch Map of the Church Green and Parsonage Lane

The vicar had several disputes with Mr Davis of The Cedars. The latter claimed that Thistlethwaite had impeded his entry down Church Lane from the main road. The vicar secured the support of eleven parishioners who signed a statement in the vestry book declaring that he had never blocked the lane but had in fact repaired it. After several years of wrangling Thistlethwaite and Davis agreed to accept arbitration in December 1747. The vicar's claim to the glebe land was upheld. The *"ancient right of way"* (i.e. Parsonage Lane) through The Cedars was to be leased to Davis but the right of way was maintained. Davis' own right of way down Church Lane and across the Church Green was also preserved. In 1764/5 Mr Davis again disputed with the vicar about Church Lane, Parsonage Lane and the ownership of the piece of land at the end of Davis' garden. Davis sold up and left the parish shortly afterwards. The vicar wrote to St John's to explain his controversy with Davis and to report on the preservation of the church's right of way (ibid).

Davis was not Thistlethwaite's only opponent. In 1756 he was really angry and upset and wrote a long invective in the vestry book against wicked men who had slandered him. It began:

"Wheras the inhumanity and malice of some men has been made very
apparent in commencing and carrying on vexations and cruel lawsuits

to the disturbance of the public peace and to the ruin of the fortunes
and ease of mind of particular persons;"

and continued at length in the same vein. The names of the
evildoers were not stated but it seems that John Aldridge IV
and a Mr Bromley had accused the vicar of perjury. The exact
nature of the perjury is never made clear. The vicar's
denunciation was supported by six signatories from the vestry
including John Baber and his son. Moreover the vestry agreed
to allow the vicar to use money from poor relief to pay for his
litigation against his slanderers. The vestry:

"do consent and agree to pay out of the money to be levied for the relief
of the poor the whole expenses of all and every action at law which
shall hereafter appear to be maliciously brought against any person or
persons whatsoever residing in our said parish" (B.R.O., D/P 126
8/3-4).

There must have been a great deal of bad feeling about. On
the 22nd of August in 1763 the vicarage barn and outhouses were
burnt down. He wrote to the college explaining that there had
been an accident caused by hot ashes blowing on to the thatch.
The fire was so strong that the glass was broken in the house
windows and the lead was melted. Some locals seemed to think
that the fire was deliberate and that it was retaliation against the
vicar for his various disputes. The problems were also connected
in the vicar's mind for he wrote to St John's bursar in 1769 that:

"I am sure that my expenses in rebuilding the dwelling before the fire
and these outhouses since are very little short of £100. I have also
with very great trouble prevented a King's highway for carts, carriages
and cattle from being carried through the yards, garden and the middle
of glebe land" (S.J.C., D 74).

This reference to preventing a king's highway through church
lands sheds light on the long controversy. Davis of The Cedars
needed access down Church Lane past the vicarage and the
church. Aldridge of Eastmore would have found it very
convenient to avoid the steep and muddy Sunninghill hill. He
would also be spared the payment of a toll if he could turn down
past the church and use Parsonage Lane across to Cheapside.

This track had been used for centuries by walkers, riders and
farm carts but with the increase of carriages the wear and tear on
the surface was much more severe. Carriage riders also demanded
smoother and wider roads than did farm carts. The question at
dispute was whether the Church and Parsonage Lanes should
become carriageways.

These local arguments over access occurred at a time when there was a nation-wide demand for the improvement of paths and rights of way. It was the age of the turnpike trusts. In 1759 the Windsor Forest Turnpike trust had built the road from Blacknest Gate to Windsor improving the access from Sunninghill to Windsor and joining the earlier turnpike which transformed Brook Lane into the London Road. There were toll bars at Blacknest and on the Church Lane corner. Toll charges were used to keep the roads in good condition and local people sought ways of avoiding the charges by using other tracks.

The vicar's dispute with Aldridge and Bromley (the latter may have been Aldridge's lawyer) dragged on for several years. In 1771 Thistlethwaite took them to court for slander and they had to apologise to the vicar both in the Court of Terminer at Reading and in the vestry records (B.R.O., D/P 126 8/3). Their apologies were copied into the vestry records on no less than three occasions. Although the Aldridge family sold the manor to John Pitt in 1764, they still owned land in the area in the 1780s but they moved out of the parish during this long dispute, bowing out on a sour note. It is possible that this argument was one of the reasons for the departure of John Aldridge IV after such a long family association with Sunninghill.

All the arguments seem to focus on the right of way past the church towards Cheapside and on the use of this route by carriages. Was this why James Sibbald, who bought the estate from John Pitt, decided to site his new mansion on the opposite side of the estate where his access to the London Road would be unimpeded?

Thistlethwaite was certainly a much-troubled man and he was also plagued by problems nearer to home. In 1770 he wrote to the bursar of the college: *"Mrs T. Returned from Bath very little better for the waters, the gout is still flying about her and nothing seems able to fix it"* (S.J.C., D 74). Perhaps she had already tried the waters at the Wells.

When the Reverend Hebelthwaite took over in 1807 he chose to live outside the parish probably to avoid the controversies which had dogged his predecessor. At the start of his period of office another valuation of the living of St Michael's was made. The church income derived from the tithes and also from *"10 acres of glebe near house for horse and cow valued at £5: 5s 7d; surplice fees of £6: 5s and Easter offerings valued at £32: 11s"*. The vicar paid a rent of two pounds six shillings to St John's College for the use of the vicarage now substantially rebuilt. It was described as having a *"new part of parsonage in good condition with 2 parlours and 2 good bedrooms but no stables or barn."* These had been lost in the fire and not yet replaced (S.J.C., D 74 21-56).

Yet another contentious matter which marks the Thistlethwaite period was the sale of the Church House. The vicar and the members of the vestry committee were prepared to go to considerable lengths to relieve the parish expenses and to help their friends. In 1749 St John's College renewed a lease to Mr Yorke for the Healthy Hall estate (ibid). Mr Yorke would feature in all the controversies as the vicar's firm supporter and friend. In 1769 Yorke bought The Cedars from Thistlethwaite's old enemy Davis and ten years later he was allowed to buy the Church House and the ancient Church Green to add to his garden (B.R.O., D/P 126 8/3).

Of course Yorke paid for this considerable extension to his garden. The vestry agreed to exchange the Church House and its land for *"a piece of land the same size or larger in Sunninghill or in an adjoining parish"*. One of the signatories to the deed was John Aldridge IV acting as a trustee of the Church House. The building and the Green were sold for fourteen acres of land at Chobham and enough money to pay for an *"addition to the west end of the church as wide as the existing church and 18 feet long with a vestry room beneath and room for parishioners above in a gallery"* (ibid).

In this way Sunninghill lost its Church Green, some of which had belonged to the parish from shortly after the church was built and the rest had been granted in 1606 and 1613 from the royal forest. The Green had belonged to all the parishioners whose rights were vested in the trustees. On a map of the late eighteenth century the Church Green is still clearly shown (see page 75). It was an irregular shape and three buildings were marked around it, presumably the Church House, Mr Glynn's old house and The Cedars. By the time this map was made however Yorke owned the Healthy Hall estate (the forerunner of Tetworth Hall), The Cedars and the Church Green (P.R.O., MR 687). The old Healthy Hall had gone and a house was built on the present Tetworth Hall site by the time of the Enclosure Act in 1813.

The Age of Elegance

Sunninghill and Cheapside were not immune from the major political events of the century. From 1739 there were army encampments on Ascot Heath and after the defeat of the Scots at

Culloden in 1745 there were several regiments quartered in the district. The Soldier's Pillar on the ancient barrows was erected to commemorate the work of these men who were kept busy making carriage drives and doing major landscaping works.

The Wells Inn acted as a magnet for the officers and for their wives and daughters. In 1767 the innkeeper, Mr Robert Hodges, opened the Long Assembly Room for breakfasts and balls. It had become a fashionable and exclusive spa:

> *"anyone could go to Bath but not to Sunninghill where 200 persons in the first families of Berkshire, Surrey and Buckinghamshire were present at a Public Breakfast in September 1786".*

The Wells was famous for its Monday breakfasts held at 1 o'clock in the afternoon, for its balls in the evenings and for the bands playing martial music in the gardens (Hughes, chapter XXVI).

In the 1790s during the wars with France there were even more soldiers here including the Sunninghill Infantry (E. Harwood, Windsor Old and New). On several occasions King George III reviewed the Royal Horse Guards, the Blues, on Ascot Heath. Following the 1784 review there was a public breakfast at The Wells where the guests were entertained by a twenty-piece band drawn from the regiments. During the royal review of the Dragoon Guards in 1798, three men fell and one was killed because the heath was so swampy. From then on the royal reviews took place on Winkfield Heath and Ascot Plain. In 1800, 32,000 men were reviewed there by the king and the duke of York, the Commander-in-Chief. Afterwards the royal family dined at Cumberland Lodge. In the year before Waterloo, the duke of Wellington himself reviewed the Blues on Winkfield Plain. The presence of the army brought its own problems. In 1800, Captain Bruhl was tried by court-marshal at The Wells for being drunk on guard at Cumberland Lodge (Hughes).

The events of the Revolution in France reverberated as far as Sunninghill. On the seventh of March 1793, the son of a French émigré family was baptised at St Michael's. The parents who were staying at *"Kings Wick"* were Marc Etienne Gabriel de Beauvau, the Prince de Craôn, and Natalie Henriette Victorienne de Montmart (B.R.O., D/P 126 1/4). Lord Uxbridge who would later lose his leg at Waterloo (and whose leg would have its own tomb there) lived for a time at Sunningdale Park, now the Civil Service College. With such notable residents and all the regiments that were based here social life in Sunninghill was at its height.

The success of the Sunninghill social season was supported by the Races. These took place for only four or five days a year, and made little real contribution to the local economy. A 1739 Act of Parliament stated that any horse running at Ascot had to be kept from the time of entering to time of running at some public house within three miles of the course. The Wells was of course used for this (D.L.). Up to 1756 the rule that all the horses racing at Ascot had to have hunted with the Royal Buckhounds was upheld but after this date other horses could race as well.

The duke of Cumberland took a great interest in the races and in horse breeding. His prize horse, Eclipse, was foaled at Cranbourne in 1764. Eclipse lived to 1789, had 334 wins at the races and sired many famous successors. Until 1998 he was remembered locally in the name of an inn on the London Road at Egham (this was astonishingly changed to *"Caffe Uno"* in 1998). In 1791 the first big race, the Oaklands Stakes, with a prize of 2,950 guineas, was run for the first time at Ascot but this was not a permanent fixture. The race was moved to Newmarket and only later returned to Ascot. The great days of Royal Ascot had to wait until the nineteenth and twentieth centuries.

Another English sport that kept the gentry busy and gradually grew in popularity was cricket. On the 20th July in 1815, the players in a three-day cricket match between the gentlemen of Berkshire and the gentlemen of Buckinghamshire met at The Wells. They went off suitably refreshed to play on a pitch sited where the Ascot Grandstand is today and they competed for a prize of 2,000 guineas.

With all these social pleasures available there was a general increase in the population of Sunninghill and an even greater increase in the numbers of gentry. Gradually the parish came to be dominated by wealthy people who ran the vestry and provided employment. They built new houses and developed their parks and estates. Some of these were available to rent. By 1768 the freeholders of Sunninghill who were entitled to vote numbered twenty-four. They were named in the Poll Book as:

John Aldridge *	Thomas Draper Baber	John Baker
Thomas Elliot	Geoffrey Hatch	Thomas Hatch
William Narraway	John Slann	J. Thistlethwaite
John Biggs	Geoffrey Cacutt	Edmund Atfield
Edmund Cook	William Davis	William Dews
J. Fernhead	Thomas Grave	Robert Harris
Sam Moody	John Nash	Foster Nash
John Simmonds	J. Tindall	J. Woods

* he also had the right to vote in Cookham.

On the above list there are sixteen men who have no previous reference in the local records. There were a total number of 3,540 voters for the whole county of Berkshire.

The Making of Silwood Park

One man not on that electoral list was John Pitt who began buying Eastmore and the manorial estates from 1764 onwards. John Pitt was the Surveyor General of His Majesty's Woods and Forests and he was involved in the construction of the Virginia Water Lake. He was related to the two William Pitts who were chief ministers for the crown and came from the Pitt family of Dorset where he had another estate. With his arrival a new era in the life of Sunninghill Manor began. No longer was the manor a group of working farms. It would become a gentleman's residence and park.

Pitt paid John Aldridge IV £2,137 for Eastmore and the Sunninghill Manor estate (I.C.A.). Three years later he bought more land, some from John Aldridge and some from the sister of Henry Aldridge's widow, a Miss Jane Shipton, for £1,697. These lands were described as *"Sellmore Coppice, coppice field and part of Wapshott's Land"*. Selmore Coppice is today known as Nash's Copse and the piece of Wapshott's Land probably corresponds to parts of what was known as Nash's field and Gunnes hill, both in Silwood today.

Pitt held his first manorial court in 1767 and it was then that he claimed he was unaware of Cookham Manor's claim over Sunninghill Manor. He started to dispute the Cookham claim at length and at great cost. This vast litigation has left a hoard of records and court barons in the Imperial College Archive. The other side of the story can be found in the Cookham Manor records at the Berkshire Record Office. He was certainly not fighting for financial reasons. In 1790 the total rent due to the manor of Cookham was one pound one shilling and ten pence and for encroachments five pounds ten shillings and two pence. His legal fees must have far exceeded that. It seems to have been purely a matter of status helped on, no doubt, by the Pitt family's inordinate taste for litigation.

By 1774 Pitt's estate covered 159 acres with forty small fields. The largest field was only seven acres. There is a detailed description of the manor lands in an indenture of this date, registered in 1777 (I.C.A.). This document recorded a curious transaction whereby John Pitt sold his estates for five shillings to John Holliday of Lincoln's Inn and then leased them back at a peppercorn rent. This may have been designed to protect his possessions during his long litigation. The indenture included a survey of *"all that manor or lordship of Sunninghill and also the mansion house with the appurtenances collectively known as Eastmore or Eastmore Farm and land"*.

Nineteen fields were named. These include *"Pound field, Church mead"*, fields called after plants such as Alder, Holly, Oak, Furze and Gorse and one called the *"New Piece"* of a little over two acres which was probably a recent enclosure from the waste. There were sixty-three acres at Eastmore, nearby another nine acres known as *"Furneze Closes"* and land tenanted by John Wapshott with *"1 acre formerly known as Further Long and Further Long Dean reserved as a cartway for Selmore Farm"*. Other fields were called *"Bromefield, Slans Mead and Stony Close"* and these had been bought from Thomas Charlwood.

Grouped with Selmore Coppice and Selmore Farm there were another eight fields: *"Crooked Ash, Birch Hill, Long Hill, Barnfield, Shagbag (or Shagbog), Barnshill, Cheapside Upper Mead and Cheapside Lower Mead"*, in all about forty-three acres. All this had been part of the estate of Henry Aldridge. Pitt also owned the cottage of William Taylor and another cottage adjoining Cheapside Lower Mead where his son William Morton Pitt lived. There were references to both a water mill and a windmill on the manorial lands (B.R.O., D/E Fa T 11). In 1781 John Pitt bought a last piece of land from the Aldridge family, a wood which had belonged to George Aldridge who was by then presumed dead.

In his 1777/8 petition to Sir Frederick North, the Chancellor, over the state of his title to the manor, Pitt provided an abbreviated list of the past owners as follows: *"King Henry VI to Norris, Norris to Lane, Lane to William Day, Matthew Day to John Aldridge, and son of John Aldridge to John Pitt"*, an omission of two generations of Aldridges. It is also interesting that there was no reference to a manor existing before the reign of Henry VI (B.R.O., D/EF a Li). At the end of all his litigation Pitt was told he did indeed hold the manor of Sunninghill under the manor of Cookham and that he must continue to pay the quit-rents due to Cookham.

There are hints that during the last years of his life John Pitt began to consider major alterations to the house and landscape including the creation of a lake. A man who was involved in the grand landscaping of Virginia Water was likely to be interested in the adornment of his own land. He may well have met Humphrey Repton when the latter was employed at St Leonard's Hill, Windsor in 1783 advising Lord Harcourt, an enthusiast for the new *"picturesque"* garden design. Pitt may also have decided to move away from the Cheapside rustics and surround himself with men of his own class. In 1782 he leased out Silwood Lodge *"a pretty rustic house"* to the Hon. Henry Greville. Silwood Lodge was close to the London Road, an attraction to these gentlemen owners with their town houses and carriages.

Whatever his plans were for the estate they were certainly not apparent when he died in 1787 and the Sunninghill Manor estate of 184 acres was sold by his son, William Morton Pitt. It was bought by James Hartley and, when he went to the East Indies a year later, he sold it on to James Sibbald, the head of the banking house of Marsh, Sibbald, Stracy and Founteleroy and Co. of London.

"Sunning Hill Park House" later known as Silwood Park, from a drawing by Louisa Wale

Under Sibbald a splendid new Georgian mansion called *"Sunning Hill Park House"* was built. The speed with which this new house appeared, within a couple of years of the purchase, suggests that either Sibbald had his plans ready and waiting for a suitable site or that Pitt had already had some plans drawn up.

The architect was Mr Robert Mitchell. *"Both fronts were decorated with porticoes of Composite pillars"* (Hakewill). There was a grand staircase under a massive dome and two wings on the ground floor. *"The drawing room, breakfast room and eating room were en suite, towards the pleasure grounds, which are thrown together by folding doors forming a range of apartments of ninety feet in length"* (ibid). This was a house for a man who intended to entertain on a princely level. It was this Georgian house which survived with some modifications up to 1876.

Sibbald's naming of his house as *"Sunning Hill Park House"* suggests an ignorance of the other property nearby. This name survived for about half a century. By then the confusion with Sunninghill Park must have become onerous and it was quietly changed to Silwood Park.

The new house stood on the south eastern corner of the estate beside the wild Beggars' Bush Heath and rather too close to the junction between the London Road and the road from Windsor to Bagshot. Sibbald lost no time in remedying this situation. In 1790 he applied for the consent of the vestry to his proposal to move the Windsor Road and six years later he applied to enclose eight and a half acres of waste in front of his new *"Sunning Hill House"* (B.R.O., D/P 126 8/4).

This was all part of the transformation of the estate into a gentleman's park, and who better to help this transformation than a fashionable landscape gardener. Sir James called in Humphrey Repton (1752-1818), whose career as a landscape gardener was beginning to flourish and who, at that time, charged ten guineas for the survey. His proposals were presented in a Red Book, a most elegant way of explaining his plans. He drew a set of charming watercolours designed to overlay each other showing the site before and after his proposals. A copy of the Red Book for *"Sunning Hill Park"* still exists, now in private hands (N.M.R.).

The Red Book was dated July 1790, a year in which Repton put forward no less than two dozen plans for estate improvements in thirteen counties. Repton's letter of introduction would surely have endeared him to his new patron. He wrote that the:

"character of the grounds at Sunninghill is evidently that of an elegant Ferme-ornée, where nature has been very bountiful in diversified scenery, while great judgement and taste seem to have directed the hand of art in availing itself of its natural beauties. I hope Sir you will allow me to pay this tribute so justly due to the memory of Mr Pitt, who gave such assiduous attention to this enchanting Spot. You must also allow me Sir

to congratulate its present possessor on that good taste which lead him to the choice of such a situation, I beg you will accept my acknowledgements for the honour you do me in asking my advice on the still farther improvement of these delightful grounds".

We realise why Repton was so popular with the gentry. The reference to Mr Pitt supports the idea that Repton had had an earlier connection with the estate.

Repton's main task was to *"form a piece of water in the valley".* He was very aware of the importance of water in a landscape and his various schemes all show a decided preference for long sinuous lakes with cascades designed to enliven the parkland with the glitter and sparkle of the water.

For James Sibbald's park he proposed that *"the water will take the form of a large river"* with either one major dam or two smaller dams. He favoured two dams, the upper dam would be:

"covered with copse wood to resemble an island; tho' in fact it may be united to the south shore, and from the north shore it may appear to be separated by a weir or shelf running aslant, over which the water will continually fall as a natural cascade".

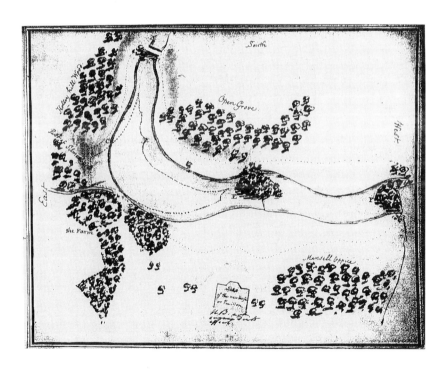

Humphrey Repton's Plan for Silwood Lake (N.M.R.)

This would then:

> *"become a pleasing object immediately before the site of the house (the white foam glittering under the shade of the Island) ... altho' it may at first appear too artificial, is by no means unnatural; for nothing is more common than to see rivers in hilly countrys checked in their course by these occasional weirs or ledges across them; yet as one great advantage from a Sheet of water is the pleasure it affords in a boat, so a communication might be made betwixt these two pieces of water, thus divided, either by a small lock concealed to the south of the island - or at less expense - an inclined plane with rollers might be there fixed which would answer the purpose (with a little mechanism) for a small pleasure boat."*

Sibbald however opted for one large piece of water and one dam and discarded the romance of the glittering foam.

Although he had been consulted primarily on *"the valley where you propose to introduce a sheet of water"* Repton proffered his opinion on the positioning of the house. He considered the location of the house of the utmost importance in the creation of a fine estate and he was not at all happy with the site of Sibbald's new house.

> *"The present house being very inconveniently situated with respect both to the Kitchen Garden and Farming Buildings, it has been proposed to build another house on the knoll which commands the valley ... and I have of course considered the effect of the water from that spot ... When the water is finished if it be thought advisable to alter or to add to the present dwelling instead of totally removing it, I should then advise at least a room be built on the knoll to take advantage of the desirable scenery which that spot would command and possibly this room might be so contrived as to form a part of some future dwelling house to be erected in this delightful situation".*

The knoll is indicated on the Plan above by the small plaque at the centre bottom. It reads *"Site of the new house or Pavillion"*. It is in fact on the hill behind the present Silwood Nurseries. From here there is still a commanding view over the lake. In other words Repton was urging Sibbald to rebuild his house on the Cheapside side of the lake close to the old Eastmore site! Sibbald ignored Repton's advice on this matter. A rather defiant note, possibly in Sibbald's hand, was added later to the Repton book. It states that *"the spot where the present new house stands was found the most eligible of any other on the estate and the water"*. Thus Sibbald placed his new house, the future Silwood, on a site from which it was impossible to view the glittering water in the desirable scenery, a major disadvantage for the estate ever since.

With the creation of Silwood Lake in the 1790s, Sibbald completed the remodelling and reorientation of the old Sunninghill manor estate. The lake flooded the old Parsonage Lane thus cutting off Cheapside from his London Road mansion. Apart from the need to secure direct access to the London Road and so avoid the Sunninghill hill, another reason for Sibbald's move was doubtless to escape the old tanneries, the timber coppices, the Parish Pound, the working farm, the cottages and the hovels of eighteenth century Cheapside.

As a result of this transfer of the manor house the future of Cheapside was dramatically altered. It would not develop as a hamlet on the main approach of a large Georgian estate but as a distant group of cottages. If the main house had remained at this side of the estate Cheapside may well have disappeared. It might have suffered the fate of many cottages on the new estates and have been entirely demolished so as not to spoil the views from the new mansions. Some clearance did occur within Sibbald's new park. The cottages shown within the manor land shown on Jean Rocque's map of 1752 had all disappeared by 1817.

James Sibbald became sheriff of Berkshire in 1799 and in 1806 he was made a baronet. Five years after he had acquired his title, Sir James Sibbald sold the estate to George Simson. Had the acquisition of a great estate been seen as a prerequisite for a title? By the time of the sale, the estate of *"Sunning Hill Park"* was about twice the size it had been when Sibbald had first bought it.

Gentry Houses

A plan of *"Sunning Hill Park"* made about 1817 shows the development of the neighbouring estates and houses (I.C.A.). Opposite to Sibbald's new house on what is now the Buckhurst Road there was the Harewood estate with a large ornamental garden. Beyond Harewood lay the Mill with the large millpond and five cottages between the Mill and the Tun Inn. Today's Heronsbrook House was drawn with ornamental gardens and on the north side of the Brook, where April Place is today, there were two cottages and some outbuildings. More cottages and the *"Thatch Tavern"* were indicated on the north side of Cheapside Road and two cottages were shown on the south side where Elm Bank and Wisteria Cottage are now. A lane led down from Cheapside to Silwood Farm, shown as a cluster of buildings. Elaborate gardens were indicated at Tetworth Hall, The Cedars and Oakleigh. Several houses were shown along the London Road east of the Church Lane but there were no small cottages near *Sunning Hill Park House* as there were on earlier maps.

In 1822 William Cobbett noted that *"Sunninghill is a spot all made into grounds and gardens by tax-eaters"*. Most of these grounds and gardens were made in the last years of the eighteenth and the first decades of the nineteenth centuries. The most attractive properties were those with a good access to the London Road such as Beechgrove and Kingswick. The older properties in Church Lane continued to change hands and develop during this period. All these estates showed a fairly rapid change of ownership contributing to the reputation of Berkshire estates for *"skittishness"*. The frequent transfer of these properties and the sort of people who lived in them reflect the changing society of Sunninghill in this epoch.

"Stoneylands" and The Cedars had developed into fine small estates. *"Stonylands"* covered the present day Ashurst and Oakleigh and included land on the south side of the London Road. The first brick house in the parish had been built on this property by Draper in the seventeenth century. *"The Brick House"* had passed into the hands of the Hatch family even before Lady Ashurst, after whom it was renamed, had left it. In 1735 the will of Thomas Hatch referred to his land at *"Stonylands where Lady Elizabeth Ashurst still lives"*. He left it to his wife and after her death to his son Lane Hatch, whose names suggest a marriage between the two long established local families.

Lady Ashurst left the property in 1740 and it was then sold to Captain Farrell who in 1745 negotiated with the parish over that notorious right of access into Church Lane (B.R.O., D/EF a T 30 1-4). In 1766 Farrell's son, William, sold Ashurst to Thomas Birch who sold it on to John Yorke. Yorke later bought The Cedars where, as we have seen, he enlarged the garden by his purchase of the Church Green and the Church House. The site of today's Ashurst was sold to a Mr Charlwood and Mr Spencer Schutz bought the rest from John Yorke. In 1806 the latter was advertised for sale with *"24 acres and many fishponds"* *"having been the residence of Mr Spencer Schutz"* (I.C.A.). Baron Schutz had been the Hanoverian envoy at the court of Queen Anne. George Augustus Schutz was a draughtsman and surveyor for the duke of Cumberland between 1746 and 1749 (Roberts, p. 37). The Schutz family had the Ashurst estate for more than one generation.

Of all the properties near the church, The Cedars was one of the most interesting. Benefiting from the garden extensions made by Yorke and from its secure access to the London Road it was sold in 1807 to George Ellis. On his death in 1815, he left it to his brother Charles who was created Lord Seaford in 1827.

George Ellis' death created quite a national and certainly a local stir. The Ellis memorial at St Michael's is today concealed behind the organ. It was carved by Flaxman and had an epitaph written by George Canning who was later to become Prime Minister. Canning often stayed at Southhill Park in Bracknell and he had much in common with Ellis. The government was fearful lest the infection of the French Revolution would affect England and Canning supported the anti-Jacobin and anti-revolutionary articles which Ellis wrote. There is no mention of politics in the epitaph however. It declared that George Ellis was a man whose *"name will long be cherished by the lovers of English Literature"*. This referred to his essays and to his friendship with writers including Edmund Burke and Sir Walter Scott. The latter is said to have written *"Marmion"* at The Cedars. Sir Walter enjoyed his days among the *"Windsor oaks and Ascot plains"* and described George Ellis as *"my dear friend George one of the most accomplished scholars and delightful companions I have ever known"*.

George Ellis, like James Sibbald, sought to embellish his property with the *"picturesque"*. He designed a contemplative or philosophical garden on the slope down to the Brook. It included well-placed trees and various monuments. Although now marred by a dreadful 1930s swimming pool George Ellis' philosophical walk still evokes a sense of tranquillity.

Some of the monuments remain today. There is a plinth inscribed on two sides with verses. This was probably the base of a monumental stone urn dedicated to the memory of his dog *"Tuscan"*. On the sides were the words *"Sagacity"* and *"Faithfulness"*. Nearby there is another stone inscribed with a long verse written to record Walter Scott's visits to The Cedars and at a point where a spring breaks through there is a stone basin which has a plaque bearing the verse:

> *"Behold her mark*
> *A little fountain cell*
> *Where water clear as diamond spark*
> *In a stone basin fell*
> *Above some half worn letters say,*
> *Drink weary pilgrim drink and pray"*.

Other gentry houses built by this time included Beechgrove, constructed between 1702 and 1722 and home in the late eighteenth century to General Fitzpatrick. He was the antithesis of Ellis, a friend and relative of the radical Charles James Fox and notorious as a *"libertine and atheist"*. He left his estate to his mistress, Caroline Price, for her lifetime and then to his neice, Caroline Fox. He had owned the much older Kingswick but it had to be sold to pay his debts. Nearby and also on the London Road was The Oaks built according to G. M. Hughes *"on top of the heath before Titnest wood"*.

A little way off, down the Windsor Road, was Harewood Park known earlier as *"Sunninghill House"* (Hughes, pp. 257-258). The Cowdery family sold it to a Mr Barker who was connected to the Days of Eton. In 1806 Lady Harewood moved in giving it its subsequent name. Five years later it became the residence of John Robinson the Crown Surveyor and in 1815 it was inhabited by William Towry. His father or brother had lived at Follyjohn Park between 1771 and 1798. William Towry was followed by George Edward Towry who lived there until 1843. By the 1890s Harewood was *"one of the oldest of our remaining houses"* (Hughes, p. 256).

Close to *"Sunning Hill House"* there were three smaller houses. Silwood Lodge, near Beggars' Bush was leased out in 1782 by the Hon. Henry Greville to Joseph Turner *"a yeoman"*. Oakleigh, the second, was called *"The White House"* by its builder Mr Gregory who divided the site and built the new Ashurst closer to the church, on the site of the today's Ashurst offices. The third was Silwood Cottage, home in turn of Mr Rivers, Sir Charles Wentworth, Mrs Ann Dawson, Captain Pater, Vice-Admiral Hardyman and his daughters. These were the sort of smaller houses generally used only for the season of races and summer balls and whose owners or tenants returned to London for the winter.

Nearer to Cheapside there was Tetworth Hall rebuilt possibly by Yorke. The eighteenth century house was sited closer to the Wells than the present day house and this may well explain its earlier name as *"Healthy Hall"*. Tetworth too developed into a fine small ornamental estate and passed from owner to owner and from tenant to tenant. Closer still to Cheapside Green was the new house known as Buckhurst or *"Buckett Hill"* Park. This was built at the end of the eighteenth century by James Barwell who also owned Coworth Park. He was the fourth son of William Barwell a former governor of Bengal, a friend of Warren Hastings, and one of the richest men in England.

In 1788 Barwell had a very fine new clock installed in the stable block at Buckhurst Park. It took the clockmaker six days to

"*Fix the Whole*" which cost £3 and a further £4 and 4 shillings for painting figures on the dials "*with Expenses of board and lodging and Carriage there and back*". Altogether it cost £52 and 10 shillings. For this Barwell had a "*New Thirty Hour Turrett Clock with 10 inch Great Wheels to shew Four Outside Dialls one Hours and Minutes and three Hours only and a New Bell of 1 cwt*" which was still working two centuries later (Guildhall Library, ms 6788 vol. 2 p. 34). James Barwell's brother, Mr Smyth Barwell, lived at Buckhurst Park and early in the nineteenth century it was advertised to be let or sold with stabling for ten horses and thirty acres of land. John Vernon bought it.

Sunninghill Park

Up to the late eighteenth century when all these new parks were made, the only "*mansion*" here had been Sunninghill Park. During its occupation by the Drapers, the Babers and the Draper-Babers, the Park developed into a fine Georgian estate. The house was modified several times but there remains little or no evidence for this house or for its alterations.

Sir Thomas Draper had extended his local interests by renting land on the Broomhall estate from St John's College. Between 1660 and 1697 he paid the College £45 to £50 in rent every eight years. He lived to a ripe old age dying in 1703 and his estate went to his wife who lived on to 1717. Her executor was John Aldridge II, her neighbour.

Sir Thomas and Lady Draper left two daughters, Elizabeth who married Sir Henry Ashurst and had no children and Mary who married Sir John Baber (her cousin and the son of the royal physician). They had a son, also John, born in 1684, who married Ann Stawell. They inherited Sunninghill Park.

The Babers were cultivated representatives of the enlightened classes of the age of reason. They patronised writers and aired their knowledge of the classics. In 1725 a translation was made of a poem in Latin by its author who called himself A.M. and dedicated his verses to Sir John Baber of "*Sunning-Hill*". The title of the poem was "*Heliocrene*" i.e. the fountain of the Sun, an obvious reference to Sunninghill and its famous waters. Sunninghill was described as a Parnassus whither the nine Muses had fled for shelter when Greece was spoiled and ravaged by the "*Barbarians*". It is interesting that while evoking Greek gods it was written in Latin.

In his lengthy poem describing this sacred place, the author claimed that Apollo (Helios in Greek) had given this haven of the Muses:

"its Title and his Beams
Give Healing virtues to its Streams!
Derived from Him its name has been
Since changed, and now called Heliocrene
A noble Structure do's adjoyn
Worthy your Goddess and her Nine!
A generous Patron in it lives
Who to the Muses welcome gives
The exiled Nymphs he will protect
And greet in their own Dialect"

(Reading Public Library, B/UJ 1211 7/51)

The noble structure was Sunninghill Park and the generous patron who could greet the Muses in Greek was Sir John Baber.

Sunninghill Park House in the Eighteenth Century

On a more practical level Sir John continued the tradition of renting the Broomhall lands from St John's College paying a total rent of approximately £660 between 1720 and 1751. In 1765 he died and his son Thomas Draper Baber inherited his property. Thomas Draper Baber sold Sunninghill Park four years later in 1769. It was purchased by the Crutchley family who would be prominent in our local history for nearly two centuries. Thomas

Draper Baber remained in the parish and when he died in 1783 he was buried at St Michael's Church.

Jeremiah Crutchley became the owner of Sunninghill Park at the age of twenty-four. His father had died when he was still a minor and one of his guardians was Mr Thrale a brewer of Streatham. The Thrales were friends of Dr Samuel Johnson and the great Doctor visited Sunninghill Park with Mrs and Miss Thrale in 1781. Miss Thrale gave Jeremiah a gift for his new estate in the form of a splendid gateway for the park. The stone piers of this gate still stand, near the farm.

The wealth of the new owner came from the enterprises of his grandfather, John Crutchley, a brewer, dyer and merchant at Southwark in London. It is possible that there was some connection with the Aldridges who did business with tanners in that part of London. John Crutchley died in 1727 and his heir was his fifth son Jeremiah, who married Alice Jackson in 1741. Their son, the future owner of Sunninghill Park was born in 1745. They also had a daughter called Alice who married Michael Duffield in 1767. It was the son of this marriage, George Henry Duffield, born in 1778, who took the name of Crutchley in 1806 and eventually inherited the estate from Jeremiah Crutchley.

The Crutchleys could trace their family back for many generations. Their family crest was *"a mount vert, a Talbot sejant argent, collared and line reflexed over the back"*. After they had absorbed the Duffield connection in 1806 they added *"the dexter forepaw on a torteau"*.

The Crutchley Arms

As the owner of Sunninghill Park, Crutchley also took over the tenancy of the farms on the Broomhall estate and he bought more land to add to the south of the park. By the time of the Windsor Forest Enclosure Act of 1813 the estate had been extended in several directions.

He also had Sunninghill Park House totally rebuilt. The side wings were pulled down and the central building was remodelled and extended under the direction of James Wyatt, 1747-1813, an architect who pulled down and remodelled so many old buildings that he became known as *"The Destroyer"*. The inside was equally splendid with carvings by Flaxman commissioned by Jeremiah's mother in 1769.

Jeremiah Crutchley took a very active part in the life of the parish, serving on the vestry committee and acting as a trustee of the local charities. He began a long tradition of public service that was carried on by his successors. Although the Crutchleys were never the Lords of the Manor, they were often regarded as such because they were so active in local affairs. Jeremiah became Member of Parliament for Horsham and later for Grampound and St Mawes. He was appointed sheriff of Berkshire in 1773.

Rural Life

While the gentry were rebuilding their houses and laying out their parks the poorer people found work on the new estates or in the royal forest and parks as woodsmen, gamekeepers or labourers. They were all dependent on the forest for fuel and food. The great storm of January 1735 brought down many trees and provided plenty of wood for the fires of the poor.

In the second half of the century there was some employment on the landscape changes in Windsor Great Park though some of this was done by soldiers. In 1753 a dam was completed to form the Virginia Water Lake. This was destroyed by a great storm in 1768 and replaced by a more easterly dam between 1781 and 1791 under the second duke of Cumberland, Henry Frederick, the nephew of the former duke, who served as Ranger up to 1791. The Royal Surveyors who made the lake included John Pitt of Sunninghill Manor, and John Robinson of Harewood Park. During the construction new plantations were established around the lake and some land close to the Mill was added to the Great Park.

Between 1790 and 1801 John Robinson had more than eleven million acorns planted in the Great Park, a number carefully recorded on his portrait now in the Royal Collection (Roberts, p. 68). This left the area with a legacy of tall oaks. Many of them came down in the storms of 1987 and 1990. Robinson also made a survey of the local roads, recording two roads to Windsor: the first by the Turnpike from Blacknest, from a spot known as *"Crocks Hole on Beggarsbush"* to Mill Gate and the second from beside Sunninghill Park and through the Great Park by Sandpit Gate. There was a steady and accelerating growth of traffic using the roads due both to the increased economic activity and to the rise in population.

By the end of the century the population of Sunninghill was almost four times larger than it had been at the beginning.

Population Figures for Sunninghill 1748 to 1811

Date	Population	Houses/Cottages
1748	247	
1750		65
1760	About 500 *"mostly legally settled"*	
1767	428	107
1780		115
1801	629	138
1811	913	

The figures up to 1780 are taken from Thistlethwaite's memorandum in the parish records (B.R.O., D/P 126 1/3). Those for 1801 and 1811 are taken from the national census. At the time of the 1801 census the total acreage of the parish was reckoned to be 3,173 acres.

In 1801 four houses had two families living in them and twenty houses were uninhabited. This was the highest proportion of empty properties anywhere in the whole of Berkshire and was due to the seasonal use of Sunninghill by families who chiefly resided in London. The vicar noted: *"At this time of year, i.e. March and through the greatest part of the winter, the largest families reside in London reducing the number of parishioners by about 200".*

The growth in the population of Sunninghill was about twice the national average. Some of the names on the 1766 *"List for Maintenance of the Church Rails"*, such as Attlee, Elliot, Slann, Baker and Lane had appeared in earlier records but there were many new names including Sir John Elwill, Bart. who lived in the parish but not on any of the old familiar properties.

There was always also a large unregistered population. The wild heaths and forests had a regular population of gypsies who were most prominent during the race weeks. The wasteland was also used by vagrants and wanderers who would put together a few branches and set up a *"bender"*. They would be chased off if they were found on private land but there was still plenty of hidden valleys where they might stay several months without detection. None of these people would be recorded in the estimates made by the vicars or later in the national censuses.

Up to 1750 there was no sign of an increased birth rate in the parish. In the middle of the century there was an average of about fifteen baptisms a year at St Michael's. Five foundling infants were buried in the churchyard in 1759 and in the two decades before and after this date there seems to be a disproportionate number of infant deaths for a parish of this size. It seems likely that some of the poor women of Sunninghill acted as wet-nurses for London families and others took in orphans with the encouragement of philanthropists like the Reverend Thistlethwaite. Two children buried at Sunninghill have been identified as nurse children from London (Gillian Clark in *"London's first evacuees: a population study of nurse children"*, The Local Historian vol. 19 no. 3 1989 pp. 100-106). This practice provided a small income for the women and a country upbringing for the children that was considered healthier than the city.

The Parish Poor and the Cheapside Cottages

The miseries of rural poverty cannot be exaggerated and Cheapside was where the poor lived. Their standard of life seldom rose above the very basic necessary for survival. Throughout the century the more responsible wealthy parishioners continued to support local charities. In his will of 1714 Edward Lane left an annuity of two pounds based on income from his Cowarth lands for the poor of Sunninghill. It was distributed up to 1929 when the charity charge was redeemed by Edward Villiers, the earl of Derby, who then owned Cowarth, for £80 of stock. In 1786 Samuel Moody left the rent of one pound per annum from a cottage at Blacknest Gate for the poor of the parish. This cottage was actually inhabited by a pauper in

1803 but it was sold off by 1831. It eventually came into the possession of the crown and the rent was lost by the failure to claim it over a number of years (for this and following see B.R.O., D/P 126 8/1-5).

In 1733 Elizabeth Squires left a legacy of £200 for the poor, the old and the sick of Sunninghill and she named Elizabeth Northcote as her sole executor. This money was used to buy nine acres including Barn Close and Hill Close near the Mill from William May. It was leased back to him free of rent on the condition that May and his heirs paid seven pounds per annum to the church for the poor. The money was to be distributed by the churchwardens. Eventually this land became part of the estate of Buckhurst Park and as late as the 1920s Sir James Savory continued to pay the same sum to the church.

In the parish records there are several transactions concerning leases by the parish trustees of cottages and land, which had been given or bought by the parish either to house the poor or to provide an income for their maintenance. For example in 1775, when Thomas Draper Baber, Joseph Thistlethwaite and John Pitt were trustees, they leased the cottages and land in Mill Lane to Thomas Narraway, a labourer, for five shillings. This land had been in the possession of the parish in 1680. Thomas Narraway was a timber merchant and a carpenter, probably from Egham. His lease included a clause protecting some of the timber. Narraway was involved in various local land deals from about 1770 to 1790 including the purchase from the parish trustees of a meadow at Chobham, the one which Yorke had sold them in exchange for the Church House and Green.

In 1789, just when the French Revolution, was beginning, the parish trustees, then James Sibbald, Thistlethwaite and Spencer Schutz, leased parish land to Jeremiah Crutchley. This included forty acres at Chobham and:

> *"Mill land cottage and woodland, also another cottage in the possession of William Lawrence a labourer"* (land which had been leased to Narraway) and *"cottages situated at a place called Cheapside with land or garden of the said two cottages and a piece of meadow belonging an acre, more or less, known as Hain's Platt"* (ibid 13/2).

This was near Pound Hill and had been mentioned in a document of 1680.

The Cheapside parish cottages were again mentioned in the vestry minutes of 1807, when they were transferred to new trustees, George Crutchley, George Ellis, Augustus Schutz and George Lee. They were described as *"2 several cottages in a place called Cheapside formerly in the occupation of the widow Slann and John Pickering"* (the coachman) and later in the occupation *"of Robert Hare, the widow Pickering and John Hudson".*

There were two almshouses in Cheapside and one more in Mill Lane *"lately built on a plot of meadow by Thomas Narraway and now in the occupation of John Borrington"* (ibid 8/4). In 1806 the Cheapside and Mill Lane cottages and the parish land in Chobham brought in an income of £58.

The vestry was permanently concerned about the burden of the poor on the rates which rose steadily throughout the century. In 1715 there was a levy of two pence in the pound of rateable value but by 1738 it had doubled. Those in charge of the vestry committees were the wealthiest men in the parish and they had to pay the highest rates. In 1768 Mr Schutz and Mr Edmund Cook were overseers of the poor and seven years later John Pitt and Jeremiah Crutchley had the same responsibility. They tried hard to keep people out of dependency on the parish. In 1736 the overseers of the poor ordered William, Edith, John and Thomas Lloyd, Sarah Humphreys and John Cordey *"to appear and show cause why they don't go into service"* (ibid 13/1).

The overseers had a constant anxiety about having to pay for paupers from other parishes and tried to have all vagrants moved on as soon as possible. Throughout the eighteenth century workmen had to have permission to move in case they or their families might become a burden and paupers could be sent back to their original parish. This inhumane practice continued into the mid-nineteenth century. The vestry also tried to make sure that no cottages, which might house the poor, were built without the consent of the parish.

In spite of all their efforts the numbers of paupers being supported by the parish grew, especially after 1780, reflecting the economic hardship of the period.

1777	13 paupers
1780	15 paupers
1782	20 paupers
1786	26 paupers
1787	24 paupers
1797	29 paupers

Only the very poor who had been resident in the parish for most of their lives were eligible. In 1788 the parish poor included twelve widows, six orphans and three men, the latter were either very old or very sick (ibid 13/3).

Each pauper received between one shilling and three shillings and sixpence per week. With free kindling from the forest this would have been a meagre but adequate provision. There were higher payments in exceptional cases: one widow with several children got as much as five shillings. In addition they were given clothing.

The growing costs of maintaining the poor encouraged the richer parishioners to look for cheaper ways of managing the problem. By the 1782 Act of Parliament, parishes were obliged to build workhouses where the poor could be kept and, in theory, work for their living. In 1791 the vestry committee agreed to build a parish workhouse for twenty-five paupers but it was not until 1799 that the plans were finally approved. The workhouse was completed in the August of that year and stood for many years near the old Sunninghill school, though it was in use for less than half a century.

In 1834 by the Poor Law Amendment Act, boards of guardians were set up to run workhouses and the parish responsibility was ended. The Windsor Union was established and Sunninghill, Thorpe and Egham were grouped together in the Egham district with a total population of 6,914. The Sunninghill workhouse was closed in 1840. Thereafter, local paupers were sent to Windsor and the parish paid its contribution to the Windsor workhouse (ibid 13/5).

To alleviate their poverty some of the poorer cottagers turned to poaching. In 1723 Walpole's government passed the infamous Black Acts cracking down on poaching and making fifty new capital offences. The vestry kept an eye on the minor offenders. In 1749 Thomas Lloyd was summoned to appear before the vestry committee for keeping lurchers, dogs used for poaching deer and rabbits (ibid 8/2). The major offenders were punished by the county courts.

William Augustus, duke of Cumberland (1721-1765), uncle of King George III, became Ranger of the Great Park. He took up his office in 1746 three months after the English victory at Culloden where he had been nominally in command of the army. The duke lived at Cranbourne Lodge and at the Great Lodge, later to be known as Cumberland Lodge.

His improvements in the Great Park, including the first lake at Virginia Water and a major tree-planting programme provided some employment but his action in seriously limiting the access to the park made life more difficult for the poor. He had all the locks changed to keep out poachers and the fences were restored and reinforced. One of his last acts just before his death in 1765 was to restrict access even more strictly. Nobody was to be permitted to pick up and take away wood or timber without a licence and these licences were to be given only to women and children. The duke was trying to prevent damage to his new plantings but he also wanted to keep all adult males, who might be poachers, out of the Great Park altogether.

Throughout the late eighteenth and the early nineteenth centuries the laws punishing poachers became ever more severe. In 1800 the punishment for taking game was one year's imprisonment with hard labour. Seven years later Parliament passed an act sentencing to death anyone offering armed resistance to arrest for poaching and ten years later, a conviction for poaching was to be punished by transportation for seven years. The harsh treatment of poachers was only eased after 1881. The effect of this draconian legislation was to cut the poor cottagers off from any easy way of supplementing their vegetable diet. The larger estates all had gamekeepers, many of whom used mantraps, and the locals were rigorously excluded even from catching rabbits.

The Vestry, Enclosures and the Land Market

The ten or so men who ran the parish vestry fulfilled many of the responsibilities now discharged by the large bureaucracy of local government. For example they supervised the use of all the wasteland in the parish. In 1723 the parishioners were reminded that it was forbidden to dig peat on the manor without consent from the vestry and the Cookham Manor Court. The vestry also gave permission for enclosures from the waste and, since they could charge for their permission, consent was usually easy to obtain. By 1790 the charge for enclosure at Sunninghill was £12 per acre. In the neighbouring parishes it was up to £28 (Hughes, chapter XIV). This low cost reflected the poor quality of most of the local waste and its easy availability.

The vestry was jealous of its right to control building on the waste. For example in 1723 they ordered a certain John Robinson to pull down the cottage which he was building on the waste (this, of course, was not John Robinson the royal surveyor). Again in 1761 Edward Brown bought land beside Beggars' Bush

Heath and built a house of two storeys with four rooms. He dug a well on the common for himself and other neighbours. He was prosecuted for building and digging the well without the consent of the parish. Two years later the vestry committee put out a public notice to remind the parishioners that no cottages were to be erected without a licence (B.R.O., D/P 126 8/3).

Sometimes there were large sums of money to be made by licensing the use of the waste. In 1793 the crown surveyors proposed building new boathouses at Virginia Water. This would involve the acquisition of some parish waste near today's Blacknest Gate. In November the vestry decided that they would charge 100 guineas but the scheme was never carried out and the money was never paid. The crown's surveyor was a Mr Everett and his plans for a new bridge and for boat-keepers' cottages on the lake within *"Millgate"* still exist (P.R.O., MF c 81-3 MPE 1080). In the same year the duke of Cumberland was reminded that he should have paid £100 guineas for enclosing two or three acres near his dog kennels in Ascot. This was paid (B.R.O., D/P 126 8/4).

Towards the end of the century, enclosure of the waste, especially by the gentry, increased. Six years after Sibbald had acquired a slice of Beggars' Bush, John Robinson, the surveyor, secured parish consent to enclose a piece of waste into *"his Park* (i.e. Harewood) *near Mill Gate"* (ibid).

Vestry consent was also required for road diversions. In 1790 James Sibbald obtained the vestry's permission to move the Windsor Road *"from the south corner of the land of John Charlwood to the south corner of the land of John Clode"* so it would pass on *"the south side of the ancient gravel pit on the said heath"* i.e. Beggars' Bush Heath near the present Cannon Public House. In 1796 he enclosed a further eight and a half acres of waste in front of *"Sillwood House"* paying £100 to the parish. He thus realigned the road from Windsor further from his house and to its present position (ibid and I.C.A. has registration documents dating to 1807).

If it was comparatively plain sailing for the larger landowners, lesser landowners were also granted permits to enclose but with conditions attached. In 1806 Mr L. Thorn applied to the vestry to enclose a small piece of waste *"adjoining his premises in Cheapside"*. The vestry agreed but recorded that he must take *"no more than is agreeable to Mr Crutchley's wishes"*, i.e. he must not infringe on the interests of the Sunninghill Park estate. He was also instructed to remake the road in a good condition after the enclosure (ibid). In 1816 however, Mr Simson, who bought the manor estate from

Sibbald, was permitted *"to alter the One Tun path to enter his land at the Iron Gate cross his lands to the end of the copse behind Mr Wilkins' stables"* and there were no conditions attached (ibid). This Iron Gate and its successor stood next to the entry to today's Heronsbrook House on the Buckhurst Road until very recently when it was allowed to fall into ruin.

The vestry was not always concerned with such solemn matters however. In 1755 a lengthy litigation with the parish of Egham over the ownership of the Broomhall estate finally came to an end. The estate was in the Old Windsor parish but its tithes etc were due to St Michael's. The gentlemen of the vestry were so delighted that they ordered the church bells to be rung for two days with *"refreshers for the ringers at the Wells"* (B.R.O., D/P 126 8/2).

The Definition of the Community: Eighteenth Century Maps

Two surveys made in the second half of the eighteenth century illustrate the development that was taking place. The earliest of these, in 1752, was made by Jean Rocque, a very competent French map-maker of Huguenot descent who worked for the crown (E.B.; B.R.O.; Royal Collections Windsor). In the preamble he described Sunninghill as *"24 miles from London in Windsor Great Park"*. His survey, made by J. Ballard, showed *"Sunninghill Park"* with its main house, ponds and streams and a few cottages or farms lying between the Great Park and Ascot Heath (see following page). *"Sunninghill"* was named on a large round area which was basically the manor estate and included all the land enclosed by today's Cheapside Road, London Road and Buckhurst Road.

Sunninghill was a set of scattered hamlets with a surprising number of marked buildings. There were clusters of houses on the north-east side of the manor estate, around *"Sunninghill Wells"* and along the London Road. A considerable settlement lay along what is now Buckhurst Road between its junctions with Mill Lane and Watersplash Lane. This was Cheapside or Cheape Green and the settlement extended north to Bucket Hill and south across the hill towards the present Silwood Lake. Today's Cheapside triangle was indicated north of the Brook. Apart from Wells Lane there were few houses south of the London Road. Of all the houses in the parish of Sunninghill about one third lay in Cheapside.

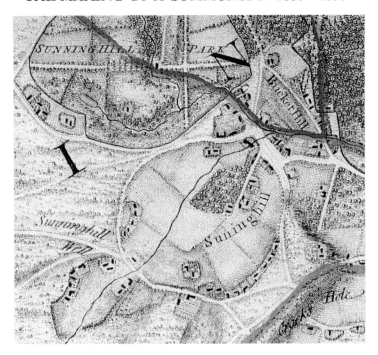

Detail of Jean Rocque's Map showing Sunninghill

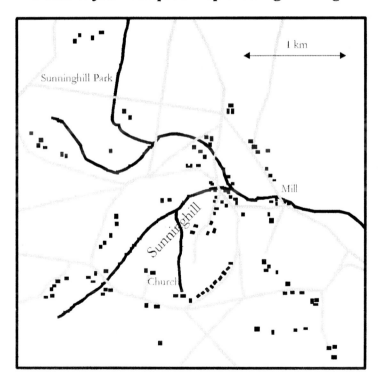

Buildings shown on the Rocque Map

William Faden's survey, made between 1788 and 1791, was called the *"Windsor Plan of the Forest"* (P.R.O., MR 687). On this and its successor of 1799-1800 (P.R.O., MR 1481) the main London Road was shown running from what is now Ascot to *"Sunninghill Wells"* where there was a group of buildings and the words *"mineral water"*. South of this road there were several houses around today's Wells Lane. A few houses were also marked along what is now the Oriental Road, and around the Upper and Lower Village roads of Sunninghill. This map was the first to show any real settlement south of the main London Road, in the area known as Bogside and Sunninghill Common.

To the east of Church Lane lay the estate of John Charlwood with a house close to the London Road. He had more land where Titness is today and was one of the major landowners at that time. By 1813 Spencer Schutz had bought the Charlwood estate and had rebuilt Ashurst there, removing the older house and developing ornamental gardens. On the west of the Church Lane there was Beechgrove and north of this was the Parsonage opposite St Michael's Church. The church lay at the south side of the Church Green, still clearly visible but not named. The old Green now belonged to Yorke who also owned the large estate opposite the Sunninghill Wells, now Tetworth Hall.

From the church, the lane still went through Silwood Park to the *"Parish Pound"* which lay near today's junction of Watersplash Lane and Cheapside Road. This map had been made very shortly before Silwood Lake was made. There were three buildings to the north-east side of this lane. The lower building near the Brook was surely today's Silwood Farm and the two higher ones were presumably the old Farrants or Eastmore. The gardens, now Silwood Park Nurseries, were not marked. The new *"Sibbald's House"* was marked close to the Windsor Road but with none of the enclosures from Beggars' Bush Heath.

Close to Sibbald's new house there were a row of houses stretching along today's Buckhurst Road. At the corner where the Cannon is today there was a blacksmith's forge, already owned by the Morton family. There were more houses along the London Road and on towards the *"Corn Mill called Lord's Mill"*. North of Sibbald's new house was the house of Mr Clode and on the opposite side of today's Buckhurst Road lay Dalton's large estate of Harewood Park. Buckhurst Park belonged to Mr Barwell on the later map with Mr Emberline owning land on the north side of the Millpond.

The group of houses that Rocque had shown on the north-east of the manor estate had all gone, cleared by Sibbald and his predecessors as they developed their park. Perhaps the cottagers had moved to *"Buckets Hill"* in Winkfield parish or to south of the London Road where there were many more buildings in 1790 than in 1752. Buckets Hill in Winkfield parish, across the Cheapside Stream, was a substantial hamlet in its own right. Cheapside Green was named as the *"Tun Green"* in front of the *"Tun Inn"* and there were two more houses marked around the Green.

The Windsor Road then went through Buckhurst Park and through today's Windsor Great Park crossing the Brook to the east of the mill and rejoining today's route close to today's Ascot Gate, then marked as *"Milton's Lodge"* and *"Sawyer's Gate"*.

Cheapside was not marked at all but the familiar triangle was divided into four distinctive blocks, two of which were labelled *"Pound Hill"*. On the smallest of the four sections at the west end there were one or two cottages. The middle plot was the largest, with several buildings marked and half of it belonging to Sam Sawyer. The *"Thatched Tavern"* was named on a section divided from the rest by what is now Green Lane.

Apart from a few cottages near the Thatched Tavern most of the buildings in this section were on the northern side, close to the fourth section which included today's Pump Lane. This was all part of Bucket Hill hamlet. South of the present Cheapside Road there were just four buildings: today's Heronsbrook House and its cottage, and two other cottages where today's Elm Bank and Wisteria Cottage stand. All four were owned by Dalton.

Between 1752 and 1790 there was a steady increase of housing in other parts of the parish and more land was being farmed. There were political and economic reasons for this development. During the French and Napoleonic wars, it was necessary to produce more food in England and so more land was enclosed. In Sunninghill the best arable land was at Coworth, Broothall and Cheapside. As more land went under the plough more labourers were needed and more cottages were built.

During the second half of the eighteenth century land was changing hands more often and some men, like Dalton and Charlwood, were buying up large holdings in Sunninghill. This active land market was stimulated by the increased profits from farming and also by the preparations for the Act of the Enclosure of Windsor Forest. There were many speculators who were hoping to profit from this act.

The increase in the small estates and large parks was also due to the popularity of Sunninghill as a fashionable place. With its own Spa, the Ascot Races, the newly constructed Carriage Rides, the new lake of Virginia Water, the Court nearby at Windsor and all the regiments billeted in the vicinity, Sunninghill attracted rich people who bought or rented houses to use during the summer season. By the end of the eighteenth century Sunninghill was a growing village with several very fine properties and Cheapside was a very recognisable part of it.

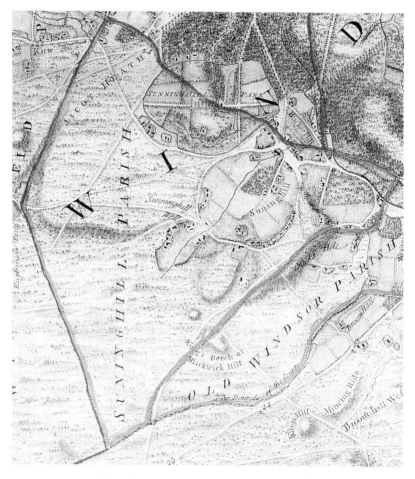

The Parish of Sunninghill in 1752

THE GROWTH OF A COMMUNITY : 1800 - 1900

"Some years ago, ere Time and Taste
Had turned our Parish topsy-turvy
When Silwood Park was Sunning Waste
And roads as little known as Scurvy
The man who lost his way between
The Bucket Hill and Sandy Thicket
Was always shown across the green
And guided to the parson's wicket."
W. M. Praed in 1864

The Enclosure of Windsor Forest

The Act of Parliament for the Enclosure of the Windsor Forest was passed in 1813 with the award of land completed in 1817. It had far reaching consequences for the whole of Sunninghill and Cheapside. Enclosure by Act of Parliament had increased since 1740 and was a way of reorganising landholding in the interests of the larger landowners. In the 1790s grain prices were at their height and farming was a very prosperous business. During this period all the more fertile wastelands and heaths of Berkshire, Surrey and Middlesex were enclosed. Although they benefited, enclosure involved all the landowners in heavy costs for fencing, and hedging. St John's College paid out £185 for enclosure and fencing at Sunninghill in 1817 (lease books at S.J.C.). The holly trees and hawthorns on the south side of the Cheapside road are likely survivors from an enclosure hedge.

Prior to the Windsor Forest Act, enclosure had gone on in a piecemeal fashion. Large parts of the waste had been assarted with the consent of the parish and with the payment of quit-rents to Cookham Manor. The manorial records show this type of enclosure peaking between 1790 and 1810. In 1790 Cookham notified Sunninghill that one pound one shilling and ten pence were due in old quit-rents and a further five pounds ten shillings and two pence for new encroachments. This might be compared with Cookham town where twenty pounds ten shillings and seven pence were due. The tenants of the manor liable to pay quit-rents were named as:

James Sibbald
the late John Yorke
the late John Charnwood

the Rev. John Hand of Windsor and his tenant George Platt
Mr Samuel Dalton and his tenant Thomas Rous
the late George Hatch, now Rev. Hatch, and his tenant
Benjamin Strange
the late Edward Price
the late Mr Benjamin Walker and Mrs Mary Walker, widow of
William Walker and her tenant the late Edward Hatch
Mrs Mary Dolby, now Mr Wherling, of Hatchet Lane, and
their tenant Mrs Dolby and Stephen Hough
Wilmot Maythis *"himself cannot be found"*
Daniel Agace
Mr John Charlwood
Mr John Clode, now the Rev. Clode of Windsor
Mr Thomas Pearman
James Brewer
Mr Knight Brewer, of Bagshot
William Walker
Jeremiah Crutchley
(B.R.O., D/E AR m 9)

Twelve years later, in 1802, Sunninghill had the highest number of encroachments in the manor of Cookham. The encroachers included John Walker, Edmund Blackman and Mr Holland *"a yeoman pucker"* (a yeoman *"pucker"* or *"pricker"* rounded up deer). The list recorded old assarts such as *"a close called Newlands, Wapshotts land and a tan yard"* which *"John Walker owned and Edmund Blackman was the tenant of five poles in Cheapside and Mr Holland had half an acre at Buckets Hill"* (ibid m. 10). It is interesting to note that the tan yard was still in existence even though the Aldridge family had left.

The Cookham manor list of Michaelmas 1809 demonstrated how rapidly the larger landowners were acquiring the parish waste. George Simson, then the owner of *"Sunning Hill"* (i.e. Silwood Park), was liable for the quit-rents on Newlands, Selmore Farm and all the lands which had belonged to the late widow Dredges, the Slanns and the Wapshotts. These pieces had all been incorporated into the estate by Pitt and Sibbald and reflect the disappearance of the small houses on the estate. Simson was also due to pay for the assarted land leased out to the late Morton and James Slann (the former owners of this land were George Clode and William Morton), and for a half an acre near Beggars' Bush. Sir James Sibbald's eight acres *"newly enclosed at the south front of his house"* were now registered to Simson and he owed for another acre opposite the Tun Inn. This last had been part of the old Cheape Green (ibid m. 11).

The late Jeremiah Crutchley had acquired land beyond the limits of Sunninghill Park and his heir, George Crutchley, had to pay for one acre *"partly dug for bricks"*, Brick Farm on the Ascot side of the Park. The *"late Right Hon. John Yorke"* paid for lands which had earlier belonged to John Aldridge, Mr Lane and William Davis, including the *"late Birches"*, the *"yard"*, *"the land of Mrs Elizabeth Squires"* and his own *"lately enclosed"* piece *"opposite the Wells about 110 poles"*.

It was not only the gentry like Simson, Yorke and Crutchley who were acquiring the waste. John Morton paid for a plot near the Tun Inn and a *"turf house"*. William Morton, the blacksmith, had enclosed half an acre near Beggars' Bush. William Slann paid for the land used by his timber yards, workshop and saw-pit and William Keep for half an acre he had taken in on the heath near the racecourse (ibid).

In Cheapside the *"late Mr John Hand"* was due to pay quit-rents for land tenanted by George Platt and the *"late Gearys, the tavern"* which was the Thatched Tavern, built about 1760. William Walker, Mr Baker, William Cooper and John Rous had also made enclosures. Walker and Baker owed for several properties: *"a house in Sunninghill, five poles in Cheapside at sixpence, half an acre in Cheapside at one shilling and six poles near Cheapside for sixpence"* (ibid).

These documents suggest that quit-rents were difficult to collect. Keeping up with all the changes of ownership was not easy and there were many people involved. In 1815 the Cookham administrators simply ordered all those owing quit-rents to assemble at Sunninghill Wells on the seventh of August. In that year the mighty sum of fifteen shillings was collected from the whole of Sunninghill Manor. It was hardly worth the effort to collect such a paltry sum. Both Cookham Manor and the local landowners wanted to see change and the solution was the Enclosure.

Another motive for enclosure was to prevent trespass and poaching. The Commissioners reported that *"The inhabitants of all the Parishes around the forest live in widely scattered dwellings, affording means of committing their various depredations with the least chance of detection"*. Only 318 deer remained in the forest and the royal hunt had been discontinued. In September 1813, a troop of the Royal Horseguards and a detachment of the Fifth Infantry assisted the *"yeomen prickers"* to sweep across the heath, over the commons and through the bogs and valleys herding all the remaining deer into the royal parks (Hughes, p. 85). The forest was no longer to be browsed by deer and domestic livestock and this allowed saplings to grow. The landscape changed dramatically after the enclosure. As Hughes pointed out, by 1890 *"Many old men are now struck with its altered aspect; where, in their boyhood, they could see for miles, now thick foliage shuts in the view"* (ibid p. 7).

The decision to enclose (or *"inclose"* as it was written then) by Act of Parliament was made by 1805. A Commission was set up and began meeting in 1806. It was authorised to regularise all the encroachments and enclosures that had gone on for centuries and allot all land to registered owners. Some of their sessions were held at the Wells Inn. The Commissioners produced a series of annual reports between 1807 and 1810. Imperial College Archive has the report on Sunninghill Manor and the complete set is in the Public Record Offices at Kew and Reading (P.R.O., T/PCa 2A and 2B; B.R.O., D/P 126/26 AB).

The Commissioners faced a formidable task. They dealt with twenty parishes and thirty-five manors. 340 encroachments had been made and 500 acres had been enclosed without authority. The Windsor Forest Enclosure Act finally registered the enclosure of 60,000 acres. 36,000 acres including the racecourse went to the crown and other large landowners. 24,000 acres were divided among all the parishes and smaller owners.

The Award of the Allotments was not published until 1817. It took time to complete all the detailed map-making, the legal transactions and the land transfers. Many claims and counter claims had to be settled. Daniel Agace who owned Ascot Manor in Winkfield put in a claim to lands in Sunninghill. He failed. There was much swapping and trading of small pieces of land to rationalise property holdings. In Cheapside the parish exchanged a piece of land which adjoined Pound Hill and Sunninghill Park, known as the Plat (the old Hain's Plat), with George Crutchley in return for land in Sunninghill Bog which, in 1855, they sold off to the Staines and Wokingham Railway Company. The parish also exchanged a piece of land with John Vernon of Buckhurst. This piece *"abutted Lords Green or Cheapside Green"*. It was in fact part of the old Green. It was exchanged for a plot of land and a cottage near the Sunninghill workhouse. This was also sold later and the parish made £111 and 1 shilling for the two pieces of land. The money was invested in Consols and later used to build parish cottages in Sunninghill Bog (Hughes, chapter VI) and rebuild a pair of cottages in Cheapside which were occupied for a long time by the widows Kidd and Turner.

The chief beneficiaries of the Enclosure Act were the crown and the major landowners. The signatories to the award included George Crutchley, George Simson, George Ellis, James Mann and John Vernon. St John's College was also represented and the Reverend William Ainger signed on behalf of the parish. The main losers were the poor cottagers who lost their ancient rights of pannage, grazing and turbary. The Fuel Allotment Trust was set up to compensate them for their loss of timber and peat. A hundred and twelve acres of useless land in Sunninghill Bog were allocated for *"turves, fern and fuel"*. The old gravel pits were put into the care of the surveyors of the highways. No land was nominated as commons for parish use and there were no longer any refuges for squatters and gypsies.

George Crutchley acquired land along Watersplash Lane, Winkfield Road and New Mile Road squaring off the old circle of the original royal park. George Simson secured the lands enclosed from Beggars' Bush Heath and two small pieces in Cheapside; one was at the junction between today's Cheapside Road and Watersplash Lane, and the other was part of the *"One Tun Green"*. The remainder of the old Green was shared between Simson and Dalton. In addition Simson registered a large piece of land lying south of the London Road.

Samuel Dalton owned Harewood Park, Brook Lodge, *"Sellmore or Eastmore farm"* and all the land north-east and east of Silwood Lake. He acquired small pieces in Mill Lane and a tiny piece along the south side of Cheapside road near the entry to his farm. Samuel's brother William was the head carpenter at the Prince Consort's workshops in 1837 (Roberts, p. 306). He was descended from Prince Dalton who had been gamekeeper and huntsman for the duke of Cumberland in the 1750s and whose lodge was destroyed when the first Virginia Water dam gave way (Roberts, p. 462). Samuel called his own son Prince and the family owned Brook Lodge, today's Heronsbrook, for a large part of the nineteenth century.

John Vernon at Buckhurst gained pieces of land on the corner of Mill Lane and Buckhurst Road and along Mill Lane. He had already bought the Mill property and fifteen acres lying between Buckhurst Hill and Mill Lane, nine acres from Henry Emblin and a cottage and garden in Mill Lane near the Green. St John's College registered land in Mill Lane and along Buckhurst Road, including most of today's Royal Berkshire Hotel and the Titness estate. The Countess of Hartington shared in the allotments along Buckhurst Lane with Samuel Dalton and Jane Churchill.

Augustus Schutz of Ashurst registered his large piece of land south of today's London Road and Lady Caroline Price of Beechgrove had the land on the south-west of today's Sunninghill crossroads, which had belonged to Kingswick. James Mann of Tetworth Hall, or *"Healthy Hall"* as it was then called, was allocated several pieces of land including plots along Cheapside Road and south of the One Mile course. He also acquired a piece at the end of his garden which had belonged to the vicar who was awarded in its place a plot lying some distance away, along the south side of the One Mile course. The vicar lost another piece of land alongside the vicarage to George Ellis of The Cedars.

The map of the Enclosure for Sunninghill Parish is the first surviving map which has *"Cheap Side"* written on it. *"Cheapside Wood, Cheapside Meadow"* and *"Cheapside Green"* are marked on another contemporary map of Sunninghill Manor that survives in the Cookham Manor records (B.R.O., D/EX 126/9).

Within its familiar triangle, Cheapside was still divided into three blocks, the most westerly lying within Watersplash Lane, Cheapside Road and a lane running along the side of the Long Gardens Cottages. Traces of this last lane still exist. The central block lay between this path and what is now Green Lane and Dorian Drive and the third ran from there to the Buckhurst Road and the boundary with the parish of Winkfield.

Land at the corner of Cheapside Road and Watersplash Lane, now Barberry Cottage, was allocated to Joseph Cannell. The next plot along Cheapside Road was allotted jointly to Benjamin Harding and Leonard Thorn. The latter held other plots along Watersplash Lane and on the corner of the Winkfield Road where the Durning Library is today. Benjamin Harding was related to Richard Harding who owned land along Watersplash Lane and the Hardings lived in Long Gardens Cottages. These were marked on the Enclosure Map and were the only buildings shown in the western section of the Cheapside triangle.

Leonard Thorn owned a large piece of central Cheapside and he was allocated all the land along Watersplash Lane on the north side of his holding. There were four or five cottages in the central block. William Walker had a plot along Watersplash Lane. He had another plot down in the Sunninghill Bog, in what is now St George's Lane, Ascot.

At the east of Cheapside, between Green Lane and Buckhurst Road, two allocations, one along Watersplash Lane and another along Green Lane went to Murrell Wright. He shared another large plot that went from the junction of the Cheapside and

Buckhurst Roads as far as today's Pump Lane. His co-owner was William Portchmouth (called Portsmouth on the Winkfield Parish map) the owner of the Dairy Farm. There were two buildings marked within this block and six more along Cheapside Road, one of which was the Thatched Tavern. To the south of the junction of Cheapside and Buckhurst Roads lay Brook Cottage, now known as April Place and Brook Lodge. The cottage was surrounded by large outbuildings probably used as a timber yard or a tannery and all this was owned by Samuel Dalton.

Cheapside at the Enclosure, 1817

1 Long Garden Cottages   2 Thatched Tavern
3 Tun Inn   4 Brook Lodge   5 Silwood Farm

On the Winkfield enclosure map the hamlet of Bucket Hill was shown, bounded on the east by *"Bucket Hill"*, on the north by today's Watersplash Lane and on the south by the stream. It was then under separate ecclesiastical and civil administrations to Cheapside. This small section was divided into a number of plots some with houses, cottages or barns. Here lived many cottagers on tiny plots all taken in from the waste. It was typical of the sort of settlement that would be impossible after the Enclosure Act.

Two plots along Watersplash Lane went to H. Platt and another large piece along the stream went to William Portsmouth. David and Sarah Portsmouth and Hannah Cook had cottages, orchards and gardens here.

Thus by 1818 the whole of Cheapside including the old Cheape Green had been allotted to landowners. Some of the Green was enclosed but a large piece of it outside the Tun Inn was left unfenced until the early twentieth century. The great landowners aggrandised their estates and ordinary folk were either the owners of small plots or the tenants of local entrepreneurs like Joseph Cannell and William Portsmouth. By the early nineteenth century this was a much more settled and consolidated district than it had been when Queen Anne died in 1714. Many would look back to the days before the Enclosure Act as the good old days.

Sunninghill in the Age of Victoria

The period between the battle of Waterloo and the outbreak of the Great War was one of the most peaceful for Britain. Wars fought by the British army were far away in the Crimea, Africa and India. Regiments were no longer stationed around this area and apart from retired admirals, generals and other army and navy officers, Sunninghill no longer saw much of military life. The Wells Inn lost its attractions as a spa but was still used as a staging post for coaches and carriages. In a Directory of 1863 it was described as *"The Wells, two chalybeate springs, formerly great objects of resort."* In 1885 the old inn was demolished and rebuilt. Later still the springs were covered over as being a hazard to the public.

The importance of the royal forest as a resource for food and fuel had ended. Throughout the nineteenth century access to crown lands was very limited. There was a royal menagerie at Sandpit Gate where the first giraffe to be brought to England died in 1829 but it was not open to the public. In 1830 this royal zoo was removed to Regent's Park and became part of the foundation of the London Zoological Gardens.

The Races attracted many visitors but neither Queen Victoria nor Prince Albert was interested and after his death the queen rarely attended. Edward Prince of Wales, however, was very keen on the Races and the social life they engendered. He and his wife often took Sunninghill houses for the week. In 1866 they stayed at Titness Park. The Race Week, held in July in the mid-nineteenth century, was one of the main events in the social calendar and there was a major influx of residents. In 1826 a new luxury food called ice cream was introduced to the wealthy guests who attended in their carriages which they drew up at the side of the course to watch the races.

The less wealthy gathered on the heath where they played cards, hawked their wares and watched prize fighting. There were many less official fights too. As a result of the lawlessness the first police court was established in 1851 to be kept in session during Race Week. At first it sat in the Paddock but was later removed to the Court House. In spite of the growing police force there were many thefts and in 1907 someone even managed to steal the Gold Cup. In 1887 a golf course was made, which meant that for the first time Ascot Heath was used for something other than horse racing.

For the rural community of Cheapside there was little real change between 1818 and 1914. The main employment was still in the forest, on the farms or in service. There was a gradual increase in the numbers of tradesmen serving the growing population and an equivalent increase in the provision of small houses for them to live in. The most significant changes of the century were the arrival of the railway with a major feat of engineering across Sunninghill Bog, the opening of the first national schools in Sunninghill and Cheapside and the complete remodelling of the ancient church of St Michael's.

Population figures for Sunninghill 1821 to 1901

1821	1125
1831	1520
1841	2062 (536 visitors)
1851 *	1350
1861	1596
1871	2236
1881	3042
1891	3939
1901	4724

* Sunningdale had become a separate Census District
(Cheapside saw a similar increase from about 100 in 1821 to
200 in 1851 to over 400 in 1901)

The population of Sunninghill grew steadily in spite of the removal of Sunningdale from the local figures in 1841. During the

1850s the population was increased by the presence of gangs of navvies working on the construction of the railway. This opened up the land south of the London Road and resulted in the development of modern Sunninghill, Sunningdale and South Ascot.

For most of this century the vestry was still the main organ of local administration. They had to collect the Poor Rate which both supported the almshouses and made a contribution to the Windsor Workhouse. In 1844 the Poor Rate was fixed at half a penny in the pound, a great reduction on the rates of the previous century. There were more people contributing to the cost.

By 1876 there were several parish charities including the old ones such as Lane's or the Coworth charity and Elizabeth Squire's or the Mill charity. These still provided a few pounds per year. In addition there was the Fuel Allotment Parish Trust set up after the Enclosure Act. This trust dealt with all the Bog allocated to the parish for peat digging. In 1844 the vestry committee appointed a bog warden to see that nobody took peat without a licence. The vestry used the parish trusts to donate money to various good causes such as the Sunday School, the Berkshire Hospital and the Clewer Convalescent House as well as to provide sacks of coal for the poor. In 1894, when the parish charities were regulated by the newly formed Charities Commission, the consolidated charities were invested in Consols and yielded a gross income of £900 per year (B.R.O., D/P 126 25/2). As well as this income there were the four parish cottages which were used for the elderly or leased out to raise money.

The parish was run by a mixture of landowners, farmers, timber men and tradesmen. Between 1841 and 1849 those whose names appeared regularly as vestrymen included Nash a blacksmith, Pither a bricklayer, Watkins a carpenter, Todd a plumber and glazier and Slann a carpenter. Of these, Alfred Todd came from Cheapside. By 1851 he lived in Barberry Cottage on Pound Hill with his wife, who came from Norfolk, and five children. He passed his business to one of his sons and there were still Todds working in the area in the twentieth century.

A generation later the vestry was run by the vicar, Alexander Wale, Sir F. W. Grey (the tenant of a local property), General Crutchley, J. Toller Esq. and Messrs Longhurst, Watkins, Pickett, Prince and King, all local tradesmen (B.R.O., D/P 126 8/5). The Longhursts were a prominent family in Sunninghill and Ascot up to the Second World War. In 1851 Joseph Longhurst, who came from Egham, was the innkeeper at the Thatched Tavern. He was a widower and lived with his two teenage sons, Thomas and Joseph and they had two servants. A William Watkins also lived in Cheapside in 1851 with his wife and two daughters. He was an agricultural labourer so it is unlikely that he would be the Watkins on the vestry committee. John Prince, however, was certainly the sort of man to be invited to sit on the vestry. In 1871 he was a master baker with his shop close to the Thatched Tavern. He had been brought up by his stepfather, John Simkins, a Cheapside farmer who had ten pigs and six cows. John Prince had a wife, a son, two daughters and a business large enough to employ an assistant baker (this and the following information on Cheapside residents is from the Census Returns for Sunninghill Parish from 1841 to 1891 P.R.O. and from the Tithing list of 1818, B.R.O., D/P 126/31).

A major change in the way the parish was run came in 1894 when all the administrative duties of the non-elected and self-nominating vestry were transferred to the newly instituted parish council. This was elected by a very limited franchise excluding all women and most working men so in many ways the old system remained intact. Throughout the nineteenth century Sunninghill Manor was still under the manor of Cookham. There were still quit-rents to pay when pieces of the Bog were sold off. In 1884 Henry Duncan Skrine of Claverton Manor in Somerset became the lord of the manor of Cookham. The Skrine family was the last to operate the old medieval system and their family papers relating to the history of the manor are in the Berkshire Public Record Office.

The New Church

The nineteenth century saw the end of our ancient Norman Church, which was demolished with a ruthlessness that would be admired by our modern developers. When Joseph Thistlethwaite died in 1807 he left £500 for the repair of the church, which was, according to him and to the vestry, in a very dilapidated state and too small for the parishioners. The vestry wanted a new north aisle and a new west end with a room on the ground floor and a gallery above. This became a music loft with a barrel organ, played by *"James Dunster of the Thatched Cottage, Cheapside"* (Searle).

In 1808 the contract for these extensions was awarded to John Milton, George Lee and James Slann. It cost £827 to erect *"one gallery with 5 seats and a pew under and 18 new pews and part of the north aisle".* There were *"faculty"* pews for the use of Sir James Sibbald, George Ellis, James Mann and Lady Harewood. The work was done but two years later there was a serious problem at the north east corner of the church tower. An architect was consulted and he recommended a buttress (B.R.O., D/P 126 8/4). It seems that the whole structure had been damaged by the alterations.

The Old Church from the North-East (Hughes)

In 1817 William Ainger succeeded Hebelthwaite and from then on the vicars resided permanently in the parish. Ainger was followed in 1830 by Wale who served the parish until he died, aged eighty-six, in 1884. During his last years Wale lived with his two unmarried daughters, Louisa and Caroline, both born in Sunninghill. Louisa painted some charming watercolours of the old church and the vicar himself made an interesting drawing from the top of the church tower. There was a succession of young curates, two of whom lodged in Cheapside. Christopher Wilkes and his brother, a barrister, stayed with Nathaniel and Eliza Lewarn at Laburnum Cottage in 1871 and ten years later another curate, Charles Dupuis, lodged with Henry and Ann Chitty. Nathaniel Lewarn was a retired grocer and Henry Chitty was a coachman.

During Ainger's incumbency a campaign was launched to raise money to improve the church. In January 1825, St John's College promised £60 to repair the church, a donation increased within a few months to £105 (S.J.C., Fines and Rents pp. 241, 243). Augustus Schutz of Ashurst then offered to put up £1,500 if this sum could be matched by an equal amount from other donors. He became the mainstay of the campaign and as the vestry reports put it, the money was raised by the *"munificence of Augustus Schutz and the liberal donations of His Majesty and the Inhabitants"*. King George IV gave £100 (B.R.O., D/P 126 8/5).

Between 1827 and 1828 most of the old church was demolished. Only the Norman chancel was left intact. During the building work, church services were held in the ballroom at the Wells. The new nave, aisles and west-end cost £3,000 and 5d. The work was done by Mr Hayter using local craftsmen such as Messrs Slann, Pither and Todd. The church could now seat 500 and almost half the seats were appropriated by the major families for themselves and their servants. The rest were free. The new church extended further to the west and north and was thus much closer to the ancient yew in the churchyard. Sadly the finished church was of no great architectural merit. The best that could be said of it in the Dutton, Allen and Co. Directory of 1863 was that it was a *"neat Brick structure rebuilt in 1828"*.

The New Church about 1870 by Louisa Wale

The rebuilding of the nave was in fact just another stage of reconstruction and alterations. The second half of the century saw a steady and relentless *"improvement"* of the church. At the vestry meetings church maintenance and improvements were endlessly discussed. In 1861 the north wall of the chancel was set back to accommodate a two manual organ provided and played by Miss Hargreaves of Silwood Park. Six years later one of the church bells cracked and had to be replaced. A small stove was installed to provide the first heating and the font was moved to the west end.

There were seemingly always plenty of donors willing to pay and there were also gifts of new church plate. In 1876 a silver mounted glass flagon was given to the church and in 1904 a chalice and silver spoon were donated. In 1877 they were debating how to pay for a new and larger organ, how to improve the seating and how to warm the church more efficiently. In 1899 a new organ was installed by the firm of Gray and Davison and by then the last parts of the old church had disappeared (ibid and 6/1). When Thomas Holloway of Tittenhurst Park died in 1887, his relatives wanted a substantial memorial and they decided to build a new chancel, side chapel and organ chamber in his memory. Thomas Holloway was one of the new men of the Victorian age. He made a vast fortune by his brilliant and very modern advertising methods through which he sold vast quantities of largely ineffective but generally harmless pills, ointments and lotions. He had no children and his wife had died before him. His greatest legacies were the Royal Holloway College for the education of young women at Egham and the Holloway Hospital for the mentally ill at Virginia Water.

During his lifetime he showed little interest in the church but his sister-in-law and her husband, Mr and Mrs Driver, were more pious and they resolved to give him a major memorial in the parish church and a large tomb in the churchyard. The new chancel was designed by the architect W. H. Crossland whom Thomas Holloway had employed to create the splendid chateau of Royal Holloway College. He used some of the same building materials in the church and its elegant iron columns were typical of the age.

The chancel was completed by 1888 and as a final touch Mrs Driver presented the church with its fine east window and three other windows in the side chapel. They were made between 1890 and 1891 by John Hardman and Co. of Birmingham and the artist may have been Henry Holiday (sadly all the records have disappeared). The east window, which is the most splendid, depicts St Michael and All the Angels triumphing over the Devil who has been totally eliminated. The archangels Gabriel and Raphael are supported by blue winged cherubim, red winged seraphim and golden winged angels and they all shine radiantly in the morning light. Christ is triumphantly enthroned above St Michael. The four apostles are represented by their symbols and the dove of the Holy Spirit dives in a sunburst from the highest point. It is an accomplished piece of pre-Raphaelite design and Victorian craftsmanship appropriate as a memorial for a man who bought such a fine collection of paintings for the edification of the young ladies of Holloway College.

With the Holloway chancel the last stones of old church finally disappeared. The ancient inscriptions were obliterated and the best of the stone disappeared into neighbouring gardens. The rest of it was put to a more prosaic use. At about the same time, or shortly after the old Norman church was demolished, the London Road was altered to reduce the gradient on the hill and so help the increasing coach and carriage traffic. In the course of the road works, stone from the old church was used to shore up the embankments. It was still easy to see large blocks until the construction of the roundabout in 1997. Now there are still just a few pieces of the old heathstone visible.

By 1827 there was a toll-bar and tollhouse at the Sunninghill crossroads; today this tollhouse is in the grounds of Beechgrove. There was another toll on the Windsor Road at today's Cannon crossroads. A stagecoach plied regularly from Reading to London, stopping at the Wells Inn. As the traffic increased along the London Road, the owners of Beechgrove found it necessary to build the Iron Bridge to link the south section of their garden with the house. This survived until the second half of the twentieth century. The vicars of the nineteenth and twentieth centuries had good cause to thank the Reverend Thistlethwaite who had preserved the Church Lane as a quiet cul-de-sac and stopped it becoming a thoroughfare leading to Cheapside.

As the population increased more space was needed for burials. In 1852 the parish paid St John's College £25 for one rood in the *"close called the Church paddock"* (S.J.C.). In 1870 they bought a field from the owner of The Cedars for £86. They were in fact buying back part of the old Church Green (B.R.O., D/P 126 8/5). Two years later there was another extension of the burial ground by a gift of land from St John's College (S.J.C.).

There were substantial changes in the administration of the church. In 1836, during Wale's incumbency, the parish of Sunninghill was transferred from the diocese of Salisbury to that of Oxford. In 1865 the Buckhurst Hill hamlet and that part of Cheapside which was in Winkfield was transferred from the Chapelry of Cranbourne in Winkfield Parish to the parish of Sunninghill for *"ecclesiastical purposes only"* (S.J.C., Deed Book p. 222). This little section of Cheapside had then a population of 130 about a tenth of the total population of Sunninghill. Buckhurst Park itself remained in Winkfield.

According to the 1847 Tithe Map the glebe lands covered eleven acres. They were exempt from paying tithes as was all the St John's College property including Broomhall Farm and Titness Park. The crown was exempt for the 504 acres it owned in the parish including parts of the Great Park. Sunninghill Park's 287 acres, once crown land, were also tithe free but the Crutchleys still made the customary annual payment of 13s 4d directly to the vicar. In the rest of the parish all the land was liable to tithes. The land was calculated as a total of 2,489 acres of which 505 were arable, 886 acres were meadow or pasture, 792 acres were wooded and 306 acres were waste (B.R.O., DP 126/3/1).

The connections with St. John's College were diminished after the 1858 University Estates Act allowed the college to sell off some of its property. The college decided to dispose of the northern part of the Broomhall estate including Titness and Coworth. In 1865 the lease of Titness Park was surrendered for £6,000 by the Riccardo family who held the 98 acres. The property was sublet to a Mr Samson. The college then sold the estate for £26,000 to Albert Riccardo and Alfred Keyser (S.J.C., Deed Book p. 243). Their aim was to get rid of their holdings of poorer agricultural land but they retained the Broomhall area hoping to benefit from the development in Sunningdale nearer to the railway. A map of 1863 showed a house at Broomhall Farm in the vicinity of the ancient priory but no other houses on the Broomhall estate.

Methodism, Congregationalism and the Salvation Army

By the second half of the century the monopoly which St Michael's had held over the religious life of the parish was coming to an end. The old system was challenged both by the creation of new Anglican churches and by churches of rival denominations.

Two new Anglican churches were developed. General Charles Crutchley gave land for the erection of All Souls Church in South Ascot, consecrated in 1897, and the new church of the Holy Trinity at Sunningdale was completed by 1888.

The biggest jolt to the old order came with the arrival of alternative churches. A small Methodist church or chapel was opened in Windsor in 1816 and a larger one followed in Peascod Street in 1835. Before the great chapel in Alma Road was built in 1877 there was a Methodist chapel in Cheapside. Some Sunninghill men featured as trustees of the Windsor chapels: Jeremiah Baldwinson in 1840, George Bawden, who was a local preacher, Henry Whiteman and Joseph Norris in 1877. Whiteman and Norris were leaders of the Cheapside Chapel in the 1870s.

Methodist services were held in houses in Sunninghill from 1836. In November 1840 a piece of land in Cheapside was leased and there may have been a temporary building there since services were being held on a regular basis from 1841. In 1847 another plot in Cheapside was leased to William Pither and James Whitehead who later bought it. These two men together with a Mr Holmes were the local Methodist activists.

Cheapside Chapel about 1900

The Pither family had been in Sunninghill since the sixteenth century. William Pither had land in Wells Lane beyond its junction with St George's Lane and a house near Ascot station, used for services during the building of the new Chapel. In 1862 the foundation stone of the Cheapside Chapel was laid by Thomas Gurney of London. After the ceremony a public tea was held at William Pither's house. His son, John Caleb Pither, a draper of Ascot, was a trustee of the Alma Road chapel in 1892, 1905, 1918 and 1928. By 1918 he was registered in the census returns as a *"gentleman and living at Prospect House in Ascot"*.

The Cheapside Chapel was the only Methodist chapel in the parish and it was therefore known as the Sunninghill Chapel. It was not until 1911 that a second Methodist chapel was established at the old Mission Hall in the Terrace in Sunninghill. By 1866 the Cheapside Chapel had a regular congregation of forty members drawn chiefly from the families who lived on Pound Hill, Cheapside Road, Smith's Green and Bucket Hill hamlet. There might be as many as two hundred for special services like Harvest Festival. Preachers were sent out from the Windsor circuit and included local men such as W. Munday of Sunninghill. The members of the congregation were tradesmen, artisans, farm labourers and gardeners who preferred the Chapel to the Church of St Michael's which was seen as belonging to the gentry.

The Methodist and Congregationalist movement drew its most fervent supporters from the newly literate who had benefited from the development of education. The first national school in the parish was established in 1818 on a site near today's Sunninghill School. The main benefactors were Augustus and Elizabeth Schutz. It was the only school in the parish and children from Cheapside would walk across the church fields to attend. By the 1870s the number of pupils had outgrown the building and in 1883 the present school was built. It was opened by Princess Christian whose husband was the High Steward of the Royal Borough of Windsor. By the time this was opened there was also a school in Cheapside.

In 1865 Mrs William Pither opened a small school in the vestry room at the Chapel. This was later transferred to a temporary wood and brick building in the grounds of today's Pemberton Lodge at the east end of Cheapside Road. After the Cheapside School was established regular Sunday schools continued at the Chapel. These were closely inspected by dedicated inspectors who cycled around from one Methodist church to the next.

In 1881 the Mission Hall on the Terrace at Sunninghill, now the Sunninghill Methodist Chapel, was opened by the Marquis of Hamilton as a meeting place for the Congregationalist Independent Mission. It was paid for by subscription and the movement to set it up was led by Mr Searle and other local tradesmen. After about ten years the congregation split and half of them joined the Salvation Army at the Gospel Hall, also in the Terrace. Eventually both groups declined in numbers. The Gospel Hall was used for various purposes and by 1963 was a furniture store. It was finally knocked down and its site behind today's library in Sunninghill was used for a new house. The Mission Hall became a public hall and meeting place but after the building of Cordes Hall it too went into decline. In 1911 it was bought by the Windsor and Maidenhead circuit and reopened as a Methodist Chapel (Mr and Mrs Prince, Margaret Brown and Eileen Fenton provided the information on the Chapel).

The growth of the non-conformist churches in the second half of the century reflected the reaction among respectable tradesmen and artisans to the lawlessness which prevailed among the navvies working on the railway, the itinerants who came for seasonal work and the wilder men of the parish. Sunninghill, especially south of the London Road, was notoriously ill-behaved. There were a series of missions to convert the sinful and some of the local worthies such as Joseph Savory of Buckhurst Park supported evangelical and reforming movements.

A typical local reaction to the reformers was the activity of the *"Skeleton Army"* in the early 1890s. Five or six hundred hooligans, including men from Egham and Wokingham, would gather at the pubs and then march out to attack the Salvation Army meetings held at The Mission. The *"Skeleton Army"* louts were supported by local publicans who opposed the efforts of the Salvationists to persuade local men to sign the pledge. Extra police had to be drafted in and one man was killed. This was part of a general struggle between the forces of temperance and their opponents. In 1883 the *"Yellow Ribbon Army"* had attacked the *"Yellow Ribbon Temperance Brigade"* in Maidenhead.

In 1978 an independent film company decided to make a film called *"Rachel and the Beelzebub Army"* about the Sunninghill disturbances. It was eventually shown on BBC 2 and Channel 4 and included three members of the Quince players in the cast. It was made on location chiefly in Cranbourne Church and Binfield because the traffic in Sunninghill was too busy.

Roads, Paths and Local History

The coming of the railway opened up the Bog south of the London Road. Between 1865 and 1867 a road was built through Sunninghill Bog to Ascot railway station using some of the land which had belonged to the Parish Trust. In the same year as this road was completed, the Windsor Forest Turnpike was abolished and that road was opened to free use.

The nineteenth century saw many alterations to old paths and some curtailments of public access. In 1878 the vestry was very concerned about the closure of the gate at the east end of the New Mile Course by the racecourse managers. Eventually free access on foot was secured (B.R.O., D/P 126 8/5). Today's Cheapside Road was marked on contemporary maps as *"Tun Lane"* and ran all the way round from the Wells Inn to the Cannon Inn. Cheapside Green was marked as *"Tun Green"*.

In 1845 there was a long discussion about erecting a bridge over the watersplash between Sunninghill Park and Smith's Green, near today's Dorian Drive, but nothing came of it (ibid). Only small amounts of money were paid out by the vestry barely enough for the essential repairs of roads and bridges.

One of the members of the vestry who was particularly interested in the condition and accessibility of the local paths and roads was G. M. Hughes. In 1890 his massive work *"A History of Windsor Forest Sunninghill and the Great Park"* was published. It remains the first and the best secondary source available. It was published by subscription and the list of subscribers provides a useful survey of the Sunninghill community at that date. They included: Lord Harlech at Tetworth Hall, General Crutchley at Sunninghill Park, Colonel Blundell MP at Ashurst, Thomas Cordes Esq. at Silwood Park, the Rev. J. Snowdon vicar of Sunninghill, Mrs Matthew Wylie at the Mains, Mr J. Pither, Miss Margaret Thacker at Queens Hill, Joseph Savory Esq. at Buckhurst Park, William Farmer Esq. at Coworth Park, Sir G. Martin Holloway and Miss Driver at Tittenhurst, Colonel the Hon. C. R. Hay at Harewood Lodge, J. K. Hitchins Esq. at Beechgrove, Edward Pott Esq. at The Cedars, Mrs Entwhistle at The Oaks, the Misses Hardyman at Silwood Cottage, and Albert Chancellor Esq. M.S.A. of Ascot.

The last decades of the century were a good time for philanthropic activity in Sunninghill. In 1882 Miss Jemima Durning Smith provided the first free library for the district. It has continued in the house she gave to the parish and contains a valuable local history archive. The Durning Trust has used the income from her other property here to fund a wide range of educational projects for the benefit of Ascot and the surrounding area. Later in 1901, Thomas Cordes gave the site of Cordes Hall to the village of Sunninghill. After his death his widow had the hall built in a lively arts and crafts architecture designed by Mr Morris of Reading. This became the centre for the social activities of the parish and, until the building of the Village Hall in Cheapside, the Cordes Hall was the only social centre for the whole parish.

"The Rich Man in his Castle"

As could be seen by the list of subscribers to the G. M. Hughes history, the farms and lodges were long gone and the *"parks"* had arrived in their places. Wealthy men who came to live in Sunninghill had made their fortunes elsewhere and were living here off their private incomes, pensions and dividends. They were never local farmers nor were they local manufacturers. Wealth was not made in Sunninghill, it was attracted to it. The residents of the largest houses fell into four categories: people of high social status who wanted a house near to the court at Windsor, those who had retired from the service of the crown in the army, navy or government service, those who had made money in the city of London and those who had made their fortune in the manufacturing industries of the Midlands, the North or the West.

Typical of the society group was Charles Churchill who died in 1829. He lived at The Oaks on the London Road, now the site of the Royal Berkshire Hotel, a house built before the manor house had been relocated by James Sibbald. Charles Churchill was a grandnephew of the first duke of Marlborough, John Churchill. His mother was a daughter of Sir Robert Walpole the *"first Prime Minister"*. Charles Churchill's widow lived at The Oaks until her death in 1846 aged ninety-five. Another who died a year later than Charles Churchill was of the same courtly origins. Augustus Schutz of Ashurst was *"a man of cultivated mind, sound understanding, unaffected piety, unblemished integrity and enlarged benevolence"* according to his memorial in the church. Certainly he and his wife Elizabeth were generous in their support of the church and the school.

Typical of the second category was Admiral Sir Home Riggs Popham, who died in 1820 and whose large memorial dominates

St Michael's graveyard. Popham was famous as the developer of the naval flag communications system. He lived on the opposite side of London Road to Titness. He was one of the many high ranking service officers who retired to Sunninghill.

Only Sunninghill Park remained in the hands of the same family throughout the period. The Crutchley family had originally bought the Park from the profits of their London businesses. For a couple of centuries they acquired more land in and around Sunninghill. After the death of Jeremiah Crutchley in 1805 the property passed to his nephew George Henry Duffield who took the name of Crutchley in 1806. He became the sheriff of Berkshire a year later. During the Victorian age the family provided the country with two generals, an admiral, county sheriffs and justices of the peace and it is strange that they were never granted a baronetcy. In 1868 Percy Henry Crutchley (1807-1876), the eldest son of George Henry, inherited Sunninghill Park. Percy Henry became a J.P. in 1863, also served as sheriff of Berkshire and died unmarried. His brother General Sir Charles Crutchley (1810-1898) succeeded to the family estates.

Charles Crutchley purchased his commission in the Royal Welsh Fusiliers when he was sixteen years old and rose steadily to the rank of Lieutenant Colonel in 1849. He managed to avoid the Crimean War but after a spell as the Commandant of the Royal Military Hospital at Chelsea he returned to active service and commanded the brigade in Gibraltar. He became a general in 1877. He had married Eliza Bayfield in 1851 and had six surviving children. Three were sons, the eldest being Percy Edward (1855-1940) who inherited the Sunninghill estates which by then included Brook Lodge (today's Heronsbrook) in 1898.

Percy Edward was educated at Harrow and Trinity College Cambridge and, in 1890, he married Frederica Louisa FitzRoy who had been a lady-in-waiting to Queen Victoria. They lived at Sunninghill Lodge for many years while his father was at Sunninghill Park House. The Crutchleys had an income from renting out property in Cheapside and Sunninghill, from the farms on the estate and for a large part of the century they owned other farms around here.

General Charles' younger son, also Charles (1856-1940), followed a military career like his father. He became Major General Sir Charles Crutchley and married Sybil Mary Coke the only daughter of the Hon. Henry and Lady Katherine Coke who were related to the earls of Leicester. Sir Charles had a distinguished military career serving in the Egyptian and Sudan campaign. He was severely injured in Sudan. His eldest son was Gerald Edward Victor (1895-1969) and his children included two sons, Edward and Richard and the actress Rosalie Crutchley.

Unlike Sunninghill Park, Silwood Park had a succession of owners drawn chiefly from the world of commerce and industry. George Simson had the estate after Sibbald's death. Simson sold to Michie Forbes in 1824 because he was in financial difficulties. The estate was described as *"all that manor of Sunninghill called Silwood Farm and Eastmore farm Sellmore Coppice and Sellmore Mead"*. It included a path which went *"to a gate or style so leading to a place called Cheapside"*, two fields called *"Cheapside Upper and Lower meads with a cottage belonging to William Martin and land called Wapshotts"* (B.R.O., D/ER T 80/6/7). When Michie Forbes of Silwood Park died in 1839 the estate was offered for sale but there were no buyers and Mr Forbes' widow continued to own the estate and to lease out the land and the houses until 1854/5.

The next three owners were men who had done very well out of the great industrial revolution. A document entered into the Cookham manor records recorded the transfer of ownership: *"Silwood Park, or Sellmore alias Eastmore Farm, was held as a Suithold Estate of the Manor of Cookham, belonged to Michie Forbes of King William Street, London, whose widow, Mary Forbes of Portland Place sold part to John Hargreaves of Sea View House, Southport, Lancs., the transfer taking place on 22 Feb. 1855"*. The price was £30,000. Hargreaves disposed of some 612 acres of outlying land to the south including Belleview and King's Beech farms. He retained about 250 acres including the present Imperial College holding. He later bought Silwood Lodge as well (I.C.A.).

John Hargreaves' wealth came from his engineering factories in Staffordshire (Hick Hargreaves Engine Co. made pumps). When he died in 1874, he left his estate to his trustees. The estate was sold a year later for £80,000 to Charles Patrick Stewart of 92 Lancaster Gate. This sale included the *"Main House, Silwood Lodge, Oakleigh,"* and *"Fairfield and a large stretch of land behind the latter"* (B.R.O., D/E Fa).

The conveyance included a map showing the owners of the properties adjacent to Silwood Park. They were: Colonel the Hon. W. F. Hay at Harewood House, Mrs Blane at The Oaks, a Post Office on the main road beside the Cannon Public House, Joseph Savory Esq. at Buckhurst Lodge Estate, Percy H. Crutchley at Sunninghill Park, Colonel Gore at Tetworth Hall, Miss Thacker at The Mount, Major Parry at The Cedars, Lieut. Col. Blundell at Ashurst, Miss Hardyman at Silwood Cottage and Col. Crutchley

(Percy's brother) at Brook House. The land in front of the Tun Inn was still an open green and there was a path at *"Gunnes's Bridge"* but none at Cascade Bridge (I.C.A.). Parsonage Lane had disappeared.

Charles Stewart was born in Dublin in 1823. He was educated at Cambridge and became an apprentice engineer with Seward and Cappel. In 1852 he was made a partner in the firm of Sharp Brothers and Co. who owned the famous Atlas Works in Manchester and he worked in and around Manchester until 1863. In spite of being deaf he was an able and enthusiastic engineer who supported new developments and the latest ideas. In 1875, the same year that he bought the estate, he became the Vice President of the Institution of Mechanical Engineers. His energy and intelligence were soon expressed at Silwood Park and though he was there only a relatively short time he left his stamp on the estate. It is appropriate that a building erected by such a major engineer should today belong to Imperial College, one of the premier engineering universities.

In 1876 Sibbald's Georgian mansion and Silwood Lodge were demolished and Stewart began to build the *"free Tudor"* house which stands there today. It was an ambitious project and the final clock tower was completed in 1878. The architect was Alfred Waterhouse, 1830-1905, who also designed four lodges and the garden cottage, making lavish use of the blue brick so popular at the time.

The "free-Tudor" Silwood Park

Waterhouse was already known as the architect of the Natural History Museum in Kensington, built 1873-81, and of the new university buildings in London and Manchester. It was his use of brick that gave the name *"red-brick"* to these institutions. His use of red and blue brick was copied by other builders and appeared locally on Joseph Savory's new buildings in Pump Lane and Pemberton Lodge.

Stewart may have found his famous architect rather too expensive. His new house cost £27,500. In 1878 he raised mortgages on the estate: £37,000 from the Silwood estate, £6,000 from the kitchen gardens, £5,000 from Fairfield and £2,000 from Oakleigh (B.R.O., D/EFa; I.C.A.).

As well as rebuilding the house Stewart made many changes on the estate including realigning the paths. In 1877 he diverted the old lane across the Park to Cheapside. It was moved:

"from the spot near the gravel pit about 120 yards from where the said footpath leaves the public carriage way at Pound Hill Stile, Cheapside and turning the said footpath in an easterly direction on the other side of Lower Farm (Silwood Farm) *for a distance of 412 yards along a new footpath to be made by C. P. Stewart across his land".*

Nearer to the lake this path joined a cart-track which led back up the hill to the site of the old Eastmore *"and through Nash's copse until the new footpath will enter the old footpath at the junction with the path leading from the One Tun Road".*

He also diverted:

"the first mentioned footpath or highway at a spot about 80 yards from Gunners Bridge and turning the said path in a southerly direction in a straight course through the land of C P Stewart called Church field along a new footpath made by the said C P Stewart until the said new footpath will reach the Church stile" (B.R.O., D/P 126 8/5).

These changes created the routes followed by today's rights of way from the Cheapside and Buckhurst Roads through the Silwood property.

When Charles Stewart died in 1882 he left the Silwood estate to his trustees including *"John Robinson* (his partner), *Engineer, of Atlas Works, Manchester and of Westwood, Staffordshire and Henry Chapman* (friend) *Engineer, of 113 Victoria Street Westminster"* (R.S.P.). A year later the Silwood estate was for sale. Once again the sale map listed the nearby landowners: Lord Harlech had replaced Colonel Gore at Tetworth Hall, Mrs Entwhistle had replaced Mrs Blane at The Oaks but Lieutenant Colonel Blundell was still at Ashurst and Major Parry was still at The Cedars. All the property from Silwood Farm to today's Heronsbrook was owned by General Crutchley. The overflow at the end of the lake was indicated on the sales map and also the kitchen and fruit gardens, today's Silwood Nursery. In the greenhouse there was a famous vine, over 120 feet long, a near equal to the great vine at Hampton Court (Hughes, p. 217).

It was yet another industrialist who bought the estate in 1888. Mr Thomas Cordes was a steelmaster from Newport, Monmouthshire. His family was of Huguenot extraction, and had moved from Spain to France in the fifteenth century (R.S.P.). His wife was a daughter of Admiral Sir Alexander Milne. The Cordes established a deer-park of a hundred acres with about 120 fallow deer. This was the first time there had been a deer-park at Sunninghill Manor. The venison from the park used to be hung in a shed by the house of the head gardener Mr Ross at the Garden Lodge adjacent to Tetworth Hall. The Cordes' ownership would see the property into the twentieth century.

Buckhurst Park had several owners and tenants before it came into the hands of the banker Joseph Savory in 1864. Vernon sold it to the Reverend George Hunt and the latter was the host on the eleventh of June 1833 when the author Greville recorded a visit to Buckhurst Park for the Ascot Races. This estate included 127 acres of land on the east side of Buckhurst Road and also land on the west side between the junction with Cheapside Road and Watersplash Lane stretching up to the Thatched Tavern and the stream.

Buckhurst Park

Joseph Savory, 1808-1879, came from a long line of London goldsmiths. He married Mary Caroline Braithwaite of Kendal,

1818-1887 and they had eight children. Both he and his wife were strongly religious and interested in reform. Joseph was a manager of Day Schools and he taught in Sunday Schools. He and his wife became close friends with Colonel and Mrs Hay at Harewood. In 1879 he fell from his horse and died after five years of illness. His estate passed to his son also called Joseph Savory, 1843-1921.

The second Joseph Savory also had broad business interests in the City of London. He was a member of five livery companies and on several boards. In 1882 he was appointed sheriff of Middlesex and London and a year later he was elected an alderman of the City. He served as Lord Mayor of London in 1890-1891. As was customary for the holder of the mayoral office, he was created a baronet.

Like his parents Sir Joseph was very devout. Licensed as a lay reader he took morning services at Chavey Down and preached in South Ascot. He was closely involved with the establishment of St. Saviour's Mission Church there. In 1888, a year after his mother's death, he married Helen Pemberton Loach (hence Pemberton Lodge in Cheapside). Percy Crutchley was the best man at their wedding.

The Savorys had no children but his marriage brought him new interests in Westmoreland. In 1892 he was elected MP for North Westmoreland and bought land near Appleby and Kirkby Stephen. In the same year he gave up the family goldsmith's business in London which was henceforth run by a cousin. He became a JP serving on the bench in both Westmoreland and Berkshire. Sir Joseph was a personal friend of both Thomas Holloway and Holloway's brother-in-law and was made a governor of Holloway Sanatorium and Royal Holloway College. From 1914 to 1920 he was chairman of the governors at the College.

Savory made many alterations to the estate. In the 1870s and 1880s the landscape was improved by the addition of many trees including the large redwoods along today's Buckhurst Road. The millpond was enlarged to form a decorative lake. At the same time the old cottages in Bucket Hill hamlet began to disappear. New estate cottages were built, including some in Pump Lane and others were remodelled to provide the *"comfort of our people at Buckhurst"* (this and most of the information on the Savory family comes from a copy of Helen P. Savory's book published in 1924, entitled *"Sir Joseph Savory"* and given by her to Frederick and Isabella Grindell of *"Grindles Cottage"*, now amazingly renamed Stag Lodge). Also for the comfort of his people Sir Joseph provided lantern slides in the barn on the farm estate, much enjoyed by the local children (C.S.).

Sir Joseph features less favourably in some of the local records and in some local memories. There were complaints to the parish and district councils about his encroachment on the Green outside the Tun Inn. It was claimed that ancient village fairs used to be held there (there is alas no supporting evidence for this) and maps were produced showing it to be *"a parish waste"*. Sir Joseph Savory was ordered to abate the encroachment. There were also tales of his miserliness. Percy Franklin, who lived at the Mill cottages and was employed to dig out the extensions to the millpond, left the estate after a disagreement with Savory over his wages.

The presence of these large estates obviously affected the growth of Cheapside, but apart from Silwood, Buckhurst and Sunninghill Parks they did not provide regular or reliable employment for local people. Since the owners were only intermittently in residence, local suppliers could not depend on them for their livelihoods. More significantly most of the larger households had their own servants who came with them. They employed very few Cheapsiders, and then only in lowly capacities as general servants, laundresses and gardeners.

At The Cedars, in 1881, Baroness Rivers had a staff of seven, none of whom were local. Another large household was the Foley family at Tetworth Hall. In 1851 Captain Henry Foley was there with his wife, six daughters and one son. They were supported by ten staff all of whom had come with the Foleys from far away. Four of the children had been born abroad in Italy, France, Switzerland and Germany and some of the staff also came from abroad. Foley had bought Tetworth Hall from a Mr Meyrick Fowler and by 1890 he had sold it to Lord Harlech.

Within Cheapside itself there were a couple of larger houses occupied by the gentry but these were tenanted by families who stayed only for a few seasons. They too brought their staff with them and did not employ local people. One of these houses was *"Brook Lodge"* also known as *"Brookside"* and *"Brook House"*. This was today's Heronsbrook House. This estate included the cottage (today's April Place), the stables and coachhouse (today's Heronsbrook Farm), gardens, orchards and farmland (today's Heronsbrook Cottage and all the land where Hilltop Close is now). Prince Dalton owned it in 1847 but by the late nineteenth century it had been sold to the Crutchleys. It was leased to a succession of tenants. In 1863 the Reverend Thomas Whateley was at Brook Lodge as was his widow six years later.

By 1891 John H Schneider was renting *"Brookside"* from General Crutchley. Schneider was a retired Lieutenant Colonel of the 3rd Battalion Lancashire Rifles. His wife Mary came from Ireland. They had three children and his sister Rose lived with them. They had ten servants living in and a gardener at Brookside Cottage. Two of their servants, the cook and the kitchen maid, had come from Germany. Not one of them was local. The Schneiders were still there in 1895 but had left by 1901. In 1906 Sir John Croker Bulteel, the Clerk of the Racecourse, was living there. It is said that his famous racehorse Manifesto was buried in the orchard, now the garden of Heronsbrook Cottage.

Pemberton Lodge was the other large house at the east end of Cheapside Road. It had been built by Sir Joseph Savory after his marriage and his widow Helen Pemberton Savory lived there after his death.

Pemberton Lodge

During Sir Joseph's lifetime the house was leased out and most of the residents stayed for the usual season or two. The Stanhopes were an exception and they were there for at least ten years. The Hon. Lincoln Edwin Stanhope had a wife who had been born in Dresden and an infant daughter. The Stanhopes brought all their servants with them. There was a cook, two housemaids, a kitchenmaid, a lady's maid, a nurse, a valet, and a page living in the house and a coachman, watchman and gardener who lived above the coach-house, where Mare's Nest is today. The house had a very fine terraced garden and occupied all the land up to the junction of Cheapside Road and Buckhurst Road and along Buckhurst Road as far as today's Cheapside Court. In 1903 Patrick Grant who had been at Tetworth Hall moved to Pemberton Lodge and four years later in 1907 his widow was there.

The long tenure of the Crutchleys and even the two generations of the Savory family were exceptional. A glance at the local directories shows the general mobility. In the Dutton Allen and Co. Directory of 1863 the owners of the more valuable properties were:

Percy Henry Crutchley J.P. at Sunninghill Park
John Hargreaves at Silwood Park
Mrs Charlotte Hardyman at Selwood Cottage
Thomas Holloway at Tittenhurst Park
D. W. Chapman at Titness Park
Mrs Hunt, the widow of the Reverend Hunt, at Buckhurst Park
Lord William Powlett at Harewood
Right Hon. the earl of Yarborough at The Cedars
Lady Dixie at *"Selwood"* Lodge
Hon. Mrs Hare at Tetworth Hall
Lady Corbet at Queens Hill
Lady Murray at Ashurst
(B.R.O., D/E A R/M12/2)

Six years later there were many changes. Only Crutchley (down in the Kelly's Directory as *"Lord of the Manor"* though he was not), Hargreaves, Holloway and Hardyman were at the same addresses. Lord Annaly was now at Titness Park, Joseph Savory at Buckhurst Park, Lieutenant Colonel C. R. Drummond Hay at Harewood, Mrs Calverley at The Cedars, Edward Johnstone at Silwood Lodge, the Hon. Ladies Murray at Ashurst and Major General Ormesby Gore at Tetworth Hall. When Lord Harlech bought Tetworth Hall in 1890, the previous owners were listed from Mr James Mann, Mr Desborough, Mr Carter, Mr Meyrick Fowler, Rev. Mr Peart, to Capt. Foley *"who, having had an estate called Tetworth gave that name to this house"* (Hughes, p. 257).

When a property changed hands, as well as a renaming, there was often a major refurbishment and redevelopment. As a result many Stuart and Georgian houses vanished under Victorian extensions. This happened at Brook Lodge, at The Cedars,

Ashurst and Harewood. This last house was dramatically enlarged by Colonel Hay and sold in 1885 by Mr Albert Chancellor, the first generation of the firm of the local estate agents. The house was advertised in *"The Times"* of the 6th July as being *"in a neighbourhood celebrated for its healthy character and beauty"*. The details of the sale emphasised that Harewood had been recently enlarged and had nineteen bedrooms and seven reception rooms. Its gardens *"beautifully undulating parklike grounds"* of about forty acres had *"vineries, peach-house, stove and plant houses"*.

In the 1895 Kelly's Directory, which described Sunninghill with its 3,207 acres as *"principally gentlemen's parks and heath"*, with a total *"rateable value of £32,099"*, there were only five properties remaining in the hands of the same families who owned them in 1869. Percy Edward Crutchley was at Sunninghill Park Lodge with General Charles Crutchley at Sunninghill Park, Sir George Martin-Holloway was at Tittenhurst with Miss Driver, Thomas Holloway's niece, at Tittenhurst Lodge and Sir Joseph Savory Bart. at Buckhurst Park. Everywhere else the properties had been sold and the ownership had changed. There was little continuity in the upper levels of society.

"The Poor Man at his Gate"

In 1840, 183 cottages, 85 houses, 7 lodges, a workhouse, a schoolroom and 2 mansions were listed in the Sunninghill Rate Book. There were two toll bars at *"Beggars Bush"* and *"Blackness"* and six shops. These included Slann's carpenter shop at *"Beggars Bush"*, David Nash's shop at *"One Tun"*, probably a saddlery, and four more in *"Sunninghill Common"* and *"Beggars Bush"*. There were 40 cottages and houses in our district which was listed under *"Cheapside, Smith's Green, One Tun and Pound Hill"*. There would be another twenty or so cottages over the Stream in *"Bucket Hill hamlet"* which was in the parish of Winkfield. *"Pound Hill"* was all the settlement to the west of Green Lane. The old manorial pound for keeping stray animals was out of use by the mid-nineteenth century but the name remained. *"Cheapside and One Tun"* lay between Green Lane and Mill Lane. This was described in the censuses of the later nineteenth century as *"Windsor Road, Cheapside"*.

"Smith's Green" included today's Dorian Drive. Henry Smith (1853-1947) and his family lived at *"The Bungalow"*, now Wisteria Cottage. He was a gamekeeper and the dog keeper for the Queen

(the Queen's private kennels were at Frogmore and the Buckhounds were kept in North Ascot). His older brother William Thomas (1845-1911) was a gamekeeper for the Crutchleys. The Smith family had been in crown service for many years, first as keepers in the New Forest and from 1820 in Windsor Great Park. Joseph Smith was gatekeeper at Milton's Lodge (Ascot Gate today) and senior woodman from 1820 to 1860. *"Smiths Green"* was named on the ordnance survey maps of the nineteenth century and was also defined in the census returns. It may have been named after this family who were well known in Cheapside for over a century. Fifteen members of the family are buried at St Michael's churchyard (C.S.).

These two sets of figures taken from the census returns give a rough profile of Cheapside's inhabitants during the second half of the century:

	1851	1891
Houses	41	60
Total Inhabitants	146	268
Children	57	58
Adults born in Sunninghill	23	25
Numbers employed	70	111
Servants/gardeners/laundresses	20	65
Agricultural and general labourers	24	14
Food trades	9	12
Trades/crafts	15	18
Others	2	2
Employers	6	5

The local population fluctuated depending on whether Sunninghill Park, Silwood Park, Buckhurst Park, Tetworth Hall and Brook Lodge were fully occupied or not. For example at Brook Lodge there were fifteen people on the 1891 census returns and only one housekeeper in 1881 and at Tetworth Hall there were fifteen in 1851 and only two in 1871. Most Cheapsiders lived in the cottages on Pound Hill, Cheapside Road, Smith's Green and Bucket Hill and about a quarter of them were children. Less than half of the residents had actually been born in Cheapside or Sunninghill. The rest had moved into Cheapside from all over the country.

Almost all the local labour was employed at Silwood, Sunninghill and Buckhurst Parks with a small number of Cheapsiders employed in the Royal Park. Some households supplemented their income by taking lodgers. How this was managed in the small cottages is hard to imagine.

There was a tiny group of professional people living in Cheapside but the only long term resident was the schoolmistress. From time to time between 1841 and 1891 there were another teacher, a couple of curates, a nurse, a barrister's clerk, and a photographer. The latter was Charles Bew's son. He provides the rarity of one of the new professions appearing in the local census returns. It would be interesting if any of his photographs of Cheapside had survived.

All the other Cheapsiders were poor cottagers who lived in rented properties that were sold from one absentee landlord to another. The landowners named on the 1847 Sunninghill Tithe map included several who had owned the land at the time of the Enclosure thirty years earlier. Eight plots, almost all the land in Pound Hill, still belonged to Joseph Cannell. Isaac Cannell owned the single plot that was eventually the site for the chapel, and he held two other plots jointly with John Bretton. The Cannell family lived in Cheapside up to the 1840s but by 1851 they had almost disappeared from Cheapside either as owners or residents. Benjamin Cannell was its only local representative left. He was the sixteen-year-old stepson of John Harris, the tailor, and he was a gardener. By that time Murrell Wright owned large parts of Pound Hill. He had a house in Wells Lane where he lived with his wife Mary, their daughter and servant. He was listed on the census as a retired coal merchant. He had several other pieces of land in Sunninghill including a farm when he died aged 81 in 1865.

The Cannell property had included the Long Gardens Cottages, two of which were, in 1841 and 1851, rented by Joseph Turner and Charles Chance. Joseph Turner was forty-five years old in 1851. An agricultural worker he lived with his wife, five daughters and a son and the family ran a beer shop. Charles Chance, another agricultural worker, was an older man of sixty-two with a wife and two daughters still at home. These two were typical of the people who lived in Cheapside.

Although Cheapside had a small population it managed to support two public houses, the Thatch and the Tun, and at least one beer shop. No doubt some locals would use the Wells Inn too. There were also two grocer's shops and at least two bakeries for most of the second half of the century. These were generally run by people who had come to Cheapside from far afield.

The Lewarn family is a good example. Nathaniel came from Cornwall and by 1851 he had a grocery and drapery business. He lived with his wife and son George, born in Sunninghill. Their shop was on Pound Hill where Thatcher's hairdressing business is now. Twenty years later the son George was thirty-three years old and he had taken over the business. His wife, Rachel, also came from Cornwall. By then his parents, Nathaniel and Eliza, were living next door at Laburnum Cottage and taking in lodgers including the local curate and his brother. Ten years later Rachel Lewarn was a widow and she employed Michael Hartridge from Staines as a shop assistant. The Post Office was installed in the late 1880s (E.B.). Nathaniel and Eliza were still at Laburnum Cottage and, at the time of the census, they had a visitor from York. By 1891 Nathaniel and Eliza had vanished and their cottage was empty but Rachel was still in business, with Michael as her assistant. She employed an extra boy in the shop called Edward Martin and his sister Maria was her domestic servant. Her business was listed as a grocery and drapery.

The other Cheapside grocer was Robert Cubitt who had come from Suffolk and married Ann Bew, a local girl. Her parents had started a shop at Rose Cottage next to the Thatched Tavern. Throughout the 1870s and 1880s Robert Cubitt was listed in the Kelly's Directory as a *"grocer and day waiter"*. By 1899 his son Herbert had bought the Lewarn's shop and was listed in Kelly's as *"Grocer, Butcher and Post Master"*. The Cubitts had the shop up to about 1910 when they sold out to William Steadman. The Rose Cottage shop was closed down when Herbert Cubitt left it but a new shop had opened on the opposite side of the road at Elm Bank and this flourished into the twentieth century.

In 1851 John Cottrell (or Cotterell), who came from Middlesex, was listed as a master baker employing one man. He had a wife Sarah, a son John and a daughter Ann who was five years old. His business was probably at the end of Green Lane near to the Thatched Tavern. Ten years later, Sarah was widowed and she and her son John ran the business with the help of her lodger, James Pottinger. In 1871 they had a new assistant called George Allan from Bray. By 1881 her son had left and George Allan was helping the seventy-three year old Sarah at the bakery. George Allan was still there in 1891 but now Sarah had gone and her daughter Ann had taken over the business.

The other *"master baker"* was George Simkins who was also a farmer and came from Windsor. Simkins' business was on Pound Hill. In 1861 he was sixty-one years old and ran the business with his wife. Ten years later his stepson John Prince had taken over the bakery. John Prince was then thirty-four years old and he had a wife, four children and two servants; one was Thomas Hopkins an assistant baker. His business seems to have been the larger of the two Cheapside bakeries and by 1883 he was calling himself *"a baker and confectioner"*. His son was his apprentice baker and Arthur Portsmouth was his assistant. Four years later John Prince was not only a baker but also the innkeeper at the Wells Inn.

The innkeepers of all three local inns changed frequently. Often, like John Prince, they had a supplementary income from another trade. Joseph Longhurst was innkeeper at the Thatched Tavern from 1846 to the mid-1850s. He traded as a wheelwright and builder. By 1861 Longhurst had been replaced by George Baldwin from Buckinghamshire and nine years later Joseph Brigstock from Leicester was the landlord though he had gone by 1877 when the licensee was Albert Wort. The licensee had changed again in 1881 when for the first time it was a woman, Mary Wallis, who lived at *"The Thatch"* with her nephew Charles Nichols and his family. Charles was a varnish maker. Only two years later Rees Jones had taken over to be followed in 1887 by John Allen, in 1895 by Albert Davis and in 1905 by F. Warr making a total of nine innkeepers in sixty years.

All these changes suggest that there was not a good living to be made at the Tavern. Certainly for most of this period they would have faced competition from the beer house in Long Gardens as well as from the Tun Inn and the Wells Inn. *"The Thatch"* however was a well-known landmark and it is said that Queen Victoria's royal carriage was sometimes seen outside while John Brown was fortifying himself inside.

The One Tun Inn showed a similar turnover of landlords to The Thatch. It also took in lodgers and paying guests. In 1847 Robert Batchelor was the innkeeper and his wife Elizabeth had taken over by 1863. She was followed by Henry Cox and then Alfred Hitchcock who was also a poor-rate collector. Frederick Stevens was there in the late 1880s. There were two innkeepers in the 1890s, Benjamin Westlake and William Roach. The last innkeeper was W. Collins and in 1908 the old Tun Inn, which had been in business for about three hundred years, was closed down. Many pubs ceased business at this time since an Act of Parliament encouraged closures by giving compensation to landlords who went out of business. The fact that it was on Sir Joseph Savory's land and he was an eager religious reformer may have been the main reason for the closure. The Tun, as can be seen from the

Bobby's notebook (see later), was always a scene of more rowdiness than The Thatch.

The One Tun and the Tun or Cheapside Green about 1900

By the middle of the nineteenth century the Wells Inn had lost much of its old glamour. It was run by Robert Dilly as a family hotel and posting house. Some of the Dilly family lived in Cheapside. Robert supplemented his income by trading in corn and coal. The Wells was the starting point for the Sunninghill to Slough coach which left every day, except Sunday, at twenty minutes past nine in the morning and returned at seven in the evening. Keck's coach to Holborn in London also went daily, leaving the Wells at nine o'clock in the morning and returned at seven o'clock in the evening to the Thatched Tavern. The age of commuting had arrived. By 1863 W. M. Barker was the innkeeper at the Wells and he took over the Dilly's corn and coal business as well. He was also an estate agent, truly a man of all trades, but he had gone by 1877. After a series of licensees Henry Wyard took over in the 1890s and his widow Mrs Wyard still ran the business in 1916.

The largest business in Cheapside was the coach building firm belonging to William Norwood. This operated from today's Buckhurst Cottage, then on the side of Tun Green next to Braisher's saddlery shop. William Norwood's son Charles was a coach painter and Edward Cannon another coach painter lodged at the Tun Inn. There would have been no room for him at the Norwoods for they had six children who were, in 1881, between the ages of ten and twenty-six. One of Norwood's daughters was a pupil teacher. By 1899 Charles Norwood had taken over the business but by 1903 his widow Mrs Charles Norwood was running it.

The only other business of any size operating from Cheapside was run by Thomas Eales who was a corn merchant and coal dealer. His yard was at Smith's Green from 1869 for more than twenty years and he employed three men. It was a forerunner of the haulage firm that operated from the same site in the twentieth century (Cheapside Court Offices today). By 1895 Mrs Eales was a widow and living in retirement at The White House in Cheapside.

Cheapside had a number of self-employed tradesmen who prospered with the growth of Sunninghill. As the century passed some of the older craftsmen and workers such as the hurdle-maker, the cow-boy and the shepherd-boy disappeared along with the tripe-dealer. Some local rural crafts survived. James King, who lived on Pound Hill from the 1880s to 1916, was blind and a basket-maker. Presumably he used the osiers and hazels growing along the Brook as had Mrs Briller who was the last hurdle-maker listed in 1851.

The Todds were the local plumbers, painters and glaziers. They lived on Pound Hill, Isaac Todd in the 1860s and 1870s and later his son Alfred. Alfred Todd's daughter, Mary, married Mr Francis, the organist at St Michael's from 1868 for 25 years. Francis was also a rate collector from 1886 to 1926 and clerk to the parish council from its formation in 1894 for 40 years. Albert J. Goodall had replaced the Todds as a general builder, plumber and decorator by 1910. He lived next to the Post Office and was still there in 1915. His board appears on old postcards of Cheapside.

William Canning of Providence Villas was the local stone mason from 1870 to the 1890s and the Hicks family provided two generations of bricklayers, Thomas in the 1850s and 1860s and Francis in the later part of the century. Another bricklayer was George Harding, his family lived in Cheapside for many years. The Kidd family were the local carpenters, John Kidd from 1861 to 1891 and his sons later. There was another carpenter in 1851, John Walter, but like several other craftsmen who are mentioned in only one census he may have been here on a temporary job.

Every community needed a boot maker. Although many poor children and even women might go barefoot every worker needed a pair of boots which would be patched many times. Boots and clothing were a major expense for the poor and by the middle of the nineteenth century the parish no longer provided clothes and shoes on the poor relief. Richard Toms was the local boot and shoemaker. He lived in Long Gardens Cottages in the last decade of the nineteenth and first decade of the twentieth centuries. His son Robert Toms followed his father in the trade up to and during the First World War. Robert's son was accidentally shot and killed by the Sunninghill Park gamekeeper, Mr Benstead, shortly before the Second World War. Robert had by then moved from Long Gardens to one of the Sunninghill Park lodges and he later moved to Pump Lane. There was a second local shoemaker at the end of the century, John Moulton.

Most poor people would make their own clothes or depend on *"pass-ons"* from their employers. For Sunday best or for special occasions the better off among them might turn to a dressmaker. Caroline Webb, who later became the schoolmistress, started her working life as a dressmaker. In 1851 and 1861 she was listed in the census as a seamstress living with her mother Mary Ann who was the schoolmistress. By 1881 however, Caroline was teaching in the Cheapside school. Ten years later she was once again entered in the census as *"a plain needlewoman"*. There was another dressmaker, a Mrs Woodley, and the few local men who could afford it were catered for by Martin Woodruff, a tailor, who lived near the Thatched Tavern. He was succeeded in the years before the First World War by another tailor called appropriately Mr Taylor.

In an age when all cooking and heating depended on the one fire there was plenty of work for the chimney sweep, William Dean in the 1870s and James Wilson from the mid-1880s to 1910. Similarly in the age of leather there was trade for the saddler, William Stevens from 1877 to 1887 and the Braishier family from 1890 to 1916. There were several coachmen working for the larger estates and Thomas Lloyd, a freelance carman and fly proprietor, lived at One Mile Cottage. Only one blacksmith was mentioned on the census returns, this was Isaac Cook who worked at the Morton's smithy on the London Road at the Cannon crossroads from 1880. There was no long term smithy in Cheapside. The Ordnance Survey map published in 1911 shows a smithy on Tun Green but this was probably either the Braisher's saddlery or the Norwood's coachworks. The latter may well have been used as a smithy for a short time.

As well as the landlord of the Wells and Mr Eales there was a third coal merchant. They could rely on business from the great houses. Mr Minchem ran his business from Brick Kiln Farm on the Sunninghill Park estate. As its name implies this was the main local brick works although there was another at Milton's Gate. Thomas Luff who lived in Cheapside was the manager of the business, other members of the Luff family had lived in Cheapside for several generations and were related to Simkins the baker.

Local brick was used in the building of the tidy cottages which were added to Cheapside in the second half of the century. The census of 1871 listed six named cottages in Cheapside: two *"Chaple Cottages"*, three *"Brooklyn Cottages"* and *"Laburnum Cottage"*. The latter, now 31 Cheapside Road, had been there since the previous century and was rebuilt as Laburnum Villas in the 1890s. *"Brooklyn Cottages"*, today's 33, 35 and 37 Cheapside Road, were new in 1871, and the *"Chaple Cottages"* had been erected near the new Chapel almost a decade earlier. These were the first of the 39 cottages that were built in Cheapside in the half-century after 1860. None of them were built or owned by the occupiers. They were either for estate workers as were the lodges and the Pump Lane cottages or built by commercial landlords and builders to be let.

Property added to Cheapside between 1847 and 1911

2 Chaple Cottages 1862-8
3 Brooklyn Cottages by 1871
2 Providence Villas by 1870
6 Savory built cottages in Pump Lane 1877/1880s
6 lodges for the estates of Buckhurst Park, Silwood Park and Sunninghill Park circa 1880
2 Laburnum Villas 1890s
2 Elysian Cottages 1890s
6 Forest View Cottages 1890s
6 Park View cottages, 4 circa 1890 and 2 later
4 Lyndale Cottages in Watersplash Lane circa 1910

These late Victorian and Edwardian houses were of a far higher structural standard than the old cottages. Solid brick walls replaced wood frames filled with straw, hair and daub. The rooms were larger and the ceilings higher but they still had no sanitation other than earth closets and several cottages might share a common water pump. The lighting was by candles or oil lamps and all food and water had to be heated over an open hearth. They did however have long gardens big enough to grow vegetables for the family, to keep a few hens or a pig.

Forest View Cottages about 1920

The Cheapside almshouses lay midway between the Chapel and the Thatched Tavern. In 1844 all the rooms were occupied and rents were coming in from *"Cripps, Booth, Widow Webb, Stubbins and Arter Lee"*. Cripps was paying £5 per year in 1858. On the 1847 Tithe map there were three plots with cottages. Each Cottage had four rooms and they had been rebuilt from the profits of the sale of fourteen acres of land at Chobham and the sale of other parish land to the railway (B.R.O., D/P 126/3/1). In 1853, the Sunninghill Parish Trust and the Fuel Allotment Trust were responsible for the cottages and 172 poles of land in Cheapside, two cottages and 91 poles near Caroline Price's land at Beechgrove, two cottages, 8 acres and 39 poles in the Sunninghill Bog, in Wells Lane, and three cottages and 27 poles near the Sunninghill workhouse. The parish fields were leased for farming or pasture and included the land in Cheapside where the allotments are today (B.R.O., D/P 126 25/1).

In 1851 the Cheapside almshouses were occupied by James Cripps, his wife and son and by three widows and their children:

Mary Ann Webb the schoolmistress and her daughter Caroline, Deborah Curtis and her daughter Jane and Catherine Portchmouth and her son John. Only Deborah Curtis was listed as a pauper. Catherine Portchmouth was an *"annuitant"* or pensioner, and James Cripps was a garden labourer. Ten years later Deborah and Jane Curtis and Mary and Caroline Webb were still there but two elderly widows had replaced the Portchmouths and the Kidds had replaced the Cripps.

In the 1871 return the Webb's almshouse was listed as a private school with Caroline as schoolmistress and her nephew Charles as one of her pupils. A year later the new school had been built and Caroline Webb lived beside it. The other almshouses were then occupied by Emma Kidd, her son and daughter, Hannah Turner and a widower Charles Poynter. Life must have changed for these pensioners with the arrival of the village school next door.

The Cheapside School

Stirred into action by the establishment of the Wesleyan school in 1865, the vestry agreed:

> *"to enlarge the room now being used by Caroline Webb as a school room in Cheapside without any expense to the Parish on the understanding that she shall continue in the occupation of the cottage in the same way as she does at present".*

This proposal was strongly supported by Percy Crutchley (ibid. 8/5). The vestry applied to the Charity Commissioners for help to establish a new National School in Cheapside. Their request was granted in 1866 but there followed a five-year delay before the cottage was transferred from the parish to the Managers and Trustees of the National school *"for the purpose of enabling them to erect a school there on"*.

From 1870 the Managers and Trustees of the National School raised money through public subscription and a government grant (ibid). This cause was not as well supported as the rebuilding of the church had been and it was not until 1874 that the Cheapside National School was built, nominally for a hundred children. This number seems to have been wildly over optimistic. The school never had as many as that on its books and it could not have accommodated them if it had. The main schoolroom was about thirty by seventeen feet and there was a second classroom of about twenty by fourteen feet.

At first Caroline Webb continued to be in charge of all the children with a young helper. However she was not a trained teacher. Her mother Mary Ann had started the dame school charging a penny a day and after her death Caroline had simply taken over. In October 1874 however, Miss J. C. White, a certificated teacher, was appointed and Caroline was demoted to two hours of teaching sewing each afternoon.

The years from 1874 to 1877 are covered in a surviving school log from which Mrs Field Smith made extracts (her notes are now at the School). Miss White did not have much success. The attendance and results were poor. *"The children are very backward and will want a great deal of attention, the Discipline is weak"* she wrote. The average daily attendance was 44. In 1875 Miss White was replaced by Mrs Humphreys but there was still little improvement. Mrs Humphreys left due to ill health and the school returned to the care of Caroline Webb with the help of a pupil teacher (F.S). Some friction between Miss Webb and her successors is indicated.

All this changed in 1878 with the appointment of the twenty-one-year-old Winifred H. Bizley, who had trained at Salisbury training college. Caroline Webb retired by 1881 when she is listed on the census returns as a *"late schoolmistress"*. The appointment of Winifred Bizley began a long and successful period at the school. The Chapel School closed down and by 1895 the Cheapside National School had an average daily attendance of 74 children. Winifred Bizley lodged with Mary Dilly at Holly Cottage, 51 Cheapside Road, and her niece Lucy also boarded there in 1891 when she was a pupil teacher at the school. Miss Bizley remained in the village for the rest of her life and was still teaching at the school after the end of the First World War. She died aged over 90 in the late 1940s.

The school was a focus for Cheapside. It was visited regularly by the vicar and other local notables such as the Savory family. The Crutchleys provided the school with a Christmas tree and gave sweets and fruit to the children. They presented the books handed out for good work and regular attendance. Most children attended Cheapside school for their first four or five years of schooling and some then went on to the Sunninghill School. It was not until 1880 that all children were compelled to attend school until they were ten years old. This was raised to eleven in 1893 and to twelve in 1899. There were exemptions for families employed in agriculture and this kept some Cheapside children out of school. Another disincentive was the charge of a penny a day. Free education only arrived in 1891.

In the 1870s there was another very small *"Ladies School"* in Cheapside. The schoolmistress was Catherine Skinner, her daughter Laura taught music and there were two boarders Emma and Margaret Hedgley who were fifteen and twelve. This appears in the 1877 Kelly's directory as the *"Ladies School in Cheapside"*

Law and Order

Not all Cheapside was as well ordered as a young ladies school and it is clear from the log of the National School that there was some wild behaviour even among the children. The 1841 notebook of an unknown policeman, our first local Bobby, gives some idea of the sort of criminal behaviour worrying the Victorian inhabitants of Cheapside. This notebook was found in the attic of a house in Pump Lane. It is endorsed several times by J. G. Rowley, Inspector, and once with the dated signature of Percy Crutchley, the local magistrate who would have appointed our Bobby. The Bobby's Notebook covers just two months in the spring of 1841, which was just three years after an Act of Parliament had enabled the magistrates to create county forces of chief and petty constables.

The policeman had a lengthy beat, which he covered twice and sometimes even three times a day on foot. All the extracts are quoted with original spelling but with modified punctuation.

"March 11th, Night, Beat: Ascot, Wells, Bog [1], Bar [2], Harewood, Titnest, Cheapside, Silwood Park, Bog, Ascot. (Time) 7 p.m. to 1 a.m.
Served a summons on Charles Stubbins [3] at Lovejoys [4] this night for digging gravel out of Sunninghill pit [5] and selling it without the consent of the surveyors. I saw John Thorn go home at 12 o'clock and George Platt [6] was about the same time in his garden he is frequently up at a late hour but I cannot find out what he is doing."

[1] The Bog was the area south of the London Road and was the local den of iniquity. On May 4th the policeman wrote:
"I have reason to believe there is not less than twenty living in the Bog who is guilty of dishonesty, the principal part of them in a petty way ... this part of the Parish I consider requires more attention than anyother".

[2] The Toll Bar on the turnpike road at what is now Sunninghill crossroads or at today's Cannon.

[3] Stubbins was fined 18s and 3d at Windsor court on March 13th. There was a rapid execution of justice in 1841.

[4] At this date the Lovejoys lived in the Bog; in 1871 Elizabeth Lovejoy, aged 53, lived in Cheapside, probably near Smith's Green, with her son and daughter.

[5] Sunninghill Pit was near Upper Village Road. There were two others, one on the present Winkfield Road and a second near the junction of Cheapside Road and Watersplash Lane.

[6] George Platt was related to Thomas Platt, journeyman butcher, who lodged in Wells Lane in 1851.

"March 15th, Morning, Beat: Ascot, Wells, Bog, Bar, Cheapside, Ascot. 11 a.m. to 1 p.m.

The inns and the beer shops [1] in order. No beggars seen and the parish is as still and quiet as if no one lived in it. At half past two I was sent for to go to Cheapside. Thos Holmes and his father [2] was fighting. he came home drunk his father was going to turn him out of the house he pulled off his shirt to fight his father and from the sons appearance some heavy blows took place the mother coming in for her share they was more reconciled when I got there. he had his cloths tied up in a bundle took his Farewell of his friends and said he whould never come into the house again. he set off for London before I left. it appeared Thos Cripps [3] was nearly as bad. he whent home and made a disturbance at the same time. they was both at the tun before Church and when they left they took some beer away with them and whent into Steers and drunk it."

[1] There were several beer shops in Ascot and Sunninghill including the Turner's beer shop in the Long Gardens Cottages. The policeman regularly checked that they were not selling spirits which they were not permitted to sell and that they were not open during *"divine service"* on Sundays.

[2] Thomas Holmes was the eldest son of the family, probably no more than sixteen in 1841. It seems that he never did return home. In the 1851 census return, his father Charles, aged fifty-four, still lived in Cheapside next door to the Cotterills on Pound Hill. He had a wife Hannah, three daughters aged between twenty and twelve years and two remaining sons, Alfred, aged eighteen, who was a bricklayer's labourer and Charles, aged sixteen, who was an agricultural labourer like his father.

[3] Thomas Cripps was a nineteen year old agricultural labourer in 1841. By 1851 he was married and had settled down with three young children. He and his wife lived near the almshouses.

"March 22nd, Morning, Beat: Ascot, Wells, Vicarage, Harewood, Cheapside, Back to Ascot. 10 a.m. to 1 p.m.

I saw a foreigner begging at Mr Wales I informed him begging was not allowed in this parish he appeared surprised and said he might beg in

150

London I said he must not do it hear he raised his hands said something in his own language and whent on for London".

The policeman spent much of his time preventing begging. On 12th April he wrote: *"I saw a little boy begging in Cheapside I took him to his father who was mending chairs nearby for Crutchleys lodge and I told him he was liable to go to goal for sending his boy begging."* He also stopped match-sellers and when he found a group of beggars he escorted them out of Sunninghill Parish and into Winkfield.

"March 30th, Afternoon, Beat: Ascot, Wells, Vicarage Bar, Mr Cotterills [1], Harewood, Back to Ascot, 3 p.m. to 5 p.m". Endorsed: *Inspected March 31 1841 P.H. Crutchley.*

"at one o'clock I was informed there was two men fighting on the turnpike road near Mr Deaths at Ascot. I whent immediately and put a stop to the fight. one mans name was Snellings from Chertsey and the other was a Bricklayer working at the queen's stabling [2] at Ascot they seemed to be desperate fellows and no doubt whould have fought a long time"

"Night, Beat: Ascot, Cheapside, Titnest, Harewood, Mr Cotterills, Bar, Bog, Wells, Ascot, 8 p.m. to 1 a.m.

I looked in at the tun tap at nine o'clock and saw the Thos Steer Henry Greener and Thos Cripps [3] I remained a long time in the Bog but saw nothing perticler".

[1] Mr Cotterill then had a shop near Beggars' Bush.

[2] New stables were being built for Queen Victoria near the racecourse and this was drawing in workers from outside the area.

[3] Thos Steer and Henry Greener lived in the Bog.

"April 5th, Beat: Ascot, Mr Pither [1], Wells, Vicarage, Sillwood Park, Titnest, Blacknest Bar [2], Cheapside, Ascot, 9 p.m. to 2 a.m.

This was benefit night at the one tun in consequence of some new articles being introduced into the club a great many members met and did not break up till a late hour no disturbance took place but some of the members after leaving made a great noise. I remained in and near Cheapside and the tun till they was all gone and quiet at 1 o'clock I saw John Woods [3] near the tun I could not see that he had anything about his person".

[1] Mr Pither was the founder of Cheapside Chapel and lived in Wells or St George's Lane.

[2] Blacknest Bar was the site of the Windsor turnpike.

[3] John Woods was another villain from the Bog.

It is evident from the notebook that the policeman's main duties were to prevent theft, begging and breaches of the peace. In March he was looking out for thefts of potatoes from potato pies in the gardens. He watched the inns and beer houses to see that there was no rowdy behaviour. On the 13th of April he was called in by Mr Batchelor at the Tun Inn who was having trouble with a servant. The policeman roused the servant from his drunken sleep and helped Batchelor to dismiss him.

Another of his duties was to see that games were not played on Sundays and he tackled Samuel Dalton for allowing a cricket match in front of his house at the time of divine service. Dalton told him to get the magistrates if he was worried and ignored our stalwart Bobby. Dalton lived at Harewood and owned Brook Lodge. Crutchley, the magistrate, would not press such a trivial matter against a man like Dalton.

Our local Bobby sums up his attitude to the local people in an entry of 29th April: *"Everything very quiet and none of the working class of people seen in any of the beer shops or inns ... I mean the lower order of people"*. No wonder Inspector Rowley could write on the 7th of April: *"A very satisfactory account of the peaceable state of the village"*.

This was of course the record of a quiet period in the 1840s at the start of Queen Victoria's reign. By the end of the century and certainly during Race Week there were more people around and consequently more crime but in such a small community any real villains would soon be discovered and removed. The good citizens of Cheapside could sleep peacefully in their beds.

The Growth of Cheapside in the Nineteenth Century

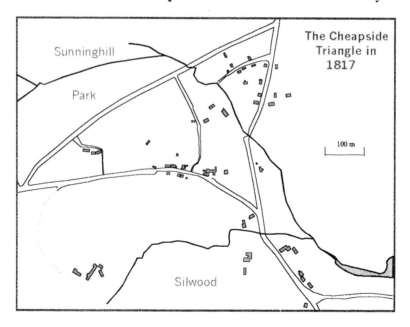

Based on the 1817 Enclosure Map

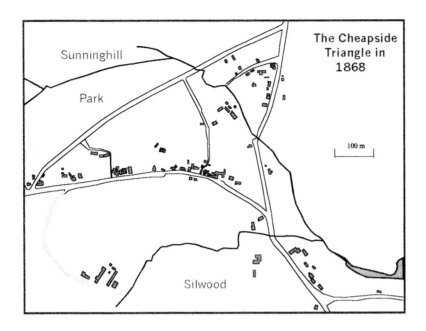

Based on the Ordnance Survey of 1868

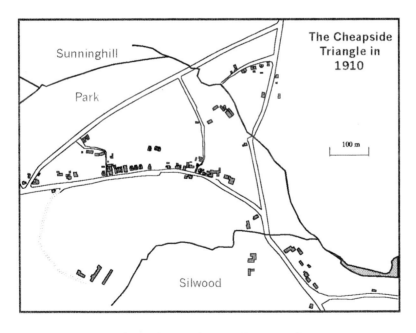

Based on the Ordnance Survey of 1910

ONLY YESTERDAY : THE TWENTIETH CENTURY

"Who-so-ever in writing a moderne historie shall follow truth
too neare the heeles, it may happily strike out his teeth."
Walter Raleigh

Cheapside in 1911

In some ways the history of our own century is the most
difficult. Detailed census material is not available for the last
hundred years. Although there is a mass of official reports, media
and private information, there are many errors in the detail.
Relying on individuals' memories is more enjoyable and
stimulating, but alas not always accurate. Where we have used oral
sources we have tried to get corroboration from two or three
people.

The last comprehensive published data for housing and
occupation in Cheapside comes from 1911. As a result of the
1909 Finance Act, a valuation of all property was made and the
owners and occupiers identified. The resulting survey provided an
excellent snapshot of what Cheapside was like at the beginning of
the century (P.R.O., IR 58/52370-52382). It would remain
virtually unchanged until the Second World War. Then there
would be a rapid and dramatic transformation from a rural hamlet
with its own shops and tradesmen into a modern residential
district dependent on a much wider community for its everyday
needs.

At the time of the 1911 survey the most valuable local
property was Sunninghill Park which, with Sunninghill Lodge, was
owned by Percy Edward Crutchley (1855-1940). The estate
consisted of more than six hundred acres of which eighty-three
acres were in the parish of Sunninghill and the remainder was in
Winkfield. In 1911 it was valued at over £73,000. The second
largest property was Silwood Park with its two hundred and
twenty-six acres. This was valued at £45,197 and belonged to Mrs
Cordes. She leased out the main house and kept a smaller house
on the estate for her own use.

Three other local estates were of high value. Buckhurst Park,
owned by Sir Joseph Savory, was valued in the £35-40,000 range.
Like Sunninghill Park this was predominantly in the parish of
Winkfield. Titness Park was then owned by the trustees of Sir
R.A.E. Cathcart who occupied the house himself. He had ninety-
eight acres and the property was worth £31,050. Its neighbour,

Harewood Lodge, belonging to Colonel the Hon. C.R. Hay Drummond, was valued at £20,050 but its acreage was not given.

The next tier of gentlemen's houses included the vicarage occupied then by the Reverend G.J. Snowden. It had three acres and was valued at £3,700. Ashurst had twenty-one acres, was owned and occupied by General R.B.H. Blundell and was valued at £10,064. The other four larger houses were all occupied by tenants. Brook Lodge was owned by Crutchley and occupied by J.G. Bullock. It had twenty-seven acres and was valued at £7,150. The Cedars, with twelve acres, was valued at £6,600, owned by Mr S. Parry and occupied in 1911 by Mr H. Kirby Port. Pemberton Lodge with only three acres was valued at £3,607 and was occupied by Mrs Grant. It was still owned by Sir Joseph Savory. There was also Tetworth Hall with less land than Brook Lodge but with a similar value. During the century these houses alternated between tenancies and owner occupations. Brook Lodge, its name changed to Heronsbrook House in the 1930s, would end the century in a very sorry and dilapidated state indeed.

The main part of Cheapside consisted of small rented cottages belonging to Crutchley and Savory. The former held most of the land on the old Pound Hill and Savory had property at the Buckhurst Road end of Cheapside, along Buckhurst Road and Mill Lane. His holding included the six cottages in today's Pump Lane, then still known as Bucket Hill Hamlet. One cottage had survived from earlier times and this was today's Pucks Cottage. This cottage and the land around it belonged to the Crutchleys. Savory also owned Grindell's Cottage (now Stag Lodge) where his butler Frederick Grindell lived and Peachy's Farm, later the Dairy Farm, where there was a small-holding of four acres, occupied by Albert Peachy and valued at £1,050. The entry to this farm was where Cheapside Court is today. There was still plenty of farming around Cheapside. A seven and a half acre piece of arable land lying along Watersplash Lane was valued at £1,058 and leased out to local farmers. It belonged to Laura Wright who also owned the six Forest View Cottages in Cheapside Road.

Interestingly Savory owned neither Norwood's coachworks, valued at £400, nor Braisher's saddlery, valued at £250, near the old Tun Green. They were both owned by Louise Jane Nash. There may be a connection here with Nash's Copse behind Heronsbrook House. Charles Norwood ran his late father's business and Raymond Braisher was still at the saddlery in 1911 but a little later he moved into a cottage in Cheapside Road.

There was no mention in this survey of the Tun Inn, which had ceased trading as a public house in 1909 and had become part of the Buckhurst estate. It was used as a *"bothy"* or lodging house for the servants.

There were very few owner-occupied properties in Cheapside. Rose Cottage with its shop next door to the *"Thatch Tavern"* belonged to Mary Bew whose family had been there for several generations. Her grandson Herbert Cubitt owned the main shop at today's 27 Cheapside Road. He sold it to William Steadman just after the survey was made. These two shops were valued at £170 and £640 respectively. The only other owner-occupied cottage belonged to Walter Toms and was today's Elm Bank. Later it too became a shop. The school, valued at £600, the almshouses and the allotments all belonged to the parish trustees and the chapel, valued at £770, belonged to the chapel trustees.

All the rest of the property was owned by absentee landlords. The four Lyndale Cottages on Watersplash Lane, the most valuable cottages worth £210 each, belonged to Frederick Scott Hohler. They were so new that only one was occupied in 1911. He also owned the Brooklyn Cottages and Laburnum Villas, which had replaced the old Laburnum Cottage, today's numbers 31 to 37 in Cheapside Road.

The total number of houses, cottages and shops in 1911 was fifty-eight. Of these forty-two still exist today albeit with a rebuilt or extended house. The railway was too far away to have had a major impact on this side of the parish and the main development of this period was taking place in Ascot and south of the London Road. However about forty brick cottages had been added to the Cheapside housing stock between 1850 and 1911. Today they are mostly owner-occupied. The tied cottage is a thing of the past though due to the recent increase in the rental market a few of them again have absentee landlords. Some of the older cottages have been pulled down and have disappeared altogether. One vanished in Buckhurst Road south of today's Georgia Cottage, another from Mill Lane next to the White Cottage and others from Bucket Hill and Green Lane.

Since very few cottages have space for a garage, Cheapside Road has become a parking space. The most distinctive difference between the postcard views of the road in the 1930s and today is this row of parked cars. This should have at least the benefit of slowing down the passing traffic. Due to the gradual erosion of the width of Green Lane and the lane down to Park View Cottages neither of these can be used by cars today, a great change from 1911 when carts could pass easily along these tracks. The Park View Cottages have been left without any car access at all.

The situation recorded in 1911 remained a fairly accurate picture up to the Second World War. The First World War was a time of depression for Cheapside. The Royal Engineers and the Pioneer Corps were stationed at the racecourse but there were no major regiments based here. As the young men went off to the Great War the big houses and estates lost their gardeners and their servants. Many like Joseph Walsh of Blacknest Cottage never returned. Other Cheapsiders who paid the full price in this dreadful war were Jonas Hand of Providence Villas, Herbert Brind from Park View Cottages and Joseph Taylor from Forest View Cottages. Walter Shobbrook whose father was the landlord of the Thatched Tavern also lost his life and Thomas Buckland whose parents worked for Sir Joseph Savory was badly injured while serving in the Royal Berkshire Regiment.

Victor Crutchley, who had been born at Sunninghill Park, served with great distinction in the Royal Navy. He was on board the HMS Centurion at Jutland and on the HMS Brilliant and the HMS Vindictive when they played an important role in the attempt to blockade Ostend harbour. For his part in the attack on the German fleet in 1918 he was awarded the DSC, the VC and the Croix de Guerre.

In 1919 the Parish Memorial was set up in St Michael's churchyard replacing a small shrine which had been placed in the churchyard in 1917 recording the names of the Sunninghill parishioners who had lost their lives. It was paid for by local subscriptions and the surplus funds were used to buy the Victory Field.

The Church in the Twentieth Century

The changing social position of the church was typified by the removal of the vicars from the stately vicarage to a modest modern house. St Michael's itself was lovingly and carefully maintained and the burial grounds grew ever larger. All the major changes here came about after the Second World War when a new hall was added on the north side of the church.

An inventory of church property was made in 1920 when the vicar was A.R. Ingram. The old vicarage had only recently been rebuilt. It was a large house with three reception rooms, nine bedrooms, two bathrooms, a servants' hall, kitchen, larder, pantry, stables, coach-house, harness room, coal-shed and fowl house. This was a substantial house for a church still playing a very substantial role in the life of the parish. The church income however was not large: £270 from commuted tithes and not quite £50 from other income (B.R.O., D/P 126/6/1). The low income of St Michael's had resulted in the earlier vicars being men of private means but a series of reforms beginning in the 1830s made church endowments more equal and the local stipend was made up by the bishopric. Sunninghill was always fortunate in that, with its close connection to St John's College, it was served by a succession of well-educated priests.

According to the 1920 inventory the church *"built in 1827, with its chancel of 1888, could seat 680 persons"* and no part of the old church of 1120 *"which may have succeeded a Saxon church on the same site"* was left standing. Six years later however the porch arch of the old Norman church was discovered in the garden of Tetworth Hall by the daughter of the vicar and G. M. Hughes. It was recovered and inserted into the 1827 doorway so that one small part of the ancient church is again on the site. The only other substantial survival from ancient times is that old yew tree. The 1920 inventory included a list of the church plate: three silver chalices, four patens, the earliest from the reign of William IV and engraved *'IHS'*, one flagon, some wafer boxes and several alms dishes, one, which dated from the reign of George I, was engraved *'gift to Sunninghill Church'* (B.R.O., D/P 126/6/1).

One of the best-remembered vicars of this century is the Reverend Thursfield who served the parish from 1936 to 1955. Although he amused the locals by his bleating voice which earned him the nickname of Larry the Lamb he was a very able and caring man. Traditionally he is thought to have had some extraordinary psychic powers. It is reported that during the Second World War he visited Mrs Jack Franklin. She was newly married and worrying about her husband who was serving overseas with the Berkshire Regiment. Thursfield warned her that she would receive a letter reporting his death that week but that it would eventually turn out to be an error. The letter was delivered a day or two later and was indeed corrected by the War Office after a few months.

St Michael's was one of the few local buildings to suffer from bombing in the Second World War. A 500 pound bomb fell near the main door of St Michael's causing damage to the tower, south aisle, windows and ceiling and tearing holes in the vaults in the graveyard. It left a crater thirty feet across and ten feet deep stretching from the churchyard wall to the west door. Thursfield wrote in the parish magazine *"We thank God that as by a miracle our Parish Church has been preserved from serious damage"*. An appeal was launched to which there was an immediate response and within three months the parish had collected £600 towards the repairs.

Frederick Vickery who succeeded Thursfield in 1956 was a very different man. He made major changes to the church especially to the Holloway chancel where he had the pews moved round to face the newly installed altar. He also removed the reredos so that the east window could be seen in all its glory. During his incumbency the new Cheapside school was built and he gave the project his unstinting support. He opened the vicarage to the poor, providing shelter for tramps and travellers. He also suffered from clinical depression and this made him unpopular with some of his parishioners. Sadly he took his own life in 1965.

One of the most tantalising stories about the church comes from the period of his tenure in the late 1950s. It is a tale related by several informants but has proved impossible to verify in any way. During excavation for a water main or sewer, workmen including *"Brush"* Hathaway found the remains of burials outside the wall of the churchyard. A sword and buckles were found in one grave and a pair of pistols in the other. Since they lay outside consecrated ground it was thought that they were highwaymen. One informant claimed that the remains were taken to Imperial College for investigation but there is no record of them there. Some locals thought the man with the pistols was the highwayman Claude Duval, who was killed in the early eighteenth century, but he was hanged at Tyburn. Others suggested that this was the highwayman killed at the Wells in 1703, said to have be one of the Dibley gang.

We must consign this to the collection of unproven stories including the lead coffin reportedly discovered outside the churchyard containing the remains of a woman found guilty of witchcraft. Another tale recorded in the parish records reports a *"subterranean passage"* between the church and the *"Avenue Field"* said to have been used by *"Catholic ladies of the Court"* who were allowed to hold services in the chancel for a time following the Reformation. No evidence of this has been found.

Vickery was followed by the Reverend Edward Gibbon, a retired RAF chaplain. In 1969 the most attractive additions to the church of recent times were donated by the two Misses Herrings of Queens Hill. The two windows at the west end of the south wall of the church depict coats of arms commemorating the connection of St Michael's with St John's College and with the bishopric of Oxford. During the last months of his tenure in 1979, Gibbon moved out of the large Edwardian vicarage into a new modern house opposite the church, built in a corner of the old vicarage garden. The old vicarage and most of its land were sold.

The present incumbent Timothy Gunter is extremely popular with all his parishioners. His term of office has been marked by many improvements to the condition of the church and the building in 1984 of a new hall, a long delayed replacement for the old Church House of the eighteenth century. During this building a large corner of the graveyard was disturbed exposing graves which dated from the 1600s. The most elaborate tomb with a double arched brick lined vault was that of Mrs Mann, who had lived at Tetworth Hall when it was still known as Healthy Hall. The most interesting tomb was that of Admiral Home Riggs Popham who had died in 1820. His large memorial was opened and the admiral's sword could be seen standing upright behind the head of the coffin.

The church of St Michael and All the Angels has remained the parish church for the people of Cheapside. Its position, cut off from modern Sunninghill by the London Road, emphasises its connection to the older medieval settlements that lay to the east and north of the church. The Church Path still passes beside it leading across Silwood Park and Silwood Lake and ending either in modern Cheapside Road or opposite the vanished Cheapside Green on the Buckhurst Road. The memorials and tombstones record many of those who lived and died in this parish. The church papers at the Berkshire Record Office record their struggles, successes and failures. St Michael's is a potent witness to the continuity of the past with the present.

While the church maintained its links with the past centuries, major changes took place as far as the secular history of the parish was concerned. In 1894 the Rural District Councils were set up taking over many of the duties of the old parish councils. In 1922 all the old manorial rights, including Cookham Manor's right to take quit-rents from Sunninghill, were abolished by Act of Parliament, thus ending a feudal connection which had existed since the emergence of Sunninghill Manor in the fourteenth century.

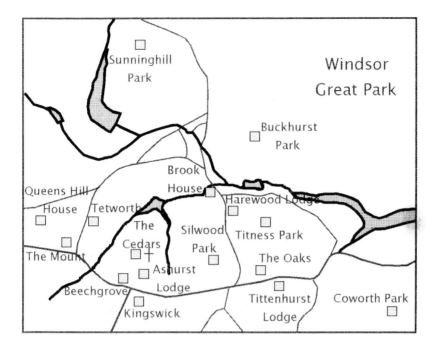

The Large Estates to 1940

Sunninghill Park

After the death of his father, General Charles, in 1898, Percy Edward Crutchley inherited the estate. He lived at Sunninghill Lodge in New Mile Road. He was an exceptionally responsible and concerned landowner, a magistrate and the chairman of the new Windsor Rural District Council. He and his son, Admiral Crutchley, continued the Crutchley tradition of giving a Christmas gift of an apple, orange and sweets to each of the children at Cheapside School and awarding books for school prizes. A number of Cheapsiders were Crutchley servants and estate workers such as Mr Elliot, the coachman, who lived at Barberry Cottage.

The main house at Sunninghill Park was occupied by a series of distinguished tenants including, it is said, Paul Mellon the American millionaire whose great art collection became the core of the National Gallery in Washington. In 1936, four years after the death of his wife, Percy and his son bought Mappercombe Manor near Bridport in Dorset. Admiral Victor Crutchley went to live there with his family. Percy Crutchley remained at

161

Sunninghill Lodge until 1940 although in 1936 he sold the twenty-five-room mansion and the 668-acre Sunninghill Park estate to the banker Philip Hill, later Sir Philip Hill, for £150,000.

Percy Crutchley died at the age of eighty-five in October 1940. Several people thought that his death was accelerated by his distress over the bombing of St Michael's Church. Thursfield wrote his obituary in the parish magazine. Mr Crutchley had been *"a valued member of so many committees"* and *"a very great and noble gentleman honoured alike by all classes"*. Only the Sunday before he died he had been *"at his accustomed place in the Holloway chapel"*. With Percy Edward's death, the hundred and seventy-one years of Crutchley residence in Sunninghill Park came to an end.

During the three years before the Second World War, Sir Philip Hill spent over £100,000 on extensive alterations at Sunninghill Park. He installed a marble bathroom and a tapestry room, both stripped out during the war. He built a new walled garden with hot houses for peaches and nectarines and a *"bothy"* for the gardener. This was where the duke of York's new house stands today. Major improvements were made to the farms and cottages on the estate and a new model dairy was built.

The Hills took over the old Crutchley interest in Cheapside providing presents for the Cheapside children at Christmas. Philip Hill's butler, Mr Gwilt, lived at Holly Cottage and later became a very active member of the committee which established the Cheapside Village Hall. The gardener Mr Owen lived in the house at the top of the lake. It seemed that life would go on as before although the Crutchleys had left. However, although Hill invested heavily in the estate, Sunninghill Park was not destined to remain private property for long. Shortly after the outbreak of war the estate was requisitioned and handed over to the Air Ministry.

Silwood Park, The Cedars, Brook Lodge, Ashurst and Harewood

The story at Silwood Park was very similar. Margaret Cordes sold off parts of the estate between 1925 and 1928, after the death of her husband. The Cordes had been generous landlords and had financed several projects for the benefit of the local community including the hall in Sunninghill named after them. Sir George Dolby who bought Silwood Park from Mrs Cordes had made his fortune from his tea plantations in Assam and from various commercial interests in the Americas. He continued to maintain the deer herd and extended the ornamental gardens. After his death, Lady Dolby sold the property to Philip Hill and went to live in Scotland. Silwood Park was also taken over by the War Office at the outbreak of war.

In 1940 however for a short time and for the only time in history the two biggest estates, the old manor and the old park belonged to the same owner. Hill never lived at Silwood and bought it only as an investment. With his purchase of both Silwood and Sunninghill Parks he also owned a large part of Cheapside. This included the land where the Village Hall stands today, most of the property on the old Pound Hill including Barberry, Little Barberry and Long Gardens Cottages, most of the property in Watersplash Lane and on the north side of Pump Lane.

The other larger houses in the district saw the traditional rapid sequence of tenants and owners. The Cedars had a succession of occupants one of whom installed a swimming pool that seriously damaged George Ellis' *"philosophical walk"*. It was eventually bought by Henry B. Turle in 1939 and the family still owned the property in the 1950s.

In 1923 Brook Lodge was transferred from the Crutchleys to the Westminster Bank. The Bank had it for ten years and it was sold twice in the 1930s before it reached Michael Heneage, a Scottish businessman who lived there with his young wife Dulcibel Effie, said to have been a chorus girl at the Windmill Theatre. They renamed it Heronsbrook House. By this date the property had been divided and Heneage owned only the house, its outbuildings, the cottage and the gardens. All the land where Hilltop Close would be built had been sold separately and was used by Silwood Farm. Robert Oliver, the coachman, and his family were brought down from Scotland by Heneage and installed in the cottage, now called April Place.

A well-known local family from the 1920s to the 1940s was the Archer-Shees of Ashurst. He was a Member of Parliament and Mrs Archer-Shee, a striking figure who rode her tricycle around the village wearing long flowing dresses and petticoats, was the national president of the Women's Institute in 1939. She organised various charities for *"poor and lower women"* and held many fêtes and galas at Ashurst. Their lives were shattered in the 1930s by a scandal surrounding the expulsion of their younger son from the naval college where he had been wrongly accused of theft. This incident was the source of Terence Rattigan's famous play *"The Winslow Boy"*.

The style and luxury of the larger local properties can be seen by leafing through the estate agents' leaflets. In 1919 Harewood Lodge was sold by Knight, Frank and Rutley on behalf of Algernon Hay. The estate had *"thirty-six and a quarter acres in the beautiful district of Sunningdale"*. By this date Sunningdale had grown so large and was so fashionable that the much older Sunninghill was considered as one of its appendages. Harewood was described as a red brick building with stone facings, *"the older portion is castellated in character and additions were made thereto in the year 1881"*. It had electric light, central heating, telephone and water and was thus a thoroughly modern property. There were five reception rooms including a *"billiard room and a boudoir"*, seven principal bedrooms, eight smaller bedrooms and a total of three bathrooms…. perhaps not so modern by today's standards.

Harewood like most of the estates in the parish still had farmland and farm-buildings including *"an excellent cowhouse"*, piggeries and a granary. There were two workers' cottages. The grounds were *"ornamented by beautiful clumps of rhododendrons and azaleas and many forest trees"*. There was a well-stocked lake, a tiled and timbered boathouse, a cricket pitch and pavilion and all the usual kitchen gardens, orchard and hothouses. The latter included two *"vineries"*, peach and nectarine houses, a propagating house, an orchid house and three cucumber and melon houses. It was liable to an annual tithe of nine pounds two shillings (tithes were finally abolished in 1936).

By the 1930s the Lascelles family were at Harewood which had acquired its name from an earlier owner called Lady Harewood. The house underwent various alterations and modifications. Remembered locally as *"a horrible ghostly house"* it was totally rebuilt on another site within the estate in the mid-1930s by Lady Shaw. She was still the owner after the Second World War.

Buckhurst Park

The long Savory era came to an end at Buckhurst Park when Sir Joseph Savory died in 1921. He was buried in the family vault in his parish church at Winkfield and a tablet was erected in his memory in Sunningdale Church. The Buckhurst estate was bought by Sir Henri Deterding who had, a year earlier, been knighted for war services. In the same year Deterding had given thirteen pictures to the Rijksmuseum in his native Amsterdam including *"The Small View of Delft"* by Vermeer, a Soloman

Ruysdael and a Van Goyen. They were mostly of the Dutch school but there was also a Guardi and a Pater. It was an outstanding and very valuable collection and typical of the new owner of Buckhurst.

Sir Henri Deterding, known by the press as *"the Petrol Napoleon"*, was one of the most interesting and most powerful men ever to live in Sunninghill. The son of a Dutch sea captain, Deterding became the second company chairman of the Royal Dutch Oil Company (founded in the Far East in the 1880s) and in 1907 a joint founder with Marcus Samuel, the future Lord Bearsted, of Royal Dutch Shell. He was the largest shareholder in Royal Dutch Shell after Queen Wilhelmena of the Netherlands. He wrote his autobiography called *"An International Oilman"* (Ivor Nicolson and Watson, 1934) and was himself the subject of a biography by Glyn Roberts called *"The Most Important Man in the World: the Life of Sir Henri Deterding"* (1938, reprinted 1976, Hyperion Press). Much of the following information comes from Roberts' book.

Before he came to live at Buckhurst, Deterding owned an estate at Holt near Sandringham where he lived with his first wife, who was Dutch, and their two sons and daughter. He enjoyed the life of an English country gentleman, hunting, shooting and fishing. He had enormous energy and self-discipline and took a cold swim every morning with his valet breaking the ice on the swimming pool at Buckhurst if necessary. He acquired estates in Germany and Holland and had flats in Paris and London. Two years after his purchase of Buckhurst Park he remarried. His second wife was Lydia Pavlovna Koudoyaroff, the daughter of a Czarist general. Thirty years his junior, they had met in Paris where she lived in the community of White Russians who had fled from the Bolshevik Revolution. Henri built a Russian Orthodox chapel dedicated to St John of Ease on the estate for the use of his wife. They had two daughters, the eldest called Olga and the youngest Lydia like her mother.

Due to his attachment to his young wife and due to the fact that his company had lost its control over the Russian oil wells as a result of the Bolshevik revolution, Sir Henri was strongly anti-Communist. He wrote that *"people sometimes imagine that my actions against Russia are prejudiced ... but what is being done in Russia is aimed against all the world"*. He worked hard to overthrow the Bolsheviks and gave large amounts of money to support the education of Russian émigré students. As a result of his strong opinions he sympathised with the Fascist parties in Italy and Germany and became a friend of Benito Mussolini. After 1933 he praised the aims and achievements of Hitler and helped the Nazi party financially. He did not think much of democracy; he called it the *"lazy man's Elysium"*. Sir Henri hated laziness. He would, he said, *"shoot all idlers on sight"*.

In 1936 Lydia divorced him in a Dutch court and he married his third wife, his German secretary Charlotte Minna Knaack. He moved away from Buckhurst to his estates in Mecklenberg in Prussia and in Wassenaar, near The Hague in Holland. When he died in Germany in 1939 his funeral was attended by prominent members of the Nazi government.

After the divorce settlement Lydia kept the Buckhurst property where she lived with her two daughters. Because of the support she had given the émigré movement, Lydia was made a princess by Grand Duke Cyril who ran a Russian government-in-exile from Brittany. She took the title of Princess Lydia Pavlovna de Donskoy. With her daughters she supported various Sunninghill charities in the tradition of Elizabeth Squires. Olga later went to help Albert Schweitzer in the Congo.

Under Sir Henri Deterding, the Buckhurst Park main house saw a major rebuilding and there were many alterations to the estate houses. A few new cottages were built. Lydia's initials *"LD"* can still be seen on Georgia Cottage, probably called after Georgia in the old Soviet Union. After the divorce she had his *"HD"* removed and her *"LD"* inserted there and on Buckhurst's North Lodge. The old saddlery and coachbuilders on Tun Green were acquired by the estate and were converted into today's Buckhurst Cottage. Lydia and her daughters lived there during and after the Second World War. It was eventually given to one of Lydia's Russian cousins.

Sir Henri was reported to have spent half a million on the main house making it one of the most elaborately appointed mansions in the country. He had a turbine installed at the Mill to supply electricity for the whole estate. The gardens were magnificent and on the lake there were flamingos, crested cranes and even penguins. He introduced a flock of twelve Canada Geese, then very fashionable with the gentry, unaware that they were creating the huge flocks which plague our parks today. Sir Henri also tried to close the public right of way which went into the property at a gate opposite Watersplash Lane and across to the Great Park but he was not allowed to do so. However it was closed at a later date, probably just after the Second World War.

Several Cheapsiders worked on the Buckhurst estate. The Bucklands who had come to work for Sir Joseph Savory in 1907 continued to work for the Deterdings. Mrs Buckland was the cook and housekeeper. They lived at the old Tun Inn and later at Georgia Cottage and their children lived in Pump Lane. Alfred Maycock of Park View Cottages was a gardener at Buckhurst and later from 1937 so was Edward Jakeman. During the Deterding period there was an accident at the Mill when a daughter of Newstead, the bailiff, was drowned in the millpond. After the tragedy the Newsteads left the Mill House and moved to the Brickfields bungalow. The Mill House was then divided into two smaller houses for estate workers.

"Upstairs Downstairs"

Life in service in these large houses like Buckhurst and Silwood Park was vividly described by Bertha Dollery who was in service with the Whighams at Queens Hill in the 1920s. The Whighams had renamed their large house with two lodges and large gardens. Previously it had been called *"St Aubyns"*. Mr Whigham's brother owned Tetworth Hall at the same time.

Bertha like so many of the servants in our region came from far away. The Whighams preferred staff who wouldn't take time off to visit their families. They also preferred staff who did not want to go to church on Sundays since this was their day for entertaining. Bertha had been brought up in South Shields, County Durham, where her father was a miner. After caring for the family since the death of her mother, when she was fifteen she had to look for a job bringing in money. This was in 1926 when her father was out of work due to the depression and unemployment in the mines. A friend who worked in Ascot recommended her to the Whighams so Bertha came down from County Durham by train, travelling overnight, and paying £2 for the single fare. When she arrived early in the morning, she was interviewed, taken on and put to work at once.

Bertha became part of the large staff at Queens Hill. They were all *"like a family to her"*. There were three permanent servants in the kitchen: cook, kitchenmaid and scullerymaid; four more in the pantry: butler, two footmen and hall boy; a further three housemaids, a lady's maid, a nanny and a governess. The footmen wore purple livery with yellow stripes on their waistcoats. The outside staff included three gardeners and several grooms. Sixteen to twenty people served three Whighams: the father, mother and daughter.

The staff had half a day off each week, from three in the afternoon until ten at night, but never on Sundays. They also had one full day off every month when they could go to London. The chauffeur took them to the station but they came back by themselves. Her wages in 1926 were £20 a year with a deduction for laundry. Her uniform *"kitchen prints and aprons"* was provided and so was her keep.

"It was", said Bertha, *"a very happy household"*. As kitchenmaid she rose at six in the morning and half an hour earlier on Fridays when she had to clean the kitchen flue for the four-oven kitchen range. The kitchen floors had to be scrubbed before eight in the morning and again after lunch. Lunch was prepared and the baking done ready for teatime. In addition all the pans and coppers had to be scrubbed and the glass and china kept clean and shiny. In the afternoon they changed into clean aprons for teatime and then started preparing dinner, usually a five-course meal but eight courses when they had guests. They went to bed at ten or eleven at night. As Bertha said, *"you got used to it"*.

At Christmas the Whighams joined the staff for dinner in the servants' hall and gave them all *"lovely presents"*. The family had their dinner at night and the servants had theirs at lunchtime. Ascot Races was another time of great excitement with many guests staying and many parties. There were gypsies, fortune-tellers, music and dancing. The servants were allowed to go out to watch King George V and Queen Mary ride down the course. *"He was a lovely friendly king,"* commented Bertha. Several Cheapsiders have commented on the courtesy of this king who would doff his hat to the small clusters who gathered to watch the royal procession enter the old Golden Gates. He would wink at the eager young maids who shouted *"Good old Georgie"* as the carriage went by. One year during Race Week there was a burglary at Queens Hill and some of the jewels were stolen. After that they had six watchmen, three for daytime and three for the nights during the Race Week.

Cheapside 1918 to 1939

Throughout the inter-war period Cheapside remained a small rural community with chickens and pigs kept in the cottage gardens and more than half the people still working as labourers, gardeners and servants on the farms and estates.

None of the cottages had electric light and very few had gaslight which was introduced into the area from the 1930s. The Ascot District Gas and Electricity Company started supplying some houses from 1927. The London and Home Counties Joint Electricity Authority which included Sunningdale and Sunninghill was operating from 1933. For most Cheapsiders however candles and paraffin lamps were the only forms of artificial lighting and most of the cottages had only one open fire or, if they were fortunate, a range on which all the cooking took place and where all the water would be heated. There would generally be one cold tap in the scullery, although some cottages still shared a pump outside. The almshouses were provided with electricity in 1952.

Until the mid-1930s there was no mains drainage and Cheapsiders had either cess pits or used privies which were emptied once a week. Even after the main sewer was installed many of the cottages remained unconnected and the *"wet scavenging"* carts still came around weekly.

Cheapside Cottages

From its earliest days the Windsor Rural District Council was kept busy discussing the installation of sewerage systems in Sunninghill. In 1896 there was a report from the Medical Officer of Health on the bad drainage and its health risks. A year later the council called for engineers' reports. There were many references to the open sewerage ditch at the Rise in Sunninghill and the problems of infections in the water supply. In 1901 when the council finally accepted a scheme it was opposed by local ratepayers. These were the wealthy people who had their own cesspits and objected to paying for a general system through their rates. In spite of a report by the medical officer of health demonstrating the danger of delay and the relation of the lack of sanitation to an epidemic of diphtheria in Sunninghill, the opposition continued in full force. They managed to delay the work until 1913. Then tenders went out and work started only to be stopped with the outbreak of war (B.R.O., RD/WI Ca/1/1-8).

The work resumed in the 1920s but it was a restricted scheme not including Cheapside. As late as 1923 Mrs L. Chetwynd of Pembroke Lodge was still asking how much this scheme would cost the *"poor ratepayers"*. The chairman of the council, Percy Crutchley, said he would call on her to explain. In 1925 the Blacknest Pumping Station was opened by Mr C. W. Searle. In his speech he related the sorry saga, how the work had begun thirteen years ago and thirty-three miles of sewer had been laid before the war. He appealed to all those living along the routes to get connected and so to *"help the council reduce its expenditure on the wet scavenging"*. By 1926, 559 houses were connected in Sunninghill and Ascot but it was not until 1928-9 that extensions to the system included Sunninghill Park and New Mile Road and not until 1939 that the cottages along Buckhurst Hill were connected up (ibid 9-21).

By 1939 some of the cottages in Cheapside including those belonging to Silwood Park, Sunninghill Park and Buckhurst Park had flush toilets but there was usually no electricity. The Mill cottages were exceptional for they had electricity from the mill turbine even though they still had privies. As late as the 1950s some of the cottages such as Puck Cottage, those in Park View and Long Gardens still had privies, no gas, only one cold tap and all food and water had to be heated and cooked over an open hearth. Housekeeping was very hard work in these conditions and it is this harsh domestic drudgery which remains the most vivid memory for all the women who lived through those days.

The 1930s saw several pieces of government action filtering through the local council to affect Cheapside. In 1934 the Protection of Ancient Buildings became a responsibility of local government and this was the beginning of the scheme which led to the listing of historic buildings. Cheapside contains one such house, Heronsbrook House, but its listing has not served it well and it has been falling into decay for twenty years or more. The more important council action involved the building of roads. In 1895 the Windsor Council had one surveyor of highways and four roadmen. Cheapside Road was surfaced in the early years of the century but Watersplash Lane was still earth up to the 1920s. By this date the council had taken responsibility for more roads and bridges from the crown. The bridge over the Brook in Buckhurst Road, known as the Cheapside Bridge, was rebuilt in 1895 and the stream across the road between Ascot Gate and Cheapside Road was put into a culvert at about the same time. The stream in Watersplash Lane was bridged in the late 1920s though it continued to flood across the road for many years after that.

One of the reasons why many of the Cheapside cottages were so slow to become connected to the main sewer and to the other public amenities was that only five of them were owner-occupied. Apart from the Crutchleys and the Deterdings there was an assortment of landlords including a few locals like Harry Coff who built eight cottages, some for his employees, between Pump Lane and the stream in 1934. Many of the landowners lived far from Cheapside and the rent was collected by their agents.

Cheapside still had two shops. There was no longer a bakery in the village but a van came round delivering bread. By 1915 the main shop and post office had been sold by William Steadman to William Balchin and after his death it was owned by his son Herbert. Mrs Balchin ran the Post Office and her daughter looked after the shop. The second shop *"Elmbank Stores"* was run by Horace Goodwin in 1928. When he bought the Balchins' shop in 1933, he sold *"Elmbank Stores"* to Mr Young. After his death his widow remarried and became Mrs Potter. She had the shop throughout the war and well into the 1950s.

From 1915 to the late 1930s, William Shobbrook, who originally came from Germany, was innkeeper at the Thatched Tavern and Agnes Wyard was at the Wells after the death of her husband. With the end of the Tun Inn all the local trade went to these two pubs and the Thatched Tavern became the main drinking centre in Cheapside and the main focus of much of village life. *"The Old Thatch"* is still remembered with nostalgia by older people *"the oil lamps, the condensation running down the gloss painted walls, the click of the dominoes, the knock on the table for a pass"* (R. Wigmore) and as *"a real local pub with its own darts team and no cards or dominoes on Sundays"* (W. Thomas). Mr and Mrs Shobbrook also sold the local medicine designed to cure most ills from a bad stomach to a bad cold. It consisted of *"2 penn'orth of rum and 4 penn'orth of a secret mixture known as Warmit"*. Children would be sent to buy a bottle from the window at the front of the pub and at least one witness declared that it tasted very good and was suitably efficacious (ibid). The Thatched Tavern stayed in the hands of the Shobbrook family for more than thirty years.

The Thatched Tavern

In 1939 there were still two dairies in the village. James and Sally Clarke ran their business from the Dairy House then called *"Sunnyside"*. Their son Colin was paraplegic but he managed to keep the milk round going after the war with the help of boys from the Gordon Boys Farm. The other was operated from Dairy Farm on the old Smith's Green. This farm was modernised in the 1930s. Milk was processed and delivered to customers within twenty-four hours of milking (J. Wigmore). Mr Wigmore, whose wife was the caretaker at Cheapside school for many years and whose son still lives in the village, came from Kent in the 1930s to become the deliveryman for the farm milk.

James Foggetter was the local insurance agent collecting a penny a week from many Cheapsiders and James King, the blind basket-maker, lived at the White House. Raymond Braisher, the son of the Braishers who had lived near the old Tun Inn, continued the family business as a saddler and cobbler near the Cheapside Post Office and William Taylor was the local tailor. A new arrival was the Ascot District Gas and Electricity Company with playing fields and a pavilion on Watersplash Lane where Cheapside school is today. Their field became a centre for local football and cricket matches and for the school sports days and village fêtes.

1919 saw the first Thames Valley buses linking Ascot and Sunninghill to Windsor and Maidenhead. In 1930 William Rule Jeatt established the White Bus Company and there was another Winkfield based company called the Vimmy Bus Service which sold out to Thames Valley in 1936. It was in the same year that the White Bus from Windsor was re-routed through Cheapside and on via Sunninghill to Bagshot. This was the first time there had been a local bus service. Up to the 1940s the single fare for the entire journey was one shilling and seven pence (about eight pence today). Winnie Thomas remembers that there was an alternative and superior transport available on Saturday mornings. A Rolls Royce went from the *"Seven Stars Inn"* at Blacknest Gate to Windsor and back for one shilling, so it was possible to go shopping in style.

The only holiday for most of the children of Cheapside was the Chapel's summer trip to the seaside. Families saved up throughout the year so that their children and some of the mothers could go along. The long journey by bus to the south coast took all morning after an early start. It always seemed to be a fine day and after an idyllic afternoon on the beach with their picnic, a tired and happy party made their way home again.

During the week of the Ascot Races all the children turned out from school to wave their flags and to cheer the royal procession, a practice continuing to this day. Race Week was always accompanied by the arrival of the gypsies who came through Cheapside on their way to camp out on the heath.

World War Two

In 1939 this peaceful rural life came to an end. During the course of the Second World War Cheapside was to be changed as never before. From a sleepy little hamlet where the way of life was geared to the big houses, the forest and the farms it became a place geared to the lives of thousands of American troops, to supporting the British armed forces and to defending their parish against enemy planes. The sleepy rural hamlet was truly woken up and would never sleep again.

With the outbreak of war in 1939 all sorts of military camps and institutions came into the area. Vickers assembled Wellington bombers on Smith's Lawn in Windsor Park. The RASC, the

RAOC, the Royal Artillery evacuated from their Woolwich Depot and the ATS Signals group were all billeted in and around the racecourse. The ATS were at the royal stables and in the royal apartments at the Jockey Club. The *"Diary of an ATS Girl"* told of the exciting social life available to the young women stationed among so many men. The Royal Engineers were also billeted at the racecourse. They brought their own band with them to provide entertainment for all the troops. The larger households offered tea, tennis and social life for the officers. Mrs Green of Queens Hill drove the YMCA van around the various depots bringing tea and comforts to the troops.

A rather different institution was the Number Seven Internment Camp which was established at Ascot. F. C. Wiseman, one of the leaders of the British Union of Fascists, was kept there until he was removed to the Isle of Man. There were many clashes between the fascist detainees and the foreign refugees who had come to England to escape the fascists and now found themselves, as *"suspected aliens"*, parked in the same camp.

One of the earliest impacts of the war in Cheapside was the arrival of the evacuees. Over three thousand children from London were sent into the district of Ascot, Sunninghill and Sunningdale by January 1941. Some children came with their mothers like the Johnson family who moved into Pump Lane from West London. Others were sent here on their own arriving in convoys by bus and by train.

The arrival of so many town children in the country created quite a culture clash and some of the incomers were described in a long report from Miss Archer-Shee as having *"rickets, impetigo and verminous heads"*. Miss Archer-Shee was one of the members of the Billeting Committee of the Windsor Rural District Council and she fought hard for these children, to see that they and the billeting officers who had to place them in homes had a fair deal. Some of the poor children were left like parcels on doorsteps. Edna Jakeman arrived home from work one day to find two little boys with labels around their necks waiting for her. Mrs Tyrrell and Mrs Phillips were others who gave homes to these unfortunate children. For some it was not a bad experience. They enjoyed their time here and stayed on after the war. At least one of them, Trevor Clark, married a local girl and one of Edna Jakeman's pair visited her for more than half a century later.

Some of the evacuees attended the Cheapside school where they had a mixed reception. The Londoners regarded the local children as rural and stupid; the locals regarded the evacuees as urban and ignorant. Some sort of modus vivendi was eventually worked out but there were tough times for many of them. Several entire schools were also moved out of London and into Sunninghill and Ascot. All the children from the Seven Stars Primary School in West Kensington came to Sunninghill School where they were installed in classrooms under their own teachers. In 1941 General Sir James Horlick handed over his main house of Little Paddocks to become a school and home for partially sighted girls. This school continued after the war into the late 1950s.

During the first year of the *"Phoney War"* there were many changes. The Scouts' Recreation field (now Hilltop Close) was ploughed up to grow cereals. Black-out curtains were hung up in all the windows. Everyone learned to use gas-masks and some foodstuffs were rationed (from January 1940). Cheapsiders joined the Fire Service, the ARP and the Home Guard. This last was originally called the Local Defence Volunteers, the LDV, known as *"Look, Duck and Vanish"*. Blockhouses were erected at all road junctions and tree trunks were positioned to swivel across the roads if needed (J. Wigmore). In 1941 iron railings and gates were removed supposedly to help the war effort.

Mrs Philip Hill organised a knitting group in Cheapside, meeting at the Chapel and in private homes, to provide comforts for the soldiers and sailors. They made blankets, jumpers, scarves and socks for sea-boots and many local people wrote as pen friends to the troops. Between January 1940 and June 1941, the Cheapside working party made no less than 3,214 garments, including linings for seamen's coats and clothes for evacuees and children whose homes had been bombed, and also dressings for wounds.

Just over a year after the outbreak of hostilities, Cheapside suddenly woke up to the reality of war when a series of bombs hit the parish. The old order was passing away with a bang. On the 27th of September 1940, six high explosive bombs fell in Tittenhurst Park leaving large craters. Three days later the bomb fell near the main door of St Michael's. In April 1941 a Heinkel bomber was shot down in the South Forest of the Great Park. Two members of the crew were killed and two survived (C.S.). The local story that a German pilot was found hiding under Gunnes's Bridge in Silwood Park could refer to one of the survivors.

In January 1942 a National Warship Fund was established and the nation set about raising money to pay for warships. Admiral Victor Crutchley inaugurated the local effort and a banner advertising the campaign was hung from the iron bridge across the London Road near the Sunninghill crossroads. The Windsor Rural District Council adopted the 5,450-ton Dido class cruiser, HMS Euryalus, which had been launched at John Brown's dockyard on the Clyde in 1939.

HMS Euryalus was named either after one of the argonauts or after one of the Greeks who besieged Troy. It was the fifth ship of this name in the British navy. The original HMS Euryalus had been launched in 1804 and had been the first ship to sight the combined French and Spanish navies off Cape Trafalgar. After the battle it became the flagship of Admiral Collingwood and towed the Royal Sovereign back to England for repair.

Within one week of the launch of the campaign, the people of Sunninghill, Sunningdale and Ascot had raised £1,250,000. This worked out as the highest average per head in the whole of Britain. Eventually the local fund reached two million pounds. This paid for the building of the Euryalus, completed by 1941, and for its first major refit. In recognition of the amount raised by the parish of Sunninghill a parade was held in October 1943 and the ship's battle ensign, which had already seen action in the Mediterranean, was presented to St Michael's Church. It still hangs in a corner of the nave. Captain R. Oliver-Bellasis, in command of the Euryalus, was presented with a plaque from all the people of Sunninghill, Sunningdale and Ascot.

The Euryalus sailed in 1945 to join the American Fifth fleet in the Pacific. It was off Japan when the atomic bombs were dropped and was the second ship into Hong Kong at the end of the war. It was a fortunate ship and had a *"lucky war"* with no casualties. When it was finally decommissioned the plaque was given to St Michael's Church. The contacts between the church and the old shipmates of the Euryalus have been maintained to the present day.

From the autumn of 1939 the Ministry of War requisitioned many of the larger properties including Silwood Park, Sunninghill Park (not until 1942) and Buckhurst Park. The latter became one of the centres for the Ministry of War Transport Division. Silwood Park was used as a British army hospital and rehabilitation unit and at one time the Pioneer Corps was billeted there. After the war many of the army huts were used for returning POWs and refugees. Phillip Hill tried to prevent

Sunninghill Park from being requisitioned and it was said locally that he had the electricity and plumbing removed to thwart the War Office. As a result of his delaying tactics Sunninghill Park was not handed over to the Air Ministry until 1942 just in time to provide a much needed base for our allies.

In October 1942 one of the most dramatic years in the history of Cheapside began. The United States Army Air Force, the USAAF, arrived at Sunninghill Park. The Eighth AAF took up residence in the house and outbuildings on the first of the month. A week later, British contractors were brought in to erect billets for the men and offices for the headquarters, based at the house. Another week later the Eighth Air Support Command was transferred to Sunninghill Park from Membury. The park was a hive of activity: road building, platform construction for the tent and hut encampments and electrical and plumbing services. Local labour supplemented British and American military personnel. During the construction a fire broke out in the main house causing considerable damage which had to be repaired (for this and the following: Edward A. Miller, American Air Force History Support Office, Washington DC U.S.A.).

In June 1943 all the property at Sunninghill Park was officially transferred from the Air Ministry to the USAAF. Throughout that summer more buildings were added to the camp including additional service and HQ buildings and quarters for more troops. The headquarters of the full tactical Ninth AAF replacing the Eighth Air Support Command were located here and, in October, the Ninth AAF took full control of the whole of Sunninghill Park. Even more tents and huts were erected. Eventually the American camp stretched right across the park from New Mile Road to Buckhurst Road. It was from here that the Americans prepared for their part of *"Operation Market Garden"* and for the Normandy Landings and the liberation of Europe. The Supreme Commander, General Eisenhower, used the Marist Convent in Sunninghill as a local headquarters and was often seen in the area.

The Americans overwhelmed Cheapside even though most of them never knew exactly where they were. Since the war American veterans have been found in Ascot, Sunninghill and Sunningdale searching in vain for any familiar landmarks and asking for *"The Park"*. Their morning trumpets calling the Reveille woke up all Cheapside and there were grumbles at the constant band practices and at the regular gunfire. Not all the noises however were unpleasant. Yehudi Menuhin played solo violin over the Tannoy to entertain the troops and this could be heard right across Cheapside (J. Wigmore). The American police, known as Snowdrops because of their white helmets, became well known as they collected the late revellers from the Thatched Tavern.

Fleets of lorries were always on the move. The fences along Cheapside Road and New Mile Road from the Thatched Lodge to Ascot were scored for many years with the marks of the heavy lorries and military equipment as they squeezed along the lane. The roads were full of mud and local children were issued with Wellington boots generally unobtainable during the war.

On the whole the Americans were seen as the friends and allies they were. Many locals found employment at the camp where there was a cinema, a dance hall and a beer garden. Goal posts were installed in the lake for water-polo games which impressed the natives. Local boys, whose parents would let them, spent all their spare time at the camp. So too did some of the local girls and a few of them eventually married their GIs. Gladys Buckland of Pump Lane met Thomas B. Cooke and their wedding took place at St Michael's Church in 1945. She left Cheapside to live in Washington DC. Her grandparents, Thomas and Gladys Buckland, had worked at Buckhurst Park and when they retired Lady Deterding gave them Georgia Cottage for the rest of their lives.

Some of the children living near the camp were frightened by the strange men with foreign accents. Others took full advantage of the camp with its friendly soldiers and an endless source of all the goods that were not available in the English shops. The Americans played baseball in the Gas and Electricity Company's field in Watersplash Lane. They gave used baseball equipment to the school children and helped to create a schoolboys' baseball league in Berkshire and Surrey. It was one of the first baseball leagues in this country. Some of the Americans attended St. Michael's Church or the Cheapside Methodist Chapel and they offered tea to the local children after Sunday School. They also provided hospital facilities for sick children and gave presents to children who had lost their homes and parents in the war.

Arthur *"Ginger"* Drew who lived in the Lyndale Cottages on Watersplash Lane entered the boxing ring for a demonstration lesson with the famous Joe Louis. The ring was in the field at the south front of Sunninghill Park house. It must have been one of the more unusual sights ever seen at Sunninghill Park. Joe Louis also gave a demonstration fight at the Star and Garter pub in

Windsor. Later Ginger Drew, who was about twelve years old, took part in an American broadcast telling the folks back home all about the contacts between the troops and the English children. He echoed the well-known phrase *"have you any gum, Chum?"*

American officers were billeted in houses all around Ascot and Sunninghill. Mrs Tollhurst had a club for officers' at Heronsbrook House. Her club had featured in a court case in 1941 concerning an unregistered alien who was working there. Later the house was requisitioned for the Americans and run by them as a billet. The Thatched Tavern was popular with the Yankees. In the summer evenings of 1943 these men, far from home and unsure of their future, would drink their pints in the road outside the pub and listen to the nightingales singing in the valley opposite, where Heronsbrook Cottage is today.

When the Americans left during the autumn and winter of 1943/1944 as they prepared for the invasion of France, Sunninghill Park was handed back to the RAF who used the hospital set up by the Americans along Watersplash Lane. After all the excitement Cheapside suddenly became a quiet place again. Across the village at the Silwood Park rehabilitation hospital Sergeant Denis Compton, the famous cricketer, was one of the Army Physical Training Instructors helping the injured soldiers to get fit again. In the last year of the war and afterwards some of the Dallas huts left behind by the Americans were used for housing refugees, families who had lost their homes in the bombing raids on London and locals who needed a home.

Most Cheapsiders had, what was called, a *"good war"*. The food rationing was eased by local supplies from gardens and allotments as well as from the American PX Store. The large private estates were no longer fully manned by keepers so poaching was easy and many a pheasant or pheasants' eggs supplemented the wartime rations. There was plenty of well-paid work at the military camps and a lively social life with all the troops around here.

At the end of the war some of the soldiers like Eddie Barker who had served in the Grenadiers and whose family lived in Park View Cottages came home along with Billy Holden whose father was a gardener at Buckhurst Park. But others had their names added to the 1914-1918 war memorial in St. Michael's churchyard. Not all those who died are commemorated there, such as Maurice Beasley of Park View Cottages who died in the Near East. His grave lies in Tripoli. He had joined the Coldstream guards in 1934 when he was seventeen and he was killed in 1943. He was not the only Cheapsider to pay the full price for the allied victory.

Sunninghill Park returns to the Crown

The immediate post war years saw extraordinary developments on the two biggest local estates. Sunninghill Park returned to the possession of the crown and Silwood Park became part of the Imperial College of London University. Thus both major properties passed out of private hands. The first to be sold was Sunninghill Park. When Sir Philip Hill died in 1944 all his estates including both Sunninghill Park and Silwood Park were put up for sale. Some of the sales were delayed by the fact that the property was still requisitioned by the War Office. Sunninghill Park however was bought by the Commissioners of the Crown Estates and so returned to the crown after 300 years in private hands. The farmland was at first leased out to local farmers but later it was run directly for King George VI.

In 1946 the King approved the reconstruction of the racecourse which resulted in the realignment of the straight mile course, new Golden Gates and the enlargement of the grandstands and the enclosures. The magnificent Golden Gates on Cheapside Road, built 1877-8 in black and gilded cast-iron, were no longer the royal entrance to the course. They had been erected when the racecourse was under the patronage of the Prince of Wales, later King Edward VII and they incorporated his coat-of-arms. His mother Queen Victoria had disapproved of *"the Turf"* and usually spent June at Balmoral. The fortunes of Ascot Races were always dependent on the favour of the monarch. King George VI and especially his wife, Queen Elizabeth, now the Queen Mother, took a great interest in horse racing and more money was spent on the Course. The valley in the new straight mile was levelled out and in 1955, with the completion of the new Gates, the new course was used for the first time. These Gates were much plainer than the old ones in keeping with post-war simplicity. They were flanked by lodges copied from those at Eridge Park, the home of the Marquis of Abergavenny, then the manager of the Course.

Since the 1950s there has been a great increase in the use of the racecourse both for races and for other functions. The large new grandstand was opened in 1961, the new royal box and enclosure in 1964 and the first National Hunt races took place here in 1965. Today the Race Course is almost permanently in use, a far cry from the beginning of the century when it was used for only a couple of weeks each year. The subsequent traffic has had a major impact on Cheapside.

In the years immediately after the return to the crown, Sunninghill Park House stood empty. It was not until August 22nd 1947 that a local newspaper reported:

"At Sunninghill Park which it was officially announced has been granted by the King to Princess Elizabeth, the work of clearing away military huts and tidying up the estate is in progress. It is understood a great deal of work will have to be done to the house to make it habitable but it is considered unlikely that the Princess and Lieutenant Mountbatten will take over more than a few of the 25 rooms when they move in".

Cheapsiders looked forward to welcoming the newly married couple into their first home. The house was almost ready and the decoration of the sitting rooms was nearly complete when disaster struck. There are many people still living here who remember the Sunninghill Park fire. One of those most closely involved was Wendy Humphries. Wendy was at Sunninghill Park on the evening of the fire with her husband Don, who had recently left the RAF and had been taken on as a caretaker and groundsman. They had called in to clean out their own little house near the stables ready for moving in themselves. As they were leaving Don noticed that a window in the main house was still open. He left Wendy holding their bicycles and went in. He walked right through the house checking the doors and windows but *"saw nothing and nobody and smelled nothing except new paint".*

He shut the window and left by the back door dropping the Yale lock. They left the Park at about ten o'clock to cycle back to her parent's home in Winkfield where they were staying. At eleven o'clock Mr Allan, the keeper, was disturbed by his dogs barking and looking across the lake he saw flames leaping from the house. Ted Green, who was about thirteen years old at the time, remembers seeing the fire from his home in Forest View and going down on his bike with his mother to watch. He said that the whole building was alight as if several fires had been started at once.

Mr Allan ran round to the burning house and saw a man rush out from the front of the house and run off towards Ascot. Later this man was identified as Mr Wakes who was in charge of removing the army huts from the park. He said he too had seen the fire and when he realised he could not put it out by himself he rushed off to Ascot to phone for help. This was considered odd by the locals since there were phones closer to hand in the old hospital block. The fire brigade arrived and drained nearly all the water from the lake to put out the fire but it had done enormous damage.

Sunninghill Park House before the Fire

Was the fire due to an accident caused by the builders who had been using blowlamps to clear the dry rot, or was it due to arson? The latter was rumoured at the time and is still strongly believed by some locals. There were many people here living in anything they could find. They were refugees, ex-evacuees, POWs, returning service men and people who had been bombed out of their homes. The council housing lists were long and some families had been moved by the council into the empty hospital blocks and Dallas huts along Watersplash Lane where they lived for several years.

Many people seemed to have keys to the buildings in the Park. The Humphries themselves had arrived home one day to find that an Alsatian dog had been shut into their house. After this incident they had all their own locks changed. The police and the army had been called in to evict squatters from the supposedly empty huts. Some accused these people of starting the fire. It is true that they were many who were impatient with their poor living conditions and some were doubtless angry at all the money being spent on the mansion. There was however no evidence to support these suspicions and eventually after many fruitless enquiries the fire was put down to an accident.

Accident or not it certainly changed the future of Sunninghill Park. At first Princess Elizabeth and her husband considered rebuilding and a large log cabin was considered as a temporary home while the main house was being rebuilt. But with the death of King George VI in 1952 the Princess Elizabeth was now the Queen. Sunninghill Park was no longer needed as a separate residence. It was therefore decided not to continue with the renovations and the dangerous ruin was demolished. The walled garden was let out to Walter Blom's Nurseries and two German ex-POWs, who had married English girls and settled in Sunninghill, worked there.

After 1947 the Sunninghill Park estate was farmed and managed as a shoot. In 1988 the great lake was drained so that the dam could be inspected. The lake is in three sections and each part was drained in turn so that over six tons of carp could be carefully removed. A jeep was also recovered, a relic from the wartime. The drainage exposed a causeway under the stone bridge, possibly built as part of the dam at the end of the medieval fishponds. When the lake was emptied the engineers examined the bottom outlet penstock. This cast iron penstock, about two hundred years old and dating from Jeremiah Crutchley's time, was still in excellent condition but the hardwood conduit was rotten and had to be replaced. The lake was refilled and restocked. With the rest of the park it has remained a haven for wild life. Every spring mandarin ducks join all the native birds nesting in this protected area.

The fortunes of Sunninghill Park changed again in 1987 when the Queen decided to make it the home for her son Prince Andrew the duke of York on his marriage to Sarah Ferguson. A large new house with twenty-four major rooms was built on the site of the old walled gardens of Sir Philip Hill. Sadly the new Sunninghill Park House no longer benefits from the site overlooking the lake. The house was designed by the Law and Dunbar-Nasmith Partnership, built by Simons of Ipswich and completed by September 1990. It is a low-key design presenting a monotonous façade and roofline towards Buckhurst Road with entries from there and from the Cheapside Road. The marriage of the young couple reflected the modernity of the house and Cheapsiders became all too well aware of the hordes of journalists cashing in on the breakdown of the royal marriage. The Duchess has kept her connection with Cheapside and is now the patron of the Nursery School held in the Village Hall.

Silwood Park

Like Sunninghill Park the post-war grounds of Silwood Park were filled with clusters of army huts and prefabricated buildings and as in Sunninghill Park many of the army huts were used by returning POWs and refugees. At the time Professor J.W. Munro of Imperial College London was looking around for a site suitable for a new Field Station to replace a much smaller one at Slough which the college had outgrown. Silwood seemed ideal but he found the military most reluctant to vacate the site. He had to use his considerable wiles to persuade the War Office to end the Military Requisition orders. Finally in 1947 Imperial College was able to purchase Silwood Park with eighty acres for the sum of £24,000. Some of this money came from the funds of the Empire Marketing Board.

The College bought not only the house and the land but also the four hundred years history of the Park and of the old Sunninghill Manor. The large manorial archive was eventually transferred from Sunninghill to the Imperial College centre in Kensington. A year after the purchase of Silwood, the College also bought Ashurst from the Archer-Shee family for £11,000. This began a new era for Silwood Park and Ashurst as parts of Imperial College. They were linked to the home College by the Number 701 bus which ran from Ascot at hourly intervals along the London Road calling at South Kensington en route to Gravesend.

The purchase of Silwood by Imperial College ended a whole cycle of manorial history. The earliest owners had been the tenants of courtiers, then came the men who made their wealth from timber and tanneries. Since the eighteenth century, in every generation, new wealthy families arrived to buy the estate. They were men whose wealth came from finance, commerce and industry and it was these men who had transformed the old manor into Silwood Park. The reason for this continuing influx of new men and new money was that none of the Sunninghill estates had any great agricultural value. Only the Aldridges at Sunninghill Manor and the Crutchleys at Sunninghill Park had settled here for more than two generations and neither family was entirely dependent on their Sunninghill estates for their fortune. Since the second World War both Sunninghill Park and Silwood Park have settled down to half a century of unchanging ownership, the one under the crown the other as an academic institution.

Not all the old Silwood estate went to Imperial College in 1947. Silwood Farm and its land were bought by William Perryman and his sons. They bought what had been the heart of the old manor of Sunninghill including what may have been the site of Eastmore, the first manor house. During their ownership most of the trees in Nash's and Mann's copses and on the Hall or Holly Hill were felled with no replanting. Today this land is covered with scrub, silver birch and other self-planted trees. Many of the trees felled by the Perrymans were ancient and they had been managed by pollarding for hundreds of years. Only two of the great Elizabethan oaks survived.

Silwood Farm in 1952

While the Perrymans ran the farm there were still cattle and pigs in the Cheapside fields. The family was popular with the local boys, allowing them to fish for rudd, roach and crayfish in the Brook. Within a few years however they sold out to Major Bagshaw who in turn sold the property to Imperial College in 1953 for £13,600. From this time on it was no longer a working farm. With this purchase, the College also acquired Silwood Lake. Between 1956 and 1958 they undertook the rebuilding of the outlet sluices which had been part of Humphrey Repton's original dam. Unfortunately in 1958 severe flooding was caused by the inability to shut the valve on the sluices. It was particularly severe at Heronsbrook where two small sluice boards were broken and at the Mill House where the large sluice gates were forced open by the flood. After 1959 the valve was never operated again.

Imperial College became one of the main employers for the people of Cheapside. Most worked there as scientists, technicians, skilled artisans or secretaries although a few were employed as they had been in the old days as farm labourers and gardeners. For some time after their purchase of the estate the College kept on a team of about fifteen gardeners under Mr Stringer. They maintained the Japanese garden, shrubberies and the large areas of glass houses established in Silwood Park by the Cordes and by Sir George Dolby. Functions at South Kensington were graced by flowers from Silwood and they decorated the stage at the Albert Hall for degree ceremonies (C. T. Lewis).

In 1961 Imperial College bought more land along Cheapside Road. This included a roadside strip which had been retained by Major Bagshaw as potential building land and the old gravel pit sited opposite to the junction of Cheapside Road with Watersplash Lane. Near the site of the old parish pound and gravel pit, the College installed an observatory and meteorological tower in 1963. The latter, it should be said, went up in the face of considerable opposition but it has long since disappeared behind the trees. It has now been turned into a telecommunications relay station. These two buildings may be very close to the site of the old Eastmore and Farrants, both vanished without trace.

After a period of some thirty years as a very active research centre for the physiological and behavioural studies of pests and parasitology the Ashurst laboratories were closed and the work was transferred into new buildings at Silwood Park. Ashurst was sold off and redeveloped in 1995. A new roundabout on the junction of Church Lane and London Road was made by the developers of Ashurst who were allowed to demolish the old house and replace it with an undistinguished pseudo-Georgian office block. At the same time Imperial College developed their Science Park and Technology Transfer Centre on the corner of Buckhurst Road and London Road. This was on the piece of the old Beggars' Bush Heath that Sir James Sibbald had annexed in the 1790s.

Today the College owns about 250 acres of parkland, marshland, woodland, lake and experimental grounds used for environmental research. The main university departments based at Silwood include the Pure and Applied Biology Department, part of their centre for Environmental Technology, the centre for Analytical Research in the Environment which included the University of London Reactor Centre opened in 1965 as *"the first all British research and training nuclear reactor"*, and part of the Civil Engineering Department. There are about 300 students and employees at Silwood and many other students visit the centre for specific course work.

Much has changed at Silwood Park. The Lanes, the Days and the Aldridges would not have recognised the elegant Silwood Park of the eighteenth century. Sir James Sibbald would have been startled by the neo-Gothic palace of the Stewarts. Now the gentlemen-owners would be amazed to see the students lounging on their once manicured lawns and astonished at all the new science buildings and experimental laboratories on the estate. Since the timber is no longer an important part of the estate economy, the land is now much more wooded than at any time within the last five hundred years.

In spite of these obvious changes much has stayed the same. The bulk of the estate is still intact and its use is still largely agricultural, albeit for experimental and research purposes rather than production. The herds of domestic deer have vanished but the wild roe and muntjak deer roam happily up and down the valley. The muntjak were first sighted around here in 1965 and are now very common. The herons and kingfishers still feed from the Brook and the lakes. Cheapsiders still use the estate paths, though less to cut across to church services, more to walk their dogs.

Buckhurst Park

All the old properties changed hands in the post-war years. In 1949 Buckhurst Park was put up for sale and was bought by the Maharani of Morvi, Jivansingh Jadega. Morvi is in Western India and was a small state of about 50,000 people in 1949. The Maharani, who was known as Maxi, had come to England as a schoolboy and thereafter spent half the year here. He had his family with him and his four daughters attended Cheapside school. According to the press reports he had *"made the British racecourses his playground"* and *"rarely bet less than £5,000"*. However, after being swindled by confidence tricksters, he sold off his thoroughbred horses and took up golf, hiring a professional to live at Buckhurst and teach him the finer points of the game. The Maharani was not to enjoy the property for long and in 1957 at the age of only thirty-nine years he died suddenly at Ascot. An Indian industrialist Shiv Kapoor inherited the property and put it up for sale a year later.

The sale was managed by Knight, Frank and Rutley. It included the main house with 122 acres of land. There were ornamental and kitchen gardens, with five vines and four peaches, a stone stairway and colonnade, a 25 yard swimming pool, a three acre lake with an island, summer house, boathouse and foot-bridge and also a farm with a pedigree attested Jersey herd. Within the main house were luxurious reception rooms, several kitchens, a billiard room and a nursery suite. The study was hung with oriental tapestries; the hall was carpeted in red and hung with crimson damask wallpaper. There were a dozen sumptuous bedroom suites with gold taps, gold doorknobs and a gold shower in the Italianate marble bathroom.

On the estate there were eleven sub-properties typical of the social unit that existed on the large local estates. These were listed as: *"the butler's flat occupied by Mr and Mrs Hare*

a cottage occupied by Mr Cauling

a flat occupied by Mr R. H. Hare, a farm labourer

a farm-manager's cottage occupied by Mr Baker

a gardener's cottage occupied by Mr Brown

Brickfield Cottage occupied by Mrs Woolf who paid a rent of £1 a week (the brick kiln was marked on the 1865 Ordnance Survey at the site of Buckhurst farm and may have been there earlier).

a modern bungalow occupied by Mr Talbot, the herdsman

North Lodge occupied by Mr and Mrs Jakeman the gardener

Georgia Cottage occupied by Mr Buckland, who paid a rent of 4s per week

South Lodge occupied by Mr Mitchell the lodgeman

The White Cottage which was vacant" (J.E.)

The estate did not sell and in March 1959 Buckhurst Park was advertised to be let at £1,100 for race week *"with twenty to thirty magnificently furnished rooms"* and *"a 500 ft long Dutch garden with 3 dozen cunningly clipped yews leading down to a well stocked 600 metre lake"*. Mrs Lilamani Kapoor, a Sinhalese classical dancer who *"had given up her art to marry"* told the press that she and her husband could not afford to live there and that they *"lived down the road nearby"*. The housekeeper and her husband, Mr and Mrs Edgar Cauling, lived alone in the big house.

A year later Buckhurst Park was still up for sale. There were rumours in the press that Princess Margaret would have it and, in 1961, an American, Tom Stangbye, was going to buy it for £80,000 but the deal fell through when he vanished leaving a long line of creditors. Eventually it was Rudolf Palumbo who bought the Buckhurst estate. The staff in the outlying properties such as the Jakemans had already been given notice to quit. The

Jakeman's moved to 49 Cheapside Road, bought for £1,600. Mr Jakeman went to work at Silwood Park and Edna Jakeman became the caretaker of the Village Hall, a job she filled with devotion for many years.

Rudolf Palumbo already owned Tetworth Hall where he had removed the entire third floor of the Georgian house, totally destroying its proportions. He passed this house on to his son, Peter. The third floor would be replaced and Tetworth restored to its Georgian grace by later owners, J. and A. Singh, in the 1990s. At Buckhurst, Palumbo put through a major reorganisation of the estate which took five years. Several pieces of land were sold off including the farm which was redeveloped as Ribblesdale Park. A third of the original Buckhurst house was demolished. The roof was raised to make the servants' rooms suitable for guests. The tower was knocked down, the plaster ceilings were removed, the dry rot eradicated and Spanish leather ripped out of the library. Eventually the property was acquired for the late King Hussein of Jordan who recognised the long link between Buckhurst Park and the people of Cheapside by becoming the patron of the Cheapside Village Hall.

Tetworth Hall Today

The Transformation of Cheapside

It was not only the large estates which were transformed in the second half of the twentieth century. After the war one of the most pressing problems facing the country was a shortage of housing. The rumours about arson at Sunninghill Park highlight this problem. The Dallas huts along Watersplash Lane were used for council housing and in October 1946 the Windsor Rural District Council bought ten acres of land on the south side of Cheapside Road from the Hill estates. This is the land where Hilltop Close is today. The council created the *"Cheapside Estate"* using some of the prefabricated huts, which had been left behind by the American army in Sunninghill Park and some British Nissen huts. The Estate became known locally as *"cardboard city"*. In fact these prefabricated houses were often much better to live in than the old Cheapside cottages. They were much roomier and had electricity, bathrooms and flush toilets. The creation of the Cheapside Estate almost doubled the number of houses in Cheapside. For the first time there was major housing on the south side of Cheapside Road and the open access to the fields running down to the Brook had gone forever.

The sale of the Philip Hill's estates released large areas of land along Cheapside Road and Watersplash Lane. Listed in the original sales brochures were:

"two lodges one a service tenancy, the other let to Mrs Sutton", she was the schoolmistress at Cheapside School.

"a superior lodge with walled gardens with main gas water and drainage", this was Sunninghill Lodge where the Crutchleys had lived.

"a building plot in Cheapside; a two bedroomed cottage with mains drainage water and gas let to Miss Smith", this was today's Wisteria Cottage and the site of the future village hall. Miss Smith had been a teacher at the school in the Royal Park.

"a pair of cottages opposite north lodge, (of Silwood Park) with main gas, water and drainage, one on a service tenancy, the other let to Mrs Elliot at 3s 3d per week", this was Barberry and Little Barberry.

"The White House let to Miss E. M. C. Kaye at £50 per annum, with main water, gas and drainage", Miss Kay and Miss Tisdale ran a small school for boys at the White House and the schoolroom was in the garden.

"a bungalow cottage let to Miss J. Beard at 5s per week, had main water, gas and drainage", she was a supervisor at the local telephone exchange.

"the Sports field leased to the Ascot Electricity Company at £45 per year", in 1935 it was let at £25.

"a Cottage let to Mr Kensall at 5s per week with main water and gas", this was today's Pucks Cottage and was one of the poorest cottages in the village. The Kensalls brought up a family of seven children in its four tiny rooms.

"three cottages in Cheapside Road, number 67, which had water, electric light and a bathroom, was with vacant possession, number 65 was inhabited by Mrs Moss who paid a rental of 6s 9d per week and number 63 was rented by Mr Pikulo at 7s 6d per week". Neither number 65 nor number 63 had electric light or bathrooms and they both had external WCs.

It was a golden opportunity both for people who wanted to buy a home of their own and also for investors. All the land and the old cottages were bought up and redeveloped. Many of the cottages had tenants who could stay for life so some of the cottages simply changed ownership and were redeveloped later. Major and Mrs Fellowes became the owners of Little Barberry. Wilfred Johnson bought a couple of plots and obtained the second post-war building permit from the Council to build Oakridge in 1946. This was the first of a series of owner designed and built properties in the area. John Henry Gough bought land in Watersplash Lane between Ivanhoe and Green Lane. He sold half to Barbara Laird the next day. Both of them gradually sold off plots and built houses. Mr Gough kept a field for his daughter's pony. This was where the new school would be built.

Gradually modern Cheapside was created. In the changes some of the old paths such as the one beside Long Gardens Cottages fell from use. In 1952 these old cottages were sold. They were described as a terrace of four cottages and part of an early Georgian cottage *"the latter being formerly a beer tavern"* a reference to its occupation in 1851 by Joseph Turner the beer seller. The inhabitants were all elderly. Mrs Beckett, a widow, lived rent free at number 13; Mr Cripps lived rent free at number 15; Mr Parker paid 6s a week rent at number 17; Mr Morse paid 5s at number 19; and number 21 was vacant. They were all sold for £1,952. Only two remain today. During these post-war years a similar fate befell most of the pre-Victorian properties along Cheapside Road and in Green Lane. Only a handful of houses survive from before 1800: April Place, formerly Brook Cottage, Heronsbrook House, formerly Brook Lodge and Puck Cottage are among them.

Another substantial change was in the pattern of local employment. At the start of the century most people living in Cheapside worked close to their homes. In the 1950s and 1960s apart from Imperial College, the main local employer was Harry A. Coff who supplied sand and gravel. Harry Coff was also the landlord of the New Inn in Sunninghill, later called the Three Jays. He had more than thirty lorries and a depot and offices on Buckhurst Road, now the offices of Cheapside Court built in the

1990s. The large-scale housing and road developments made plenty of work for Coff's business. Some Cheapsiders still worked on the Crown Estates in the parks and gardens of Sunninghill Park and Windsor Great Park as their predecessors had done. But with the advent of the car more Cheapsiders now worked further afield in Windsor, Bracknell and even in London. The era of Cheapside as a commuter village had begun.

The increase of motorised transport brought many changes to the village and had a big impact on the local community resulting in the loss of local shops. After the war there were still two shops in Cheapside but *"Elmbank Stores"* went out of business in the late 1960s. It had survived in the 1950s under Mrs Potter who sold it to Mr Bartlett. The last owners of this shop were Mr and Mrs Pratt who were in business as late as 1968. The Post Office Stores survived longer. After the war it was owned first by Mr and Mrs Scott, then by Mr Prew who had been in the RAF and later still by the Brooks family. The Post Office licence was lost when the Brooks were the owners. In 1980 Mr and Mrs Hines took over and the shop finally closed due to loss of business in 1996. Cheapsiders would now shop in Ascot, Windsor or Bracknell using a wide choice of superstores. During the 1980s and 1990s no less than ten new superstores were built within a five-mile radius.

The first group of brick houses to be built after the war was today's Silwood Close. In 1954 application to build opposite to the old Golden Gates was made by Warner's Ascot Development Limited. At first only four houses were approved but later five more were built and this resulted in the creation of Silwood Close. Just as the nineteenth century developers had built a block of six identical cottages at Forest View, now the twentieth century builders were also building estates of identical houses all on the same building line. The development at Silwood Close had the advantage of being small in number and the houses soon developed individually with their own gardens and extensions. In the 1950s and 1960s more individual houses were built in Watersplash Lane.

It was the construction of Hilltop Close that brought the first large block of homogenous housing into the village. Throughout the early 1950s there was pressure on the council to replace the army huts on Cheapside Estate with proper houses for the eighty families who had been living there. The council put the work out for tender and the price of £99,521 11s 6d from Messrs Halfacre and Young of Maidenhead was accepted. Hilltop Close was completed between 1956 and 1958. It provided much needed modern homes for those who had lived in the army huts and for others from Sunninghill and Cheapside who were still living in houses without electricity and hot water.

In 1959 a proposal to build twenty private houses on the land of the old Dairy Farm was strongly opposed locally. Led by Mr Showler and Mr Belvin the Cheapside Rural Preservation Society was set up and thirty-five householders joined. It seemed to them that all the open spaces were vanishing beneath bricks and tarmac and that the local facilities could not cope with more houses. The old Cheapside School was already overcrowded. The council answered some of their complaints by producing a scheme for extra temporary accommodation at the school and promised to build a new school on a site in Watersplash Lane (F. S.). After this in spite of further protests planning permission was granted for what became the 1975 Dorian Drive development. The first houses on the estate cost about £25,000. This development was on the land which had once been known as Smith's Green.

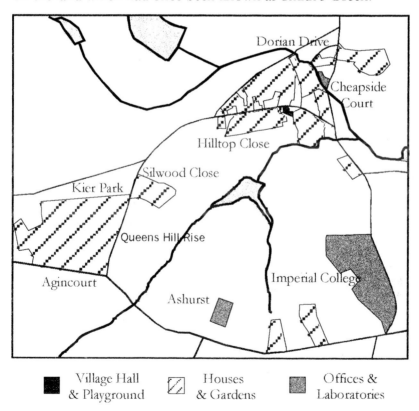

Village Hall & Playground		Houses & Gardens		Offices & Laboratories

Post 1945 Developments

There were several complaints about the style of the new developments but as the Deputy County Surveyor said, *"Cheapside is not a village of great architectural beauty"*. The point ignored by the planners however was that although not of any special architectural merit, Cheapside had a wide variety of styles of houses and had formerly had no large homogenous blocks of housing. This was permanently changed with the construction of Hilltop Close and Dorian Drive.

For thirty years Hilltop Close was part of the housing available for the tenants of Windsor and Maidenhead Council. However the 1990s saw the sale of many of these council houses. The new private owners made many modifications, some involving the removal of the old hedges, which had lined the south side of Cheapside road. Gradually the homogenous look began to disappear and the houses of Hilltop Close developed some of the same sort of variety that has affected the older sets of houses such as Forest View.

Throughout the 1960s and 1970s various private developers and speculators showed an interest in the area. These included Rudolph and Peter Palumbo, Tiny Rowland, Harold Bamberg and Patterson Cowan. Some parts of Cheapside certainly suffered from this interest. A case in point was Heronsbrook House, a listed building with its oldest parts dating from Jacobean times and the front built in Queen Anne's reign. After the war the owner Mrs Heneage remarried, to Group Captain Reginald C. Field. They had the old house transformed into seven flats and lived at Heronsbrook Cottage, having turned the Olivers out as soon as Mr Heneage died. They retained the largest part of the land and built a new bungalow in 1961 calling it Heronsbrook Cottage and renaming the old cottage April Place.

In 1963 Heronsbrook House was sold to a syndicate for £20,000. For two years this syndicate tried to get planning permission to build more houses in the grounds but they failed because this area was zoned as Green Belt. In 1965 they sold out. The property was divided and the garden cottage and stables were bought and redeveloped into Heronsbrook Farm. The freehold of the main house and some of the flats were bought by Patterson Cowan and Archibald Lee. Mr Cowan had already demolished the old workhouse in Sunninghill and he was the developer of four large constructions in Windsor. In 1970 he moved out of his flat in Heronsbrook House and four years later he bought The Cedars from Miss Turle. He remodelled the old Cedars altering the roofline, installing bathrooms and creating fewer, larger rooms. Gradually Heronsbrook House began to fall into ruin and some of the flats became empty.

In 1991 Cowan was declared bankrupt and his share in Heronsbrook House was acquired by Peter Grace of the Ascot Polo Club who in turn sold out in 1997 to Woolridge of Bagshot. Throughout the 1980s and 1990s the old house was not maintained and by 1998 it had become an empty wreck. The problem of financing the maintenance of a listed building as a small set of flats, without any development on the green belt land around it seemed to be impossible. It will be interesting to see what future there can be for the property. Certainly its listed status seems to have done more harm than good. Another Cheapside property which suffered from a lengthy period of decline was Pemberton Lodge. Empty and derelict from 1983 it was finally redeveloped into three flats retaining and restoring the old structure. It has been more fortunate than Heronsbrook House though it lost all its old gardens to new developments along Buckhurst Road and its old coach house became a separate house.

Other estates were broken up in the 1960s. The destruction of the Beechgrove estate on the death of Sir Fullerton James ultimately removed a local landmark. The old iron bridge which had linked the north and south parts of his garden across the London Road was taken down. As the bridge was only fifteen feet from the ground it was occasionally hit by lorries. It took several days to remove the solid iron construction. At the west end of Cheapside Road the extensive grounds of Queens Hill owned by Lieutenant Colonel H. P. Green were developed to create Queens Hill Rise and Kier Park. The old indoor tennis court of Queens Hill was bought by Agincourt (Ascot) Ltd., a firm headed by James McDermott and opened as a bowling club. In 1992 planning permission was sought to build a block of eighteen flats in a six-storey building. This was deferred at the time but permission for a development was eventually granted and the Agincourt estate was built in 1994.

With the building of houses and flats at Agincourt, Queens Hill Rise and Keir Park the green buffer at the west end of Cheapside Road was heavily reduced and more traffic flowed through the narrow village centre. Only the pinch point between the Thatched Tavern and Elmbank has managed to slow the cars down.

Harewood Lodge opposite to Buckhurst was developed by Mr Harold Bamberg. It had stood empty after the death of Lady

Shaw. After remodelling the house Bamberg sold it and part of the estate to Johnson's Wax when his airline Eagle Airways went into liquidation. In spite of being designated in the green belt, between 1988 and 1992 new and replacement buildings were erected at both Harewood and Titness Parks.

Throughout the 1980s more and more houses were fitted in. Some houses were built in the gardens of older houses, some old houses were replaced by more than one house, and other properties were redeveloped into blocks of flats. It seemed that the insatiable demand for more dwellings would never be checked. The parish gave notice to all allotment holders to quit, in order to put forward a scheme to sell off this land for development. They intended to use the profits to fund a new Sports Complex in South Ascot. Cheapsiders were up in arms and they supported the tenants of the allotments. They felt strongly that this was over development and there would soon be not a single patch of green left in what had been up to 1945 a very rural hamlet. Increased development had also put increased strain on the small roads. However in 1988 the process was halted. The scheme was dropped and it was hoped that the heavy redevelopment, such a dramatic feature since the war, had come to an end.

The most important changes to the appearance of Cheapside Road took place in the 1960s and involved the demolition of the old almshouses, the old school and the chapel. These had been the landmarks of the Victorian and Edwardian village. The two old almshouses were replaced by five new units in 1968 and still provide homes for older residents in the centre of the village. They are no longer next to the school. The old school was replaced because it was no longer large enough and the new school was built between Cheapside Road and Watersplash Lane, of which more later.

The chapel was removed because in the new post war world there were too few attending and it was no longer needed. The Cheapside Methodist Chapel had flourished up to the 1960s. During the Second World War several Americans worshipped there and there was a small organ, played in the 1940s by Mrs Talbot of Sunningdale. Cheapside families who attended regularly had included the Bartons of Nutbush Cottage, the Browns of Barberry Cottage and the Toms of Long Gardens Cottages. By 1969 when the Cheapside Wesleyan Chapel closed it had a congregation of less than twenty. It was sold off a year later and demolished. The swifts who had nested every year under the large high gable lost their home and Chapel House was built on the site.

The New Cheapside School

In the immediate post war years Cheapside School educated all the local children from the ages of five to eleven. The catchment area included parts of the parishes of both Sunninghill and Winkfield. With the introduction of the *"Eleven Plus"* examination, children who passed went on to either Ranelagh School at Bracknell or to the Windsor grammar schools. By the 1960s about six children a year were going to the grammar schools. The rest went on to Sunninghill School. This ceased to have children over 11 after Charters School was built.

Winifred Ross was in charge of the Infants at Cheapside School from 1950 to 1968. Her husband, George Ross, had lived at Silwood Park Garden Lodge adjacent to Tetworth Hall in the early 1900s when his father was Head Gardener to Mr Cordes (F.S.). Mr Cordes supported George's education and he became a manager at Arthur Cozens, the Electrical Engineers and Contractors, in Sunninghill. George is a good example of the enlarged opportunities opening up for the children of Cheapside.

With the additional children now coming from the Cheapside Estate, the Victorian school was soon bursting at the seams. In 1951 new cloakrooms and a refurbished kitchen were added. As the traffic built up along Cheapside Road in the 1950s it became necessary to protect the playground from the road and the fences were repaired and strengthened. In 1952 the first school badge was approved but there was still no school uniform (F.S.).

In spite of the piecemeal repairs and additions the 1957 Inspectors' Report declared that Cheapside School was *"almost a slum"*. The children ate their dinners, cooked on the premises, in the classrooms. The heating depended on two ancient stoves. Overflow classes were held in the Village Hall. By the mid-sixties there were 111 children on the roll. There were only two classrooms: the five to seven year olds were taught in the small room by Mrs Ross and the seven to eleven year olds were taught by Mrs Taylor, later by Mrs Cavanagh, and by the headmaster. The large room was divided into two sections as appropriate.

The school had many good friends. After the departure of the Crutchleys and the Hills it now received money from the Rotary Club for school prizes. These were given for academic and sporting excellence but the most important prize was *"for service before self*". One especially generous individual patron was George Jackson of Oakleigh on the London Road. He enabled the school to plant the row of poplar trees that shaded the school field; some of these survived the great storms of 1987 and 1990. He also provided books for the library. Colonel Sir James Horlick allowed the children to use the open-air pool at Little Paddocks and the older children would walk across for swimming lessons. The children did a lot of walking. Once a week they went across to St Michael's Church for a service, crossing the Brook where the quicker boys could catch crayfish en route. For their sports they used the field at the end of Watersplash Lane and they made regular nature walks along the Brook (G. Goulding).

The development of Dorian Drive bringing in more young families made the building of a larger school imperative. Plans for a new school off Green Lane were approved in 1962. It cost £23,000, had room for 85 children and was formally opened in June 1964 by Robin Woods, the Dean of Windsor (F.S.). The old school with its plot of about one tenth of an acre was sold for £4,850 and three houses were built on the site (J. E.). With the new school, Cheapside kept an important part of its life. Today there is also a playgroup in the Village Hall.

The Village Hall

During the war Cheapsiders had a variety of local entertainments at the Army Camps. The Chapel room was the centre for the Women's Social Hour and the knitting groups met there. The school might be used for meetings but it was uncomfortably small for dances and concerts. For that sort of amusement there was the Cordes Hall in Sunninghill where there were plays and variety shows, and next door to it there was a cinema.

After the war the camps closed and the war work ceased. A group of Cheapsiders came together determined to establish their own local Social Centre. They thought it would be a comparatively simple task to find a small piece of land when there was so much for sale and then to erect on it one of the many surplus army huts. But it proved to be very difficult indeed. The long struggle for the Village Hall certainly developed the community spirit of Cheapside. The tale of the Village Hall is one of local tenacity and perseverance in the face of indifference and even hostility by the local authorities.

In November 1945, Major Fellowes was elected chairman of a committee formed to establish *"a Social Centre and Institute for Cheapside"*. They wrote to ask for an army hut and they asked Mrs Philip Hill if they might have the piece of land opposite the school used by Mr Potter as an allotment. Immediately they ran into problems. Mr Gwilt of Berry Cottage, who was the Secretary, found the Air Ministry was reluctant to sell them any of the huts on Sunninghill Park and there was another long delay as the Ninety-Nine Trust Ltd acting for the Hill estate considered their proposal.

The committee looked around for alternative sites and in 1946 on the death of Michael Heneage they tried to get part of the Heronsbrook estate but once more they were unsuccessful. With support from Sir James Horlick, Mr Gwilt tried to get support for the project from the National Council of Social Service and from the Berkshire Education Committee. They also approached the Library Services suggesting that the hall might be used as a community library.

By April 1946 the Hill estates had agreed to sell them three quarters of an acre for £250. The site was an old allotment lying behind the cottage opposite the old school. The cottage was occupied by Sophia Smith, a retired teacher who had a free tenancy for life. Mrs Fellowes wrote on behalf of the committee offering to buy both the cottage and the land for £400 and in May an agreement was made.

Having failed to get an army hut and worried about getting planning permission to put one up anyway, Mr Gwilt started looking into the cost of a Colt timber framed building. This proved to be too expensive. By October 1947 they were again searching for a Nissen hut only to be told that there were no longer any huts available at Sunninghill Park or Silwood Park. Finally they were allocated Nissen hut No 155 from Woolmer Camp at Borden and this became the first Cheapside Social Centre.

The committee then launched an energetic money-raising campaign. They were still trying to get some official sponsorship but at this stage there was no help forthcoming either from Berkshire Education Committee or from the Social Services Council. In October they were told that the Crown Commissioners were considering making a donation. This gave them encouragement though it never materialised.

Nor did the planning process go smoothly. The committee was informed by the District Council that Cheapside was not an area where *"further development for communal facilities"* was thought necessary. When they persisted they were told they could go ahead but they should expect no financial support from the local authority. In all this gloom one positive backer made an appearance. In June 1948 Mrs Tufnell, who was the head of a local firm of estate agents, agreed to give the committee a mortgage.

With a site, a hut and a promise of a mortgage the committee set to work again to raise the money privately. Mr Scott of the Post Office was one of the main fund-raisers. The biggest donors were Murray Bakham of Armitage Court, Sunninghill, Sir James Horlick and Lady Deterding who sent them £50 from the south of France. Other cheques were received from Hubert Raphael of Queens Hill, Miss Kaye of the White House, S. Keen of New Mile Chase, Frank Fisher of Pemberton Lodge, the Tufnell family of Fairfield and Mr Perryman of Silwood Park Farm. There was also a donation from Mrs Mosenthal who ran the Tittenhurst Charitable Trust and another donor was Miss A. Langley who had been born in 1882 at the cottage inhabited by Miss Smith. Many unrecorded donations also came in. By September they had raised £300 which was indeed *"very creditable for a village of only 320 persons including children"* as Major Fellowes commented in a letter.

The whole village worked to raise the money. One money-maker which involved the whole community, especially Mrs Becket of Long Gardens and Mrs Potter of Elmbank Stores, was the baking and selling of meat pies. This project was part of the WVS *"Pie Money Scheme"* and it brought in about £80 a year for the Social Centre Fund. To make the pies and sell them they had to obtain a catering licence under the Rural Meals Scheme. In those heady days of rationing and British bureaucracy the committee were informed that meat pies were classified as *"main meals not light meals whether accompanied or not by a piece of cake"*. To sell these *"main meals"* they had to satisfy the government inspectors on the contents, price and conditions of sale and to make regular returns.

With all the post war regulations, the committee needed a whole sheaf of licences before they could open the hall. To install a floor they needed a timber licence and to perform concerts they needed a Performing Rights Licence. They also had to register as a Charity. The Ministry of Education granted them a permit to buy 106 square yards of linoleum, from Caleys of Windsor at 13s 3d per square yard. Finally in June 1948 they secured planning permission and by autumn they had collected eight chairs, a small card table, a piano and some crockery. In December the Berkshire Education Committee agreed to lend them fifty chairs for the Christmas period and at last the Social Centre was opened for use with a grand Christmas concert and social.

There was plenty of local talent to provide the entertainment. After the fire at Sunninghill Park, Don and Wendy Humphries had lived on in their little house near the stables which were not damaged and Don worked on the estate. He was an accomplished pianist and organised his own band. George Batt of Park View cottages was also an entertainer and a drummer. Don's band played for modern dancing and jive while George Batt's group played for old time dancing and they both joined together in the concerts and dances put on at first in the school and later in the new social centre. Mrs Becket performed monologues and Mrs Johnson, Mrs Buckland and Mrs Gwilt sang. Many of the older residents look back to the social activity of these post war years with fond memories.

Within a year of opening the Social Centre was at the heart of all village activities. Among the associations which used it were the WI, which was formed in 1963 and flourished for a decade, the Girl Guides, twenty-two of them, the Boys Club, seventeen of them, and the Youth Club, attended by twenty or more, which was run by Mr Batt. On Thursdays there was a visit from the County Library service and there were ballet lessons and on Fridays there were socials and concerts. The Centre was run by its trustees and its management body. The trustees included the vicar, Miss Kaye and Mr Pollard. Pie making continued to bring in about £90 a year towards the running costs. This helped to pay for electricity to be installed and after this the Social Centre could be used as a polling station in the election of October 1951.

As soon as the army hut had been erected the committee had to start negotiating for a more permanent building. After the death of Sophia Smith her cottage was sold to Dr E. M. Blackett and they were able repay the mortgage to Mrs Tufnell. About the same time the committee was informed by the Planning Authority that the Nissen hut was *"not suitable for permanent erection"* and that it had to be taken down by December 1956. From then on they had to obtain an annual licence granting *"Temporary Permission for the Retention of Temporary Premises"*. They also had to embark on the huge task of raising the money to build and equip the present Village Hall. The cost was estimated at £8,167 and at times this seemed an impossible amount to raise. In 1963 there was a desperate appeal asking *"Do we still want a Centre where we can meet?"* The answer was *"Yes"* and under the chairmanship of John Fowler all kinds of money raising efforts were tried: a mile of pennies, sponsored runs, annual fêtes and sports-days on the Paddock Field in Watersplash Lane.

In 1967 the new Conveyance and Deed of Trust for the Village Hall was registered. It was from then on known as the Cheapside Village Hall. The trustees were the Reverend Gibbon, Mr Wells, Air Commodore Field, Mr Johnson and Mr Elsbury. By this date the regular events taking place in the hall included the Ladies Keep Fit classes, Bingo sessions, Sunday School classes, Whist Drives, Art Classes and Horticultural Shows as well as the meetings of the WI etc.

In 1969 the Village Hall Committee was disappointed to hear that they would get nothing towards the Hall from the Department of Education and Science but they were very relieved to secure a grant from the Social Services Ministry. The Committee approached five firms making prefabricated halls and selected Youngman's of Crawley in Sussex as the most suitable. The architects, Louis Gray and Mutch of Sunningdale, gave their services free. Finally in 1971 the Nissen hut was demolished and the new building went up. It had cost £8,665. The ministry gave £3,639 and the villagers found the rest. Mrs John Fleming opened the new Cheapside Village Hall in May 1969.

In 1987 King Hussein of Jordan who owned Buckhurst Park agreed to be the patron of the Village Hall. After his death in 1999 his widow Queen Noor became patron, describing Cheapside in her letter of acceptance as an *"enchanting village"*.

There was indeed some enchantment in the air that kept the Village Hall running and also provided inspiration for a series of exhibitions on the history of Cheapside. The first was in 1977 and there was another ten years later. Finally in 1996 twelve residents agreed to prepare the Cheapside Millennium History Exhibition and worked on it steadily for the next four years. The exhibition boards would be preserved for future use and this book was written to keep a record of all the information that had been collected. The Hall is managed by a committee of Cheapsiders whose chief task is raising enough money to meet all the running expenses and the profits from this book will contribute to these.

Among the many significant events of the post war years the most positive was the creation of the Village Hall. It has kept a community spirit alive in a hamlet that has lost its Chapel, its Post Office and its shops and where most locals now work at a considerable distance from home. Even the school is less of a local focus than it once was since it is now used by children who do not live nearby and who come and go in cars rather than on foot. The villagers who worked so hard to establish a permanent Village Hall deserve the thanks of all present-day Cheapsiders. It is still very well used for Keep Fit, Art and Ballet classes and also as a daily Nursery School. The local Horticultural Shows take place three times a year and the Hall is a centre for all sorts of local celebrations and entertainments. Without it Cheapside would be just another residential district in the large Windsor conurbation. The Village Hall has certainly fulfilled the aims of the founders to provide a social centre for the Cheapside community.

Change and Continuity

Within the old triangle formed by the Cheapside and Buckhurst Roads and Watersplash Lane there are now more than double the number of houses there were in 1891. The following table demonstrates and echoes many of the national changes. Although the number of houses has more than doubled the population has only grown by a third. The number of children has almost halved proportionately while the number of those in retirement has increased eight times. Less than a sixth of the population has lived in Cheapside for all their lives whereas in 1891 this was over a third. In 1891 less than ten were born abroad and they had all come from European countries. Today twenty-five residents were born overseas and they have come from all over the world: the Americas, mainland Europe, Asia, Africa and Australia.

	1891	1998
Houses	62	145
Residents	237	311
Of which children	58	41
Born locally	85	43
Self employed/retired	7	56
Servants/gardeners	53	7
Agricultural workers/labourers	21	3
Tradesmen/shopkeepers	32	5
Employers	7	14
Others	2	109

A mere handful is now employed as gardeners, labourers and servants and there are equally few tradesmen and shopkeepers. However the numbers of employers has doubled and the employees are now in a vast array of jobs. There are film directors and hospital consultants, accountants, engineers and finance directors, oil executives and dentists, nurses, midwives and teachers, timber agents and beauty therapists. You are more likely to meet a computer programmer, a pensioner or a pilot in Cheapside Road today than a forester, a gardener or a farm labourer. Today apart from ten or twelve who work from home all the rest are employed outside the area. While most are employed in the Thames Valley or London, some travel great distances and some travel all around the world regularly in the course of their work. The global village is here.

Throughout the history of this hamlet there have been constant changes and even the landscape has altered. In spite of the great loss of trees in the storms of 1987 and 1990 Cheapside is much more wooded than at any time in the last thousand years. This is due to the end of farming and hunting as major economic activities. You will see no grazing cattle or pigsties in today's Cheapside although you can still hear a cockerel or two. You are very likely to see a roe or muntjak deer eating the roses and the camellias but you will not see a deer being hunted across the forest.

The housing stock has been transformed. A cottage that cost a thousand pounds only fifty years ago would now cost over £100,000. In the eighteenth century the larger houses were gentrified, now it is the turn of the cottages and the pubs. The Thatched Tavern is no longer the local for domino-playing labourers but a smart restaurant for race-goers and BMW drivers. The dangers facing Cheapsiders are no longer hunger, cold and disease but fast traffic and noise.

The connection with the crown has been strengthened by its repurchase of Sunninghill Park and new money continues to arrive here. In the 1980s Arabs bought several estates and now buyers are coming from Russia. No longer do the cottagers fill the pot by poaching but there are still rabbits and deer to be had and some of the pheasants which escape the royal shoots may yet end up in a Cheapside casserole. The bluebells still flower in the birch and oak woodland, the heron fishes in the Brook and the kingfisher flits along from its nest near the millpond.

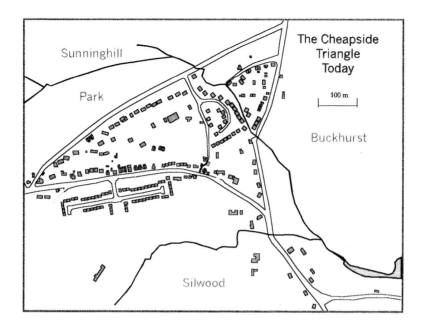

Sunninghill

Park

The Cheapside
Triangle
Today

100 m

Buckhurst

Silwood

Today's Cheapside is a far distance from the huddle of medieval cottages that lay on the edge of Sunninghill Manor between Windsor Forest and Sunninghill Park, but it has several features in common with the village of the past. The roads and paths follow the old ways and there is still the contrast between the large parks and estates and the smaller cottages and houses with their even smaller backsides. Cheapside has remained a mixed community. The hamlet is still surrounded by green spaces which set it apart and which help to give it its own identity. Long may the green spaces continue!

APPENDIX ONE

Sunninghill Manor and Silwood Park

Owners/Occupiers of Sunninghill Manor
As Part of Cookham Manor

A 1591 record of Cookham Manor (B.R.O. D/E Est 01) listed past owners and tenants of Sunninghill as:

John of Sunninghill
Adam at Dene
John at More
Robert at Dene
William Stapper
Harry Battell
John Rede
Parson at Clewer
Robert Atcombe,
Alexander Atho
Geffry West

A more accurate list would include:

1197 Gilbert de Blackman granted lands at Sunninghill by William de Cumba
1220 John de Sunninghill
1242 Ricardo de Pesemer
1252 Robert of Sunninghill, a royal keeper
From 1307 it was in the Dower of Queen Isabella
1326 John of Podenhale and wife Joanna held land in Cowarth and Sunninghill
From 1358 it was in the Dower of Queen Philippa
1362 John of Sunninghill and wife Joanna bought from John Holm
1372 William Derenford and wife Joanna held lands at Sunninghill and Cowarth
From 1399 it was settled on Humphrey, Duke of Gloucester
1410 John Wantele
1438 Thomas Haseley
1447-1483 and 1485-1487 it was in the Dower of Elizabeth Woodville, wife of Edward IV
1447 Sir John Norris and Sir Edward Grimston took over from Thomas Haseley

1448/9 Trustees for the property were Sir Edmund Hungerford, Sir John Norris, William Norris, Roger Norris, Thomas Bakham
1466 Sir William Norris
1487-1503 it was in the Dower of Elizabeth of York, wife of Henry VII
1506 Sir Edward Norris
1558 Sir Henry Norris
1567 Henry Lane bought the manor from Norris.
1582 William Day, Provost of Eton, later Bishop, bought the manor and **Eastmore** from Lane
1613 Matthew Day
1629 Phillip Farrant II bought parts of manor
1664-1669 Matthew Day II
1668 Thomas Rawlings bought Phillip Farrant II's inheritance and the manor from Day
1673 John Aldridge I bought the manor **Eastmore and Farrants** from Rawlings
1708 John Aldridge II
1737 John Aldridge III
1747 John Aldridge IV
1764 John Pitt
1787 James Hartley

Owners of *"Sunning Hill House"* later Silwood Park

1788 Sir James Sibbald *, creator of the lake and the park
1811 George Simson
1824/5 Michie Forbes and Mary Forbes
1854/5 John Hargreaves
1875 Charles P. Stewart *
1888 Thomas Cordes and Margaret Cordes
1925 Sir George Dolby
1940 Sir Phillip Hill
1947 Imperial College

* Both built new houses on the London Road site

208

APPENDIX TWO

Sunninghill Park

Occupiers when Crown Property

1376/7 Emparked by Sir Simon de Burley for King Edward III

Bailiffs:
1447 Sir William Perkins
1448-1540 The Norris family

Parkers or Keepers:
1484 William Bolton
1485 William Staverton
1486 Henry Jewet
1498 John Basket

Bailiffs:
1540-1619 The Neville family
1619-1630 Sir Alexander Levingstone
1630 Sold by the Crown

Owners when Private Property

1630 Sir Thomas Carey and family
1654 Sir Thomas Draper
1703 Sir John Baber
1765 Sir Thomas Draper Baber
1769 Jeremiah Crutchley
1805 George Henry Duffield Crutchley
1868 Percy Henry Crutchley
1878 General Sir Charles Crutchley
1898 Percy Edward Crutchley
1940 Phillip Hill

1945 Repurchased by the Crown

APPENDIX THREE

The Priests and Vicars of St Michael's Church

Appointed by the Abbess and nuns of Broomhall Priory

1297-1316	Clement Debenham
1316-1321	John de Laupar or Laufar
1321-1321	Adam be Mere
1321-1322	Richard Freemantle De Wynchcombe
1322-1338	Thomas de Schenlegh
1338-1348	Simon de Tappelewe
1348-1350	John Peckere De Swindon
1350-?	William de Neenton

No surviving records from 1350 to 1535. The Black Death occurred around 1350. The Broomhall priory records were destroyed by fire in 1321 and 1462. Broomhall Priory was closed in 1522. All would contribute to the loss of records.

Appointed by the Master and Fellows of St John's College, Cambridge

1535-1557	Joseph Gates
1557-1565	Thomas Ranerd
1565-?	Robert Sherrington
?- 1594	Maurice Serill/Sorrill
1594-1626	John Robinson
1626-1654	John Robinson (son of above)
1654-1664	Francis Sayer
1664-1700	George Dawson
1700-1702	William Forkington/Torkington
1702-1722	John Morris
1722-1748	Robert Palmer
1748-1807	Joseph Thistlethwaite
1807-1817	Samuel Hebelthwaite
1817-1830	William Ainger
1830-1884	Alexander Wale
1884-1912	John Snowden
1912-1936	Arthur Ingram
1936-1955	Gerald Thursfield
1956-1965	Frederick Vickery
1965-1979	Edward Gibbon
1980-	Timothy Gunter

APPENDIX FOUR

Transcription of the Letter from Prince Arthur to All Souls College Oxford

From the Prince

Trusty and right welbeloved we grete you well. And forasmoche as we being credibly informed that your last election is past and nowe of late devolved into the handes of the right reverend father in God our most trusty and most entirelibeloved His Holiness the cardinal of Canterbury. we desire and right affectionatley pray you that the voters for our sake and at the contemplation of this, ye thus have our right beloved William Pickering scholar of Law in so much as he is of alliammia* unto the founders of your place and that of his father also is in the most tender of our derrest modre the quene especially named in your next election. As we especially trust you whereinas moche be ye accustomed so to be unto you and your said place the most good and gracious lord in every reasonable desire herafter

Given under our signet at the manor of Sunninghill the 18th day of november.

* It means that he was a member of the University.

INDEX

INDEX